Uncomfortable Truths
Confronting Reality in Troubled Times

I0022590

Alex Bearss

Table of Contents

Copyright

Uncomfortable Truths: Confronting Reality in Troubled Times

Copyright © 2025 Alex Bearss

(Defiance Press & Publishing, LLC)

All rights reserved. No part of this publication may be reproduced, distributed, or transmitted in any form or by any means, including photocopying, recording, or other electronic or mechanical methods, without the prior written permission of the publisher, except in the case of brief quotations embodied in critical reviews and certain other noncommercial uses permitted by copyright law.

Published by Defiance Press & Publishing, LLC

Bulk orders of this book may be obtained by contacting Defiance Press & Publishing, LLC. www.defiancepress.com.

Defiance Press & Publishing, LLC

281-581-9300

info@defiancepress.com

Dedication

To my two brothers, to whom I owe everything; to my parents, to whom I owe my existence and upbringing. I wouldn't be the person I am today without them. And lastly, but most importantly, to my fellow Americans, both here and those that haven't yet reached these blessed shores; I pray for your life, liberty, and pursuit of happiness. Always let your enemies know: Come and take it.

The only color that matters to me is green. — Alex B.

Warning

Warning: The concepts and ideas you are about to read may cause you discomfort. If you feel threatened or unsafe by a diversity of ideas, please close this book immediately and contact our support staff. After providing payment information, our safety and mental health task force will* arrive on the scene, quarantine this book ($1,159.99 per incident), provide onsite counseling ($359.99 per hour, three-hour minimum), and offer a comforting stuffed animal of your choice (cost dependent on size, number of requested dyes, colors, and availability; an extra-large stuffed rainbow unicorn definitely costs extra). Legal notice: By reading past this warning, you, the reader or listener, agree not to hold the writer, ghostwriter, editor, publisher, publisher's janitor, delivery driver, audiobook distributor/voice actor, or paper fabrication plant liable for any harm caused by this work (including self-immolation, inspiration for retribution, or feelings of being offended). You have been warned.

(*Quoted prices are the minimum fees and may be subject to additional costs dependent on zip code, current rate of inflation, safety of the local area, mental state of customer, and the whims of whoever happens to pick up the phone that day. Availability of the services requested is also dependent on the whims of whoever answers the phone, so please be patient. Your call is important to us. Please stay on the line, and the next available representative will be with you shortly.)

Prologue

As a veteran, Native, Hispanic, trans lesbian of color to a single parent (VNHTLOC+) growing up, I've had unique perspectives on contemporary (that is, modern) society that no other has. "My Truth," being what I am, has led me to see and understand our world not as I wish it to be, but as it is. As all insights do, these ideas began as battles in the mind to match perceived reality and desires with the real world as it stands today. While undoubtedly the generalities made between these covers are not absolute, they represent broad truths we all do (or should) see and understand, but which are not talked about outside of hushed conversations in private sitting rooms (or bar stools, if preferred). You may not like these truths, but that's the point.

As I sit typing these words, an empty White Claw box (White Claw is an alcoholic seltzer with a good alcohol-to-calorie ratio) sits in the street as an eyesore. I wish the box weren't there or that someone (myself included) would have the decency to pick it up and throw it away, but alas, it sits there. Simply wanting it gone or putting it out of eyesight (say, by closing the blinds—mine are automated) and convincing ourselves it's not there does nothing to change that reality. If reality and words are to have meaning, we must recognize existence as it is, rather than ignore the truth because it is inconvenient or not in line with how we wish the world were. To quote actor Jared Harris from the miniseries Chernobyl, "The truth doesn't care about our needs or wants. It doesn't care about our governments, our ideologies, our religions. It will lie in wait, for all time [...] What is the cost of lies? It's not that we'll mistake them for the truth. The real danger is that if we hear enough lies, then we no longer recognize the truth at all."

My goal in writing this book is for people to understand and admit what (on some level) they already know to be true and be able to acknowledge this to themselves and others publicly. To the extent readers or listeners haven't heard or pondered these truths, they must be made aware for their own sake. Why is this important? We make decisions every day, from what clothes to wear depending on the weather and how we show ourselves to the world, to which cars to purchase and food to buy. These decisions for ourselves and others require us to realize how the world works in reality to achieve the best outcomes by making the best possible decisions.

For example, you wouldn't want a pilot flying your plane if they believed the world was flat, and you wouldn't want editors of school textbooks to believe the Holocaust didn't happen. Nor would you want newspapers that believe the United States was founded in 1619 or Supreme Court justices charged with enforcing Title IX (which prohibits discrimination on the basis of sex in higher education) unable or unwilling to define what a woman is (although this sounds like an Ivy Leaguer, my money is on unable). We need to understand and accept reality, because if we don't, we will make errors, sometimes fatal, that will make all of us worse off.

There is a phrase, originated, as best I can tell, by the intellectual Thomas Sowell: There are no solutions. There are only trade-offs. We accept and communicate untruths to each other because we feel "our side" will be the worse off if the truth is known. We know, for example, males and females think differently and want different things. But this (arguably) harms the goal of equality among the sexes. We know there are better and worse ways of living but ignore this idea because it requires judgment and acknowledging a hierarchy of human activity and cultures.

Our country is in a state in which we seem unable and/or unwilling to admit reality to each other, for fear it will be used against "our side." If we know we are wrong, we need to admit it so we can fix common problems in an effective manner, even if this means admitting the opposing side is right or at least has valid points. I'll make you a deal (which, of course, I have no way of enforcing): It takes, on average, five hours to read a 90,000-word book (which I've made) and nine to ten hours to listen to a 90,000-word audiobook (although, if you're from The University of Texas at Austin, I'd recommend giving yourself thirteen hours; Apple's audiobook app can slow the audio to .75x speed for better comprehension).

If you hear me out, at the end, I'll admit things I once believed but now think were wrong. For those questioning this work (and for those not questioning this work, you should be on some type of list... not the good ones), this is an olive branch, a promise that I'll be (overall) honest with you if you give this work an honest read.

You, as a reader or listener, have a choice. You can use the words here to build your understanding of the world for the better, or you can stop here and dismiss any further thoughts on the matter, concluding that this work was thought up by an idiotic, insensitive, illiberal philistine from a part of the country that doesn't matter (or shouldn't). But you do so at your own peril. The real world will continue to operate not as you wish it, but as it does and has. And if you are unable or unwilling to see and recognize the truth, your choices dictated by a falsely perceived reality will be for the worse in ways you may not be able to recognize until it is too late. I hope for your sake you make the right call. Best of luck and give 'em hell.

> *"No matter what happens next, don't be too hard on yourself. Even now, after all you've done, you can still go home. Lucky you."*

— Lt. Colonel John Konrad, commander, 33rd Infantry Battalion (fictional)Chapter 1

Chapter 1 Who I Am

"The question isn't who is going to let me, it's who is going to stop me."

— Ayn Rand, author, 1905–1982

Since this work's cornerstone is my perspective (which is unique and cannot be completely empathized with by others), it's important that you know who I am. As previously mentioned, I am a veteran, Native, Hispanic, transgender lesbian of color raised in a single-parent household at times (VNHTLOC+). Each of those descriptions has meaning that, as far as I know, is accurate, and I leave it to you to either know or look up what each indicates. Many readers or listeners may have never heard the term intersectionality, and if you haven't, I weep for the education system that brought you up. For those whose otherwise perfect public schooling didn't teach them, I shall.

Intersectionality is the concept that different social characteristics combined are distinct and separate from their individual pieces. A gay Hispanic man's life experience is different from that of simply a gay man or a Hispanic man. Thus, a gay Hispanic man's life experience and truth cannot be truly understood by other gay men or Hispanic men. As such, lesbians cannot understand my life experience, truth, and victimhood because of my various other social categorizations. While they understand part of that nature by, like me, being a woman and attracted to women, they cannot understand what it's like to also be a Native American veteran and the persecution this entails. Native Americans can't understand the oppression I live under, because unfortunately, nearly none (by percent) of the Native American population is transgender. Thus, as far as I know, I am unique in this world.

I bring intersectionality up because (predictably) the following chapters will be controversial (but shouldn't be). They are based on things I have observed, dealt with, felt, and lived through in ways others can never understand. You, the reader, cannot ever comprehend fully my perspective no matter how hard you try or how extremely well I describe it. You must simply take, as a matter of fact, that I've seen and felt what

I'm describing. Any attempt to belittle, downplay, or challenge this work or my character has an obvious culprit I almost need not say — sexism, homophobia, transphobia, racism, and anti-single parent hatred. We need not know exactly which one applies, so, for critics, just pick the one that best applies to you. In absence of that, I'll pick one myself, as any or all of them probably apply on some internalized level you don't even realize, you bigot.

My Struggle

Very young, I was drawn to women but couldn't understand why. At first, I cursed God for having made me this way, but then I realized it was a gift. I would never have to worry about being drugged and raped by groups of privileged, cisgender males (that is, male individuals whose gender and sex match) in frat houses whose attention I would otherwise have sought. I would never have to concern myself with the burden of societal expectations of motherhood and children unless I wanted them (but they're kind of a drag; better to just get a nicer car). I knew my life would be challenging, but I was inspired by the singer Lady Gaga's hit single, Born This Way. That is until 2010, when she wore a dress made of raw beef to the MTV Video Music Awards and made me realize she not only advocates for the murder of animals but that some of what she does might just be for attention (perhaps other celebrities do the same? No... No, that can't be the correct conclusion). Thus, I knew from that point on I'd have to inspire myself. After a few minutes of introspection, I realized I'm all the inspiration I need.

I've always somehow known that not only was I unique, but that I was the most unique of the unique. When I made this realization in 2010, I hadn't accomplished anything yet, but that didn't mean I wasn't distinctive, rare, and exceptional, with the exquisite bravery of a beautiful butterfly flying against the wind.

That being said, as a member of the 2SLGBTQPIA+ (two-spirit, lesbian, bisexual, gay, trans, queer, pansexual, intersex, asexual — or ally? I lose track after a while) community, I'm more open to new experiences and potential partners or groups of partners than the average person. In addition to being attracted to lesbian females, I'm also open to relationships with bisexual females and even pre-op trans men (if you need help with that definition, please look it up). I make a distinction between bisexual and lesbian females because, in some circles, that distinction is important. Who our intimate partners are attracted to, of course, makes a difference.

For example, after numerous conversations with cisgender straight women, most said they would prefer their partners not be intimate or attracted to other cisgender men (typically referred to as bisexual men). (Oddly, and unexplainably, straight cisgender males I polled seemed to be more accepting of their LGBTQ+ partners and their desire for same-sex experiences, as long as the event(s) was/were inclusive.) I personally am more open-minded than those bigoted cisgender women. Additionally, I highlight my attraction to pre-op trans men to showcase how inclusive I am to all members of this diverse world we live in and to therefore contrast myself against others who may be so small-minded they refuse to even consider non-traditional relationships.

I discriminate between pre-op and post-op (that is, those who have undergone gender reassignment surgery or double mastectomies) to signal my hatred of Western medicine, which has been dominated by dead White men. Those who choose to undergo surgery, to me, indicate, at best, a neutral attitude towards a system rife with homophobia, racism, and transphobia, and I will not take part. Participants are complicit, if not culpable, in supporting one of the innumerable pieces of systemic oppression. This is also the reason I refuse gender-affirming medical treatment. I know I'm woman enough, and if the world can't accept me for that, that's their problem.

By my understanding of the terms, as a woman (right now) attracted to both women and men (trans men are men), that makes me simultaneously straight, lesbian, and bisexual. If there's any doubt, I'm happy to share my internet history with any skeptics. Lastly, critics wanting to validate my claims on my gender and sexual preferences with how I've presented myself in the past (and present) must also understand I've previously come out as gender-fluid and even at times as gender-queer (that is, genders outside the traditional gender binaries of "man" and "woman"). As if in some type of strange competition with less open-minded celebrities, by my count, I've come out at least four times. First, as trans, then as lesbian, followed by gender-queer, and lastly as bisexual (after my eyes were opened to the beauty of trans men); although, truth be told, these realizations happened in quick succession.

While at first confusing, it's simple to understand once you consider I've always been a woman, lesbian, and later gender-fluid/gender-queer, with my preferred partners matching the accepted definitions of lesbian, bisexual, and straight. WebMD defines gender fluid as a person whose gender identity is not fixed. So in the past, I may have thought of and presented myself as a man using he/him pronouns. At other times in my past, I've also known that I am a woman. Presently, I'd like to highlight how I currently identify by having you reference the first paragraph of this chapter. If there are future interviews, book signings, or debates, know I may at that moment be a man, woman, or neither. I realize for many this will seem confusing, while others may understand the trauma this has created for me.

In order to allow others to effectively communicate with me in a courteous manner, I've selflessly chosen to go by Alex, which is short for either Alexis or Alexander (don't worry about which one in the moment unless you're about to sue me and require a legal name). Additionally, because at any moment I may either feel like a masc (masculine) trans woman or cisgender man, I've chosen to simply use he/him, in accordance with diversitycenterneo.org's article, "Pronouns: A How-To – The Diversity Center." "Anyone of any gender can use any pronouns that fit for them." Lacking a stricter set of rules, I'm assured I'm acting in a safe and inclusive manner. It would be insane to insist others track my gender as it changes and require them to change pronoun use in reference to me. How, after all, can someone know how to refer to me in the moment when my gender may change in an instant, potentially triggering anxiety and feelings of being unsafe by someone misgendering or potentially deadnaming me (that is, referring to me by a name I no longer go by).

As the reader or listener may note, I've left out straight cis women as potential love interests. While many straight women were drawn to my masc-trans feminine body, I abhorred straight women. The privilege they inherently held and their lack of much of the structural oppression I endured caused me jealousy. I wish they (and everyone) could understand the hardships that I as an individual endure. Despite this well-reasoned jealousy, I knew in my heart I had to be more accepting, so I have graciously not discriminated against them as intimate partners in ways others have discriminated against me. (Technically, they cease being straight once they are in an intimate relationship with me if, during the relationship, I remained a woman.)

Additionally, some critics may take issue with the term masc trans woman, as, to some, it may seem like a contradiction. I would point out that there is a long history of tomboys; that is, girls who enjoy at a young age to take part in typically male-oriented activities. But what if a tomboy is a trans woman? That is, a biological male who knows they are a woman and thus, in that moment, becomes a trans woman desiring to use she/her pronouns. What, then, if this trans woman enjoys typically masculine activities? How can we tell this individual they are anything but a trans woman who is also a tomboy (and thus, a masculine trans woman)? They know they are a woman but don't want to take part in traditionally feminine activities.

Furthermore, what of the case of a person who has undergone gender reassignment surgery but at the same time dislikes traditionally feminine dress and activity? What, after all, are feminine dress and activities except those defined by the patriarchy? We thus reach my self-identification (sometimes) of masc trans woman as a coherent, logical, well-thought-out set of ideas. I hope that clears everything up.

As happy as I was with who I discovered I am, my hopes of a happy life were torn to shreds by bigots. Lesbian women rejected me out of hand. Doctors and Planned Parenthood employees at the front desk focused on surface-level aspects of my body, like a lack of noticeable breasts or female genitals and reproductive organs. I was discriminated against by TSA agents (who demanded my gender for inspection purposes) for showing no feminine features except my feet, which I've been told appear slender, youthful, and nubile to those I've asked. Hardly anyone understood who I was, and the lack of empathy and accommodation appalled me. You, the reader, must know that not all women like pink and high heels. Some of us (women) have facial hair that the patriarchy demands we remove. Many of us don't have high-pitched valley-girl voices and instead speak how we wish to speak (such as in a low pitch) so as to convey our own strength and uniqueness. Don't let others define you; you know who and what you are, just like me.

Lastly, even if you can't see it, I know history is overwhelmed by discrimination and bigotry against me, my family, and my racial and ethnic group that was and is inescapable. Since my family sought asylum in the 1940s in the US, I knew the country would be unaccepting of me and my family, as it always has and always will be. Despite my grandfather dying at Auschwitz in World War II, hatred will continue flowing towards us. I curse the day he fell from that guard tower.

The World as I See It

Walking down the street, interacting on social platforms, making purchases at stores — everywhere I go, I feel the inescapable sting of racism, homophobia, and transphobia. Even though no one says it, I know everyone is judging me above all others around me. I can see it in their eyes when they look at me. I see it when they ignore my presence, as if I'm not a person. I feel it when store clerks mockingly ask if I need any help (as if that's the real reason they walked over) or, conversely, ignore me, allowing me to flounder in the sea of commercial goods I'm incapable of sifting through. You may not see it because, of course, you can't. I can see it because only I know the true intentions of others' thoughts and actions towards myself. I am not a victim; I am the victim. Some of you may not believe the amount of victimization I have received every minute of every hour of every day, so I will grace you with my insight.

I will not discuss this again in person. After this, I'm done having to explain my victimization to everyone else. This book is meant to open your eyes so you can do the work. I have suffered enough (in fact, as I type, I'm suffering right now). Below are clear examples of this dystopian society I have found myself cursed with being brought into. While trying to provide my deep, well-thought-out insight to the world via social platforms, I was plagued with what I consider intolerable cruelty. People disagreed with my opinion. It wasn't even that they didn't like my opinion; they hated that it was coming from someone like me. Without knowing me, around the world, bigots were targeting me and my exceptionally intelligent ideas. Why else would they so cruelly mock and pick apart my well-reasoned notions? I knew they weren't attacking my well-grounded ideas; rather they were attacking me personally.

Rather than be a supportive ally, I was violently berated with words that cut as deep as any knife. While bringing the gift of my insight to the world, I was nearly killed by strangers clacking away at their keyboards, each one sounding to me like the nails being driven into my coffin. I know what your reaction to this will be: "Why not simply leave those forums that are causing you such misery?" My response? It would be the equivalent of asking a fish to leave the ocean, a wolf to leave their pack, a New Yorker to leave the city. These networks are my life, and they provide me meaning and focus. They are what allow me to spread my ideas far and wide to be discussed, celebrated, supported, and (most importantly) be viewed by all, so that others' lives may be made better. I don't do this for myself; I do it for the benefit of the world. While you may believe this a tad egotistical, I assure you it is not. Others can't have the insight I do, and thus only I am able to bring the gift that is my thoughts to the globe.

While sitting in an airport lounge (as a good environmentalist, I refuse to travel via private jet, so I fly commercial in the coach section with the rest of the proletariat), I struck up a conversation with a stranger. I felt safe, acknowledged, supported — and then it happened. Out of nowhere, like a sniper unseen, I'm hit with it: "Where are you from?" My heart started racing. I panicked, but there was nowhere to run and no law enforcement (whom I don't trust) around that I could turn to. Worse yet, I wasn't able to record this verbal assault because I wasn't anticipating such evil to attack when I felt safest.

"Where are you from?" They might as well have said, "Go back where you came from. You don't belong here. You're not one of us." This Californian (don't think I'm prejudiced and assumed this by the way they dressed, talked, and acted; I know because I asked) had wounded me to the core; and worse, I knew they enjoyed doing it. As the appropriate response, I held them accountable by shouting them down, ensuring everyone in the airport knew an intolerant bigot was amongst us. Sadly, it seems the entire airport was made up entirely of bigots, because no one outside of airport security did anything. Luckily, security safely escorted me away from danger. One more day, one more close call.

13

In another intolerable cruelty thrust upon me, society at large has made it impossible for me to thrive and survive. Everything from my Starbucks triple venti half-sweet non-fat Caramel Macchiato to my downtown artist's loft has skyrocketed in price to the point that I'm being forced to switch from my local cruelty-free, vegetarian, minority-owned co-op bodega to the corporate monsters at Whole Foods. There's barely anything left for my trip to the dispensary.

Additionally, despite the fact that I hold a self-accredited doctorate in post-colonial trans feminism as it relates to Critical Theory, the dystopian hellscape that is the American job market has no work compatible with my skills, salary, zip code, mental health days, and paid vacation requirements. For some odd reason, my credentials and background are not good enough for the slave drivers in corporate America I refuse to associate myself with. I know what I'm worth, regardless of whether others are willing to compensate me for my skills and accomplishments. Sadly, society will not pay me what I know I'm owed.

My Vision for the Future

Imagine a world in which we are all equal; where despite caste, upbringing, skin color, sex, effort, or imagination, we have all reached perfect equity. For those less informed, there exists a beacon of hope for this glorious utopia in the fictional work, Harrison Bergeron. In this short story, nobody is smarter, stronger, quicker, or better looking than anybody else. The 211th, 212th, and 213th amendments to the constitution ensure that the "Handicapper General" (government administrator) has the legislative tools needed to enforce equity for all. This individual is charged with ensuring perfect fairness amongst everybody.

In this narrative, those deemed too good looking are required to wear masks so they look no more beautiful or ugly than anyone else. Those who are strong have weights and shackles attached to them so they can only perform at a level equal to everyone else. Those smarter than average have earpieces installed, which occasionally blare into the wearer's head, preventing them from thinking in too coherent a manner. (Spoiler alert: It turns out the punishment for removing these handicapping devices is, rightfully, execution by the Handicapper General via shotgun).

Luckily, we have people at this moment doing all that they can to help us reach equity. Self-described Marxist lesbian Emily Drabinski, current (2023) head of the American Library Association, has toured countless libraries across the country to seek out the best techniques and practices in the United States. In one notable example, she found one was a "library of things" that even loaned out, for free, steam carpet cleaners to patrons. I cheered when I heard the capitalist pigs at the local supermarket wouldn't make a dime from this public service (although I was a bit taken aback when I heard the waitlist for the machine was forty people long).

If only all our needs could be taken care of in such an inexpensive and efficient manner.

The desire for equality, the product of a western-led White supremacist mindset, produces inequitable income and wealth. In order for us to reach social, racial, and sexual equity, we must discard such racist ideas as "equality of opportunity" and instead progress to the idea that some groups deserve more equality than others. In order to be anti-racist, we must atone for the mistakes of our racist ancestors (not mine; they were all victims) by elevating certain groups above others. Only then will we live in a country worth existing in.

Just imagine it: an equal number of men and women at every job — CEOs, pilots, soldiers, garbage men people, strippers, all with perfect parity. Imagine prisons where Asians, African Americans, Pacific Islanders, Hispanics, and, of course, Whites are all incarcerated in perfect proportion to their share of the population. Envision a world in which everyone is paid equally, regardless of hours worked, difficulty of job, or education required. We could leave behind racist and sexist tests, whose very purpose is to exclude women, minorities, 2LGBTQPIA+ members, and, of course, 2SLGBTQPIA+ women minorities like myself from schooling and jobs. My most hated of screenings is the Federal Aviation Administration's (FAA) pilot tests and check rides (that is, a test of your ability to fly an airplane), which clearly has, at its heart, a desire to exclude women and minorities from high-paying commercial pilot jobs, despite increasing pilot shortages.

Additionally, I envision a world where only those worthy of praise are held up for celebration, casting aside and tearing down monuments to hate, misogyny, colonization, slavery, and those who marginalize our most overlooked citizens. While visiting the monuments of our greatest cultural contributors in Hollywood, I came across the epitome of hate and racism. In 2007, Herr (it must be read in a German accent) Trump was awarded a star on the Walk of Fame for his misogynistic Ms. Universe competition and nausea-inducing show, The Apprentice, platformed, of course, by the corporate media, in this case NBC. After nearly vomiting with rage, I could at least take heart in knowing that the monument to a fascist had been defaced, destroyed, or marred by like-minded individuals countless times. Why such a monster would be allowed next to our most famous, and therefore most moral, individuals is beyond me. Anyone, dead or alive, who doesn't adhere to our enlightened worldview must be unpersoned, removed from pedestals, and branded for what they are, lest their hatred spread.

(For some odd reason, when I asked why his star remained, the rationale was described as a "domino theory" — if one star is removed, they might as well just remove them all.)

Last and most importantly, in my vision of the future, there are no prisons or jails because there won't be a need. Once equity is reached, no one will have any reason to commit crimes, and the prison-industrial complex will collapse, with a few exceptions for reacclimating counterrevolutionaries to the New Order. Honestly, if I could, I would free all the criminals currently incarcerated in the American Gulag back into their communities with their friends, families, and neighbors who miss them dearly and would welcome their return with open arms (actual arms, not firearms).

You see, it's a known fact that those caught committing crimes are no better or worse than you; they just happened to get caught. Those sitting in jail for drug dealing, theft, murder, rape, and pedophilia (among other crimes) are only there because of a racist and bigoted system that incarcerates marginalized groups because it hates them. Even if those currently incarcerated committed crimes at a higher rate than their currently free comrades, it's only due to the poor socio-economic environment they grew up in. We should pity them, not punish them.

#Freethemall (at first, I felt I needed to explain it's "free them all" not "free the mall," but it works as a call for both liberation and a communist people's rallying cry, and I approve.)

To the extent reacclimatization is needed, I believe I've identified an archipelago in the Aleutian Islands where counterrevolutionaries can be reeducated and reformed before being brought back into this new utopia. Through labor and cultural education, these reformed American comrades will be dissuaded of their former bourgeois (read: middle class) immoral lives (the words "or die trying" come to mind).

I hope you agree with my bold, unique, and novel (that is, new) vision for the future. If not, don't worry; we'll have plenty of mental health professionals and armed diversity counselors on hand to ensure your mind has been made right. Where others have failed, we'll finally have the ideas, leaders, and societal drive to create a people's utopia.

For doubters, understand you can't make an omelet without forcefully relocating a few chickens. See you on the other side.

"Dark Humor is like food. Not everyone gets it."
— Joseph Stalin, 1837

Chapter 2 Males and Females Work Differently

Why Are Men and Women Different? It isn't just upbringing. New studies show they are born that way.

— ~~The Onion, April 1, 2022~~ Time Magazine cover, January 20, 1992

In 2010, NBC published a story concerning obesity rates of gay and lesbian Massachusetts residents versus their heterosexual counterparts. Surveying more than 67,000 people between eighteen and sixty-four, the study had two interesting findings: In that year (undoubtedly, it's gotten worse for everybody since), the obesity rate for gay men was 14%, versus 21% for straight men. Much more concerning for me, the obesity rate among lesbians was 26%, versus 17% for straight women. That begs the question: why such a large gap? But the answer is obvious and needs no focus groups, polls, or insight from health experts or psychologists. You already know the answer, and if you don't, it will take but a moment of thought to figure out why. For those who can't guess, I'll enlighten you. All others, please skip the next paragraph so I can get right to the heart of this chapter.

*In 2010, "men" was synonymous with "males" and "women" was synonymous with "females." I listed their gender instead of their sex because that is how the NBC story reported it. For the purpose of this paragraph only, assume the 2010 standards of language

Males are attracted more by visual cues. Anyone with two eyes can tell any time the camera cues on the cheerleaders during an NFL game, or when some poor soul looks the wrong way at the beach while walking with his significant other. One of the most popular memes on the internet, "Distracted Boyfriend," perfectly demonstrates this. Because males react more strongly to visual cues, they are attracted to things that are perceived as attractive, which in our time generally means being in good shape (by which I mean thin, and add muscular for males). In order to attract partners, gay males must be what other males want: someone with a good body. Thus, more gym visits and less McDonald's to meet this standard result in a lower-than-average obesity rate.

Females seeking males find themselves in the same boat as gay males. In order to attract partners (or more desired partners), it is rightly assumed they'll have a better chance if they're in good shape. This explains why straight females have a lower obesity rate than their lesbian counterparts. While lesbian females are still drawn by visual cues, it's not nearly the priority that it is for most males. Thus, since looks aren't as strong a force driving attraction, and females weigh attributes like personality more heavily than males, the need to be in better shape isn't as strong. Since having a "good body" requires effort, time, and sacrifice, if it's less necessary for attracting partners, it may fall off the priority list. This isn't meant to be criticism; if people (myself included) didn't think it was necessary to be in good shape to attract partners, fewer people would exercise and diet, at least not as much as they currently do. This is not to say that lesbians don't care about appearance or that all gay males care about is looks; it's a relative comparison between the two sexes.

This leads directly to the point I'm trying to make. Male and female minds, personalities, drives, and ways of solving problems work differently. That's not to say a randomly picked male and randomly picked female couldn't have the same desire for career advancement, for example. It means, regarding the population as a whole, that what drives the two sexes is different. Males and females (again, generally) look at the same problem and solve it in two different ways. Not all problems, of course, but many. The "pull over and ask for directions," although a tad dated with smartphones, is the cliché example of how the two sexes solve the same problem differently. These differences were honed over countless generations by evolutionary forces whose goal is to have the best chance of passing down genes.

Imagine a simple scenario: You are in charge of an ancient tribe of equal males and females. Who do you send on dangerous hunts or to combat nearby hostile tribes (and by hostile, we also mean they could just have some cool stuff we want)? You could send all males, all females, or a mixed force. Even assuming the sexes in this scenario are equal in strength (which they're not), it makes no sense to the future population of your tribe to send any females. Larger populations have more youth to take care of the old, fight enemies, and complete more complex tasks than smaller populations. This is true even today. If you have a population of ten, the spear maker could be the same person as the doctor. If you have a population of 330 million, there are specific people who can spend decades in school and training before opening your brain for surgery. Larger populations overall in human history have been a competitive strength, and you only achieve that by protecting those that bear the population.

Males, in the reproductive sense, are expendable. You could have a tribe of one male and a hundred females, and your tribe will thrive into the future (perhaps with a few genetic defects, but hey, we're just speeding up evolution). If you have a tribe with one female and a hundred males, that tribe is ultimately doomed. Its whole future relies on one female, at a time when death in childbirth, an accident, or disease is a very real threat. If that hostile tribe (or now-hostile, since you tried to take their stuff) can outbreed you, it doesn't matter how fertile that one female is; she can still only have one child per year (don't worry, I googled it). With males performing the dangerous tasks, females were kept back to care for children (or at least to not damage their important reproductive organs).

Again, put yourself back in time thousands and thousands of years. Whether consciously or subconsciously, if you were charged with staying back and taking care of the home and children (whether fair or unfair), who would you want to partner with to pass on your genes? The male with the most chiseled chin or the one who brought home the most bacon and could keep you safe? What gives you and your offspring the best chance of survival? This is a generality, and of course, we have chosen (and do choose) partners on more than just this simple quality. But these are strong, overriding desires that put other conscious and subconscious wishes second. Bottom line: females value security (to be understood as wealth, status, and/or strength of the male) over looks.

I'm not saying anything you can't look around and see yourself. Some females go towards males with awful personalities but visible physical strength. Girls in their twenties will pair up with older, dad-bod-shaped males whose main quality is being wealthy. You only need to Google wealthy (or strong) males, and you will typically find them with females well out of their league looks-wise. For those wealthy males who have partners at or below their own physical attractiveness, I question the fidelity of such relationships, as everyone does (or should).

Males, their physical attractiveness not nearly as important to the opposite sex, generally do not go through the time-consuming process of applying makeup, painting their nails, shaving their arms and legs, or other activities that improve their appearance to the same extent females do. Females could choose not to engage in these activities, but they (or their subconscious) know this will harm their goal of either finding or keeping a male partner. Males can apply more time, effort, and money to their looks, but a part of males knows that the real way to attract and keep more desirable partners is with social status, wealth, and physical strength.

Think back to high school and picture who the most attractive girls tended to date. Football stars, basketball players, water polo competitors, and the like. Why? Because they looked (and usually were) the strongest. In an evolutionary historical sense, this provided the best chance for personal security for the female, protection against other males, and genes for physical strength that would be passed down to any offspring, thus continuing the lineage. Even if you are female and don't believe this applies to you, understand two things: (1) This is one factor among others, and (2) this occurs on a subconscious level.

Growing up, I couldn't tell you why I was attracted to who I was; I simply was. Hidden in the background of our mind is another part of us that gets a vote and influences you in ways you don't see without significant introspection and maturity. Countless fortunes have been spent in psychologists' offices so people can understand their subconscious desires and actions when they come into conflict with their conscious ones.

Males have a different problem set to consider. The same goal exists: to pass along genes, but without material wealth and status (social status also aids in passing along genes—ask Nick Cannon), how do you choose a partner? Simply, males pick the one most physically appealing (what is considered physically appealing can and has changed over time), as that partner will pass along what he has perceived as good genes down to their offspring. Again, this is not the only consideration. There's a reason Tinder, a dating app, provides space for females to put interests, political affiliation, vaccination status, and astrology signs in the details below the profile picture. And in nearly all cases, this will be the very last thing any male reads through, if they read through it at all. It's like the French section of assembly instructions; they're there, but almost no male is going to read them (if males read the instructions at all... The analogy actually works better than I first thought).

A "sugar daddy" is a male females partner with for some type of material gain. It could be gifts, a place to stay, or in its most extreme form, straight-up cash (the world's oldest profession). In nearly every case, the male is older, wealthier, and less attractive than the female. Every person reading this knows of people like this, either public figures or people within their own sphere. There are almost no corresponding female equivalents to a sugar daddy. The reverse, a "sugar mama," is so rare, I've never seen or heard of it, or it is on such a low magnitude compared to the reverse it's comical to even consider. Can you imagine a good-looking young male in his prime partnering with an older, wealthier, less attractive female? I'm sure it happens, and when it does, it must turn heads, as the sight is truly a rarity, like seeing a straight male in fashionable clothing for no other reason than to feel pretty.

Apologies if you happen to be an older female searching for young male partners, but professionals may be the only practical answer to your search.

Consider a more common sight: strip clubs. I don't even have to put a qualifier in front of it like "male" strip club or "female" strip club because it is assumed that if one exists, there are probably scantily clad (or non-clad) female performers and an almost exclusively male clientele. A quick search of my area turned up two clubs with male performers and about fifteen with female ones.

What is made clear here is that, even with a population split approximately evenly between males and females, males frequent these establishments more. One who believes that males and females are the same may believe that some type of systemic sexism exists that leads to more female strip clubs than male, but the answer is simpler. Females desiring to see the male form have greater free access to it than males do for females. Males wanting to see unclad females in person must either court someone or pay professionals. Most females can simply ask the question and will be whisked away to a more intimate spot to see the male form without even stopping by an ATM.

Why Males Do What They Do

There's good reason males instinctively choose physically harder, more demanding (and higher paying) jobs. The US Bureau of Labor Statistics puts out annual reports that consistently show males work more hours per week at jobs that pay more. Why do they pay more? Some are in locations people would not choose to spend time if not for extra pay (think oil rig workers or on the road as long-haul truck drivers), and others are in environmental conditions one would not choose, all things being equal (think construction in the heat of summer and cold of winter). These jobs require higher pay because they could not attract workers otherwise. Why spend months at sea in dangerous conditions if it paid the same as being a cashier at the local supermarket?

But here is the big question… Why do males want jobs that make more money? One of the truths of our time is that males generally select jobs that are less satisfying but higher paying, while females select jobs that are more fulfilling but lower paying (if they choose to enter the job market at all). I will not go into detail or provide examples of this because you know this is accurate. I will, however, explain why this is the case. Males believe they can get what they truly want with higher paying jobs, while females believe they can get what they truly want doing the opposite.

So what do males want above all else? Females. And what do females want above all else? Security for themselves and their (potential) offspring, which in earlier times (and I would argue presently) was provided nearly exclusively by males. We were developed, from birth, to execute well-designed roles evolution (or the Creator, for those faithful) has selected for generating the best odds of successfully passing down genes. Imagine if sex was less desired by males and was simply done whenever it was decided "we" needed a larger population. It is no exaggeration that the whole of human existence would come crashing down around us.

Without needing or wanting more attractive mates or to release sexual tension, males' desire to compete with one another would be destroyed (or at least severely hampered), as the only reasons to excel would be for material gain or social prestige. My guess: males would be content, once they had reached relative comfort, to do nothing but take part in easy activities such as TV, video games, drinking, and using illicit drugs. The question (if you could call it that) would then be who would perform the less desirable tasks currently done by males...

Females are a civilizing force for males, and anyone who's seen a bachelor's home or apartment knows this. A male's general ambition, whether he realizes it or not, is driven by the desire to impress and attract the opposite sex. Sadly for males, attractiveness alone doesn't have the same pull it does for females, and thus they must find other means. The evolutionary path that led to modern humans today, via trial and error, carved traits and characteristics into the bodies and minds of males and females, the genes for which were more likely to be passed on to the next generation.

What does this have to do with our current day? The manifested mental and physical differences are comically obvious, such as males typically being stronger than females (if you doubt that, know that there aren't any rules barring females from the NFL, NBA, or MLB) and females typically being more selective when choosing a mate, as they must have established trust with the male over long periods of time to continue providing resources and (hopefully) help raise any offspring produced. Understanding that males and females are different helps explain much of what today is called sexism. Of course, sexism exists, and to the extent we can eradicate it, we should. But significant portions of what we call sexism are simply the result of evolutionary forces.

Take, for example, the "gender pay gap," which I will refer to as the sex pay gap for simplicity. According to Wikipedia and the references they cite (I don't have all day to go through that...), the current average pay females receive in a year is 79% of what males make. For activists believing females aren't treated fairly, the implication is that an average female makes 79% of males at the same job working the same number of hours. This is demonstrably false, and anyone saying this is either ignorant of reality, lying to you, or both. Males and females make different choices about the jobs they wish to participate in and the amount of time they wish to dedicate to that job. If a female with a child only wishes to work twenty-five hours per week at a job near a daycare, how can it be said that discrimination is involved when we compare her wages to a male's working sixty hours per week at whatever location pays the largest amount? As noted earlier, males and females want different things and thus make different choices. Those choices have an impact on what careers each sex seeks and, ultimately, the amount of income earned.

There is nothing stopping a male from taking a job in a more fulfilling career that helps people in deeper ways any more than there's something stopping females from taking lucrative jobs whose ultimate goal is the generation of larger amounts of wealth. The dynamic of males wanting attractive females and females desiring security has a very modern and well-understood consequence. Because males place so much value on looks, any criticism of female looks isn't just attacking their skin-level beauty; you're attacking their ability to attract more desirable male partners who can provide security and material comfort. In essence, you're attacking their ability to have what they perceive will be a happier, more secure life for themselves and their offspring.

A male's ability to provide income and protection is only marginally affected by his looks. Attacking, for example, a wealthy male's looks will result in very little personal insult, as this is actually only a skin-deep issue. It will affect his ability to attract females, but not nearly as much as other factors such as those already noted previously. Think back to any body-positivity conversation. Nearly all only involve females. Almost no one is promoting male body positivity by having body wash commercials with overweight males, fashion shows featuring plus-size males, or op-eds by morbidly obese males urging society to be more accepting of all male bodies. Even attacking a male's genital size is fair game publicly in ways that, if done to a female, would be grounds for banishment (aka "cancelling").

I'm not saying any of this is fair, as it is obviously a detriment to poorer, weaker males and physically less attractive females. Unfortunately, we must work with the cards we're dealt and not complain that society should change a game that it can't, even if it wants to. Try convincing females to look beyond a male's employment or males to completely ignore looks. You can pretend and wish it weren't so, but you're fooling yourself.

As a personal example of how males and females think differently, I was talking with a female about her experience in bars. I was naturally jealous that she could walk into any bar and instantly get the attention of anyone there she desired. Her response: "Well, of course, but how many of them will be there the next morning, having gotten what they wanted?" I hadn't thought about it from that point of view and hadn't realized the challenge she faced was different from mine. I hadn't realized our drives were different.

If you told an average young male he could walk into any bar on any night and walk out with somebody different each night without issue, he would probably wish this above all else. The questionable longevity of such relationships would fall secondary to the desires of the moment and would generally be accepted as the cost. For most females, a plethora of partners, each of whom leaves them in short order, would be a living hell (even if there was a readily accessible replacement nearby).

Why do we try to live in the fiction that males and females are the same, with the exception of our various surface-level, physical differences? Because it is thought that by acknowledging that the sexes are inherently different, we would return to an era in which females were treated as subordinate and/or unequal to males. Believing males and females think and operate the same also helps the idea that unequal outcomes between the sexes in income, wealth, and career advancement are due solely to discrimination on the basis of sex.

If, however, males and females do think and operate differently by their very nature, as is true, free of socially constructed roles, then most of that inequality is due to different choices males and females make. In one scenario, unequal outcomes are due to societally imposed norms, while in the other, outcomes are due to our very nature. Only you can determine which influence is greater, but there are objectively correct and incorrect answers, whether you want that answer or not.

Is there sexism in the twenty-first century? Of course, there is (and it goes both ways). Advancements in equality between the sexes are a very recent improvement in terms of human history. It is within one human lifetime that females gained the right to vote, became legally equal to males, and became able to enter the workforce in more similar proportions. That last statement is specifically about the US, as, according to the US Department of Labor, the male labor participation rate is approximately 68% compared to ~57% for females. According to the World Bank, globally, approximately 80% of men and 50% of women are part of the labor force.

But as barriers have fallen, our natures have become more revealed. For example, imagine if there were historical laws barring males from wearing lipstick. An assumption would be that, once this law was removed, males would wear lipstick in the same proportion as females. But if that didn't happen, there would need to be explanations. Two explanations would exist: males are still being pressured to not wear lipstick (society's fault), or males don't want to wear lipstick (somehow it's in males' nature). You may desire for males to wear lipstick in the same proportion as females, but there are natural, ingrained reasons why this isn't the case (primarily, most males don't believe they'll get what they desire by wearing lipstick).

In the same way, you may want females to desire career advancement over all other life wishes in the same proportion as males, but our desires don't work the same way. You may wish males cared about their looks and presentation to the world to the same degree that females do (trust me, that feeling fades fast), but by the male nature, this isn't the case.

In a recent World War II documentary, military historian and former US Air Force intelligence officer Reina Pennington brilliantly describes events that occurred during the Battle of Stalingrad on the Eastern Front between Germany and the Soviet Union. She takes time to highlight the contributions women made in combat operations both as pilots and front-line soldiers. She noted that many of the female Soviet snipers were good at their job because "what it took to be a good sniper is precision and patience, and women tended to be very good at that." That last part concerning patience got me thinking; in a situation involving potentially waiting for hours to shoot, which sex would wait longer, males or females? No matter what answer you believe makes more sense, I highly doubt you believe both sexes would wait an equal amount of time.

While watching the gameshow Jeopardy! (this may come as no surprise, but I get more joy rooting against someone than for someone), I noticed males almost always wagered larger amounts after getting a "daily double" (an opportunity to bet as much of their money as they want on a single question) or during "final jeopardy" (the same concept, except at the end everyone gets the same question and can wager on it). While visiting casinos with female friends, I've noticed females tend to not like gambling as much, or do not like gambling the same amounts males do. After having forgotten to change the sports channel, you may find yourself with a poker tournament on, and you'll notice nearly all the people playing are male.

The reason for this is twofold: (1) Males tend to take greater risks in hopes of getting a larger reward, and (2) females tend to value money in hand more than potential money won in a game of chance.

In my youth, I always saw stacks of scratched-off lottery tickets in my grandparents' house, since my grandmother enjoyed purchasing them for the potential win. There is no contradiction here between my experience and my belief because my belief is based on observations of a group versus an anecdote that applies to one person.

While you may believe much of this work is based almost entirely on anecdotes, know that it's easy to debunk: simply seek out those facts. In 2017, the now-famous USA *Women's National Soccer (or football if you unfortunately prefer) team scrimmaged against the high school-aged FC (football club...) Dallas Under-15s boys academy team. The result was the national team lost 5–2. One could make the argument, with more important games coming up, that the national team either weren't putting in their all or perhaps were simply allowing the teenage boys to win. The scientific thing to do would be to continuously recreate this experiment to see if we get consistent results, and then search for answers as to why these results occurred.

*My research into the women's team did not turn up any transgender women, so it is probably more accurate to say "female team" for the purpose of what I'm trying to show. They are also more well-known as the "women's national soccer team" rather than the "females national soccer team," hence my choice of words.

But the reason for this result is obvious. Males are stronger and faster, on average, than females. It is provable simply by looking at the times of the fastest runners, swimmers, and total weight lifted by weightlifters. There is no reason the most competitive females couldn't compete against the most competitive males in these fields, unless it is true that males are stronger than females. To believe otherwise is to believe our strongest, most athletic, and most competitive females (all of whom could easily best me in any contest of physical strength and agility, except potentially twelve-ounce curls) are only that way because they are not trying as hard as the boys.

This also explains why there is a larger problem with physically abusive males than physically abusive females in domestic abuse cases. While I have seen limited research that shows the quantity of physical abuse may be comparable between the sexes, the "quality" of abuse is most definitely one-sided. Because males, on average, are stronger, there is a much larger likelihood of severe injury or death in domestic disputes with females as the victim and males as the aggressors than the reverse. Believe otherwise as you like, but until we have some sort of reality TV-style MMA bouts between random couples that demonstrate otherwise, you know this to be correct.

No Means…

In 2017, billionaire CEO Warren Buffet (born August 30, 1930) was being interviewed on CNBC. The complete interview can still be found, but the exact clip of the quote further in this paragraph is suspiciously difficult to find. During the interview, a few synapses in his brain connected the conversation with an "old story," as he described it, prompting him to say that "if a diplomat says yes, he means maybe. If he says maybe, he means no. And if he says no, he's no diplomat." The conversation itself concerned ongoing negotiations over business deals. Had he stopped there, he would have probably been praised for his wit and intelligence; unfortunately, he decided to continue with his female interviewer. "And if a lady says no, she means maybe. And if she says maybe, she means yes. And if she says yes, she's no lady."

For those who may be slightly confused, he was likely not talking about a transgender woman but was referring to the fact that a stop by the ATM would probably be necessary. I had first come in contact with the US military's sexual assault prevention programs while still in college around 2008. I and hundreds of other male cadets between our sophomore and junior year of college were in training. We sat in a large auditorium because we were told to, and asked absolutely zero questions about what was going on (this also gave us a break from being yelled at or marching in circles to test our competency and obedience). As it turns out, these were presentations from various military and government departments to provide us with an assortment of knowledge our government wanted us to know. Some talked about how to report mistreatment; others simply welcomed us. One in particular was… unnecessarily hostile.

A woman got up on stage and chastised the male audience for the sin of being males. This was a member of the base's sexual assault prevention program, and that was made painfully clear. As memory serves, we were all but accused of raping and harassing females and told we needed to be diverted from our misogynistic ways. How did she know we were on the verge of these deplorable activities? Because we were young males. Every year I was in the military, we had annual sessions in which we were segregated from our female coworkers, sat down, usually in a small auditorium, and told what was acceptable and unacceptable behavior concerning how to treat females. This was in the "don't ask, don't tell" era, so the assumption was we were all straight and therefore dangerous.

For years, I had heard "no means no" and took it to heart as a cornerstone of my belief system. If pondered, it made sense; if the person you're pursuing ever turns you down for coffee, a meal, a drink, or other activities males and females engage in, if they ever say no, that is the end of it. Attempting to "not take no for an answer," say, by asking a female out a second time, amounted to unacceptable harassment. In a much more serious case, if a request for intimacy results in a no, that is the final word, and no other acceptable action can be taken except to give up and move on. Why, after all, would the person you're pursuing ever say no if there was mutual attraction?

It made sense to me that being turned down meant there was, in fact, no chance that would be consensual. Years later, a very confused coworker of mine imparted a story about events that took place the previous weekend. My friend had met a nice woman, took her on dates, and eventually invited her up to his place. As the night wore on, my friend wanted to become intimate with the female and so asked if that would be okay. Her response was no, at which point my friend gave up, having had exactly the same training I had concerning acceptable activity. Twenty seconds later, she began removing articles of clothing and, contrary to what she stated, indicated physically that no doesn't necessarily mean no.

After this, I had myriad discussions with females who found themselves in strangely similar circumstances but on the other side. They had met males they were interested in but played hard to get; they rejected the initial advance, desiring either a stronger advance or to seem more desirable by being unattainable temporarily. These same female friends then expressed disappointment that some of the males they turned down did not try again, after the females gave no overt indication whatsoever they were actually interested. I'm sure exceptions exist, but I have never met or heard of any heterosexual male playing hard to get.

Imagine a male, after having been asked out by someone he was strongly attracted to, turning them down to seem more desirable or because he wants the female to try harder. As I've seen and heard from those around me, if a male turns someone down, it is very likely because they are not attracted enough to them. If a female does the same, there is a chance they are, in fact, attracted to their male counterpart, and this is simply part of the game that must be played in order to arrive at a desired outcome. To quote the animated television show, Rick and Morty, "If it's too easy to get there, we'll never get there."

*I admit there is a version of this game that males play. They will delay overtly making a move to make the female believe they are not a typical male. Females are saturated with overt courtship, and any male not doing this sticks out, differentiating them from everyone else

**Late in my career, the sexual assault prevention courses vastly improved. By the end, I was actually amazed I wasn't called a potential rapist while at the same time maintaining the important parts of the training, including what not to do and how to intervene in situations likely to result in immoral or illegal activity. I personally would love it if we were all more open about what we're thinking, but that doesn't seem to be in our nature.

Males tend to be more straightforward about their desires, which aren't that big of a mystery anyway, and are often baffled at the mixed signals they receive from those they are courting. A quick internet search turns up hundreds of memes of females sending signals of interest that fly over males' heads. The reason for this is males are expecting what males would do in the same situation: be overt and with clear intentions such as "Would you like to come back to my place to become intimate?" instead of subtle hints such as "Would you like to see my new tattoo?" which just so happens to be bordered by rather intimate areas.

To further the main point, there is a very frowned-upon activity within courtship between the sexes, but it only goes one way. Unsolicited pictures of straight males' genitals sent to the person they are courting are usually wholly unwelcome and have a high chance of landing the offender in legal or HR trouble. Unsolicited pictures of a straight (I take that back — the sexual orientation of the sender in this case makes absolutely no difference) female's intimate areas are almost universally approved of and welcomed by the male sex, so long as it doesn't generate an issue with the male's potential current significant other. An entire book could be written about this double standard but isn't needed. Immature males do this primarily because they believe females want to see males' bodies (and particular parts) in the same way that males want to see females' bodies. After all, if males and females are the same except for the coin flip of being born into a different sex, there's no reason females wouldn't want to see the same thing that males would like to see from their potential partner. Of course, this isn't the case.

So far, I've only come across one group of people strongly desiring pictures of male genitalia to be sent to them.

While attending a meeting when I was in the military, about twenty of us were gathered around a table. To my great joy, the meeting was coming to an end, and all that was needed was for the individual leading the meeting to call a close to it. She asked if anyone had any further comments or questions, looked around the room, saw no one had anything more to add, and ended the meeting by saying, "All right, silence is consent," thus ending our gathering.

For those not understanding the issue with this statement or outlook, I hope you have a good lawyer on retainer.

Upon hearing this, my eyes went wide and I looked around to see if anyone else had caught this controversial joke (which I found hilarious), but no one even paused to consider what had been uttered. No one thought it odd because it was coming from a female, and thus not truly threatening to anybody. Had I said the same thing, I would have instantly gone onto a list of those whose minds needed to be made right, lest I corrupt others with my politically incorrect jokes. I wish I were kidding, but saying far milder jokes has landed me in at least one coworker's sights, as I had expressed "problematic" views that were not in line with hers.

The double standard existed because my coworkers knew males and females work differently and that the same thing said by the two different groups carried different levels of intent and concern.

Chapter End Notes

You already knew everything written above to be correct and probably knew it years or even decades before this book was published. For critics, if there is criticism, it is likely that so much of this relies on prohibited stereotypes those same critics don't want to be true but are. It's easier to believe in the fiction that the sexes are the same because it saves us having to ask very difficult questions many of us don't want the real answers to.

All that being said, males and females should be treated equally under the law, and we should shame sexist actions against both males and females. But being sexist is not the same thing as understanding that males and females are different and distinct. To believe otherwise is to ignore a very obvious reality and replace it with a falsehood more comforting to you. You are, of course, free to believe whatever you like, but you will only be handicapping yourself and will continue to be baffled by the actions males or females take. You may even start asking yourself why Leonardo DiCaprio doesn't date someone his own age or why those females around him don't do the same.

Men marry women with the hope they will never change. Women marry men with the hope they will change. Invariably, they are both disappointed. — Albert Einstein

2024 Translation

[Cis-gender heteronormative males] marry [cis-gender heteronormative females] with the hope they will never change. [Cis-gender

heteronormative females] marry [cis-gender heteronormative males] with the hope they will change. Invariably, they* are both disappointed.

*"They" is not an additional individual with a dissociative identity disorder (split personality), but the earlier mentioned individuals.
— Albert Einstein he/him

Chapter 3 Nearly All Crime Is Born of Want, Not Need

Outside of the killings, Washington has one of the lowest crime rates
in the country.
— Marion Barry, Mayor of the District of Columbia, 1979-1991,
1995-1999

While on the way to a liquor store in my home city, I missed an exit
ramp on the highway. In truth, I was probably distracted by a car with
thirty-two bumper stickers and only got to the ones reading "coexist," a
fish with legs (?), followed by a flag with a very strange mixture of
circles, umbrellas, triangles, and stripes I couldn't quite comprehend. So
enthralled was I by the collection of colorful, fading stickers that I missed
my exit and now had to find the next nearest liquor store. Without
question, I hopped off the next exit, diligently following Google Maps,
which had apparently led me to an economically downtrodden part of
town. Familiar with poorer parts of town, I was largely unconcerned
about the bars on the windows and odd characters lingering at
intersections. It wasn't until I stepped into the liquor store that I realized
how bad a neighborhood I was in. I had heard stories of this or that part of
town being bad but had never really experienced it in person. I believe
something in the psyche keeps males less concerned about the threat of
physical violence, primarily because historically they have been able to
meet violence with violence. While there were/are females who can do
the same, it is not on the same evolutionary and historical level. As such,
my nature prevented me from understanding the environment I had driven
myself to.

I was unable to pick up the bottles I wanted to purchase. Every item
except some non-alcoholic mixers was behind the cash register, which
was itself behind what I believed to be reinforced glass, with holes in it
just big enough for bottles and money or credit cards to fit through. I then
realized that the store owners themselves trusted their own customers so
little they would not even let them pick up the merchandise before paying

for it. I then grasped that if the store didn't trust its customers in the neighborhood, it would be wise for me to pay more attention to my property and personal safety in the area. I have never since returned to that part of town.

Of all the stores with all the variety of merchandise, why is a liquor store so concerned about theft? If poverty is about a lack of needs, such as food, shelter, and clothing, why have I never seen a store selling those items under lock and key? I've certainly seen stores that put some products behind glass and others that put theft-resistant tags (think ink) on fashionable clothing, but I've never seen a store where I couldn't pick up the clothes or pick out my groceries before purchasing them. Even jewelry, watch, and luxury sunglasses stores will largely allow you to meander through the shop, with dangerously little reinforced glass protecting the workers.

The store was as fortified as it was because that's the type of store more prone to theft in the neighborhood I was in. The truth about theft from liquor stores and of beer from gas stations, in general, is that the theft is not about need. It's a very basic, well-understood desire to get products that make us feel good without having to pay anything in return. Most of us resist this urge, as it's far easier and safer to work and pay for the items than it is to risk punishment for not paying. Even if we couldn't pay, the vast majority of us would do without rather than risk jail or fines. If there are some very open-minded individuals that consider alcohol a need on the same level as food, I would argue that the presence of a vast variety of diverse cheerleaders and supermodels in close proximity is a need someone should be providing me for my well-being.

In August of 2023, a woman by the name of Ta'Kiya Young was shot to death by police officers outside a store in an Ohio suburb. Police just happened to be in the area when someone there flagged them down over an individual still in the parking lot who had stolen from the store. Officers stated that as they approached the car of the suspect, the woman put it into gear and accelerated into one of the officers standing in front of the car. The officer she was driving towards fired a single shot, after which the car traveled a short distance before coming to a stop.

Ms. Young was twenty-one years old, six months pregnant, and left behind two sons, ages three and six. According to police, she was a member of the group responsible for the thefts that initiated the calls to the police. The items stolen? Bottles of liquor. Initial reports from national media, including USA Today, the Associated Press, and NBC focused on the fact police had killed a twenty-one-year-old pregnant woman for theft. Friends of Ms. Young described her as "the life of the party," according to local news outlets. Left out of every headline was that the woman had (allegedly) attempted to run over a first responder while stealing liquor from a neighborhood supermarket.

Absent from any commentary addressing the events was why a twenty-one-year-old with two young children and in her third trimester of pregnancy felt she needed to steal alcohol and then flee the scene — in a manner requiring her to accelerate a two-ton vehicle at a law enforcement officer. I find it silly that I have to do this, but we must understand what the difference is between a want and a need.

A need, as far as I have found definitions for, is a requirement or something essential. From my schooling, I was taught a need is something like food, water, and shelter; that if you do not get it, you will die. A want is something you would like to have but is not a requirement or essential. While a yacht provides shelter, caviar provides food, and Fiji Water provides (duh) water, they are not, in fact, needs, as there are more reasonable (and much cheaper) alternatives that would allow you to continue living. Ms. Young didn't need alcohol, and neither did her unborn offspring, may they rest in peace.

I ask you a simple question. Wherever you are in the United States (those from other places may not understand this line of questioning), look around you. Do you see emaciated — abnormally thin or weak, especially because of illness or a lack of food — people wandering the streets in your city or town? Unless you're near a hospital, drug treatment center, or vegan restaurant, the answer is probably no. For all the talk of taking care of the needs of the homeless and impoverished, in the United States, odds are they are, in fact, clothed and generally have a healthy appearance (minus the consequences of drug and alcohol abuse), if not a tad overweight (a 2012 study by the National Library of Medicine states obesity rates between the homeless and non-homeless were approximately equal). I don't say this to attack the homeless and impoverished. I say this because it is the truth and to reinforce the point I'm trying to make in this chapter.

If you have seen any homeless (or "unhoused," although this term is highly misleading) emaciated individuals, I've found fifty-pound bags of rice for $21.98. With every pound of rice containing approximately 1,648 calories, this means you have 82,400 calories per fifty-pound bag of rice. This is enough to feed a person about forty-one days (at 2,000 calories each day, per United States Food and Drug Administration recommendations) at the cost of 18 cents per meal. If you're concerned about Americans starving to death or going hungry, I recommend buying the bag, boiling the rice, and serving it to every emaciated person you see. If your response is that people need more than rice, feel free to not provide any rice to any emaciated people around you and allow them to assume room temperature. My guess: the cooked rice will go bad before you find enough emaciated people who want to consume it (although, for appearance, they may take it).

Why bring up the staggeringly low cost of rice? Because it exemplifies that the bare essentials of life are (in historical terms) inexpensive. We are what make "necessities" expensive. We desire housing in trendy areas or those that many others want. We want food that is both tasty and requires as little effort as possible, such as highly processed snacks, fast food, or meals served at restaurants prepared by cooks and delivered to us at our convenience while we sit, converse, and drink. We don't just want clothing; we want clothing that others will comment on or respect rather than simply what is cheapest and most practical. We pretend the costs of existing are high when, in fact, they can be low, but at a price.

While many complain, they don't want the solution because they know what the solution means: living where they do not want, perhaps in unfashionable areas, in a state they feel is beneath them. It is within the human condition to complain, no matter how well we have it. We have been trained not to question these complaints from others, lest our own complaints, in turn, be questioned and found wanting.

But more on my city: I have a gas station and a drug store approximately 100 yards from my home. Quite recently, before winter hit, there was a young male, twenty-five or so, sitting and shivering outside the drug store where I was going to pick up some adult beverages. Feeling altruistic (because I'm great), I told the youth if he followed me back, I would give him a coat (since, as any pragmatist would agree, winter is coming). He followed, took the coat, and I felt great, believing that as I drove and walked around my neighborhood I would occasionally see the youth wearing the coat I had provided and would feel good about my giving, altruistic nature. Oddly, when I saw him two days later, he lacked the coat. Three days later, he rang my doorbell to ask if I had another one he could have. The reason I gave him the second one was the same reason I gave him the first. I had something I didn't want and thought it could help someone else. Sadly, as with the first jacket, the second was not worn by the individual. If you must know where these coats went, visit your local pawn shop. You might find a coat owned and worn by yours truly.

Why include a story in a chapter regarding crime with a narrative that doesn't involve crime? Because the themes are the same — society wanting to feel good for the actions it takes, people taking advantage of others' emotions and pity, and lastly (and most importantly) a failure to recognize that we are tolerating deviant behavior and ultimately enabling it. My "neighbor" was selling my coats (which I didn't want), likely for drugs. For the next six months (and throughout the winter), he continued ringing my doorbell (with no coat) asking for more coats, not because he was cold, but because he needed something to trade for more drugs. After coat number two, I realized I was only fueling a drug habit, not making this individual's life any better.

I don't believe this individual wanted for food, shelter, or clothing. Even today, I frequently see him walking the streets in normal men's attire, rags, women's clothing, or whatever he(?) preferred that day. By my count, there are no less than four homeless shelters within one mile of where I sit at this moment. This individual lives as he(?) wishes and certainly doesn't seem concerned about his(?) welfare. I believe he knows where to find food, money, and clothing enough to sustain himself. He presents a good case study of where criminality starts, and one we can all understand — a desire to get what we want with as little effort as possible.

I say that to say this: if our most poverty-stricken citizens do not fear for their survival from a dearth of resources, does our criminal class? Reams of op-eds and magazine covers blame criminality on our fellow citizens' lack of material needs. But when I turn on the news or hear from my coworkers the items stolen from their cars and homes, I sulk my head. Think of the items under lock and key at your local Walgreens or Walmart: hair products, trendy clothing, Bluetooth speakers, video game systems, and alcohol. Would you die without these? Certainly, life wouldn't be as fun or fulfilling, but no serious person thinks these items are necessary to survival. But these are the items stolen. When was the last time you heard of someone being arrested or charged for stealing bread, fruit, rice, beans, cereal, or vegetables? Think back to your own life; have you ever seen such a thing? If you have, did that person appear to be starving? (That last one is rhetorical because I know you haven't seen it, but feel free to make up an example; I enjoy people's creativity.)

There exists a supermarket where I live called HEB (this is not a paid endorsement, but HEB is the world's best grocery store). They cater to what the community it serves buys. In wealthier neighborhoods, it sells caviar, sushi, and mineral water from the finest artisanal springs. In more modest neighborhoods, it supplies staples the local population can both afford and want, such as large bags of flour, rice, beans, and frozen uncooked meat products. I bring this up because we all know and can see that nice things cost money. Additionally, we (should) know that staples are generally inexpensive (unprepared rice, beans, flour, etc.). I personally thoroughly enjoy buying pre-cut watermelon (I don't like dealing with the rind or the mess; it's just very inconvenient) but also know that pound for pound, it's at least three times the cost of a whole uncut watermelon. While the nicer things in life have no limit to how high their cost can go, the most basic version of the same items are within reach of our most modest of households.

If you need an example, google what Bose Bluetooth headphones cost versus the least expensive Bluetooth headphones you can find that won't break as you pull them from the container. Of course, Bose Bluetooth sound-cancelling headsets sound better (I have some myself; I fully endorse them), but at over $200, perhaps a more modest off-brand pair may be the logical choice for those on tighter budgets.

Our criminal classes are not forced into auto theft, burglary, and armed robbery out of necessity. Simply put, it's because they have wants that are far easier (in the short term) to obtain via theft than to earn via work. The item I'd like most at the moment (a new 2022 Jeep Wrangler Unlimited, Rubicon Edition with optional lift and M2 machine gun mount) is approximately $55,000. At the median US salary, it would take a full year to earn this without any other expenses, including food. While the vast majority of individuals buy the car and pay it off over time, a minority conclude it's easier and quicker to steal.

For those commenting on the realistic and practical nature of continuing to drive a stolen car, just replace "car" with any commercial good.

To take it in a dark direction, this also explains rape. Rapists have a desire to have sex with someone (for whatever reason; take your pick) and do not want to go through the painstaking process of finding a consenting partner they would like to have sex with. There's the long(ish) legitimate route (which seems to be getting shorter every day), and there's the short, illegal, reprehensible route.

If you believe thieves only steal because they need to, it shouldn't take that much of a mental stretch to then assume rapists only rape because they have needs that will not be met in any other way. Crimes involving sexual gratification and/or children seem to be the only criminality the West doesn't wish to tolerate or explain in the same way as other criminality.

If you believe our fellow citizens are forced into criminality, I will ask you a simple question. What would you do? If you were stripped of every possession you own and thrown out onto the street with just the clothes on your back (the cheap ones — no cheating by selling Balenciaga bodysuits you may have on), what would you do? If you are a generally honest and respectable person, I guarantee you your first thought is not robbing houses and stealing cars to pay for food and motels. It's not because you know more about government social programs than those currently walking our streets; it's because you have the drive and will to do better than where you'd been placed. You would find the environment intolerable and would do everything in your power to get out of it and back to a life more familiar to you. You could spell this out in a step-by-step process and hand it out in pamphlets, and still, the criminal and destitute classes would generally ignore this pathway out.

Why? Because it requires self-control, delaying gratification, and planning for the long run versus the wants and desires of the moment. It is easy for us to see greed in the wealthy buying ever larger yachts and sprawling mansions, but what we fail to understand is the greed of all, including the poor and criminals. In truth, greed is found at all income levels and across all social classes. From Ponzi-scheme-inspired hedge fund managers to car thieves, theft is theft. The desire for more (or greed) is best harnessed in a regulated capitalistic market. In order for an individual to make more money honestly and legally, they must provide a product or service other people want or need. Greed alone does not build wealth.

To the extent that greedy people lie, cheat, or steal in order to build wealth (say, by raiding a Walgreens and selling the stolen products on the street), they should be held accountable and prosecuted in accordance with how society sees fit. You may feel the real thieves sit in boardrooms running multinational companies. To the extent there are crooks in those offices, I would recommend not buying their products or services if you feel strongly about the subject. If you feel you cannot go without the product or service, consider that what you are getting is worth the price.

Why are there those among us who believe nearly all crime stems from existential (that is, a threat to your existence) need? Because to believe otherwise means crime is a moral failing rather than a societal failing. If a car thief steals a truck, it is only to sell it for bread and pay an overpriced rent. If a pickpocket slices a purse string with a knife to make off with it, they're probably only doing so to feed their starving child. If a gang of twenty teenagers raids an Apple store, smashing items not personally pilfered onto the cement outside, it's only so they can trade the items for clothing and medicine.

If, on the other hand, these individuals were stealing these luxury items for themselves or to sell later for drugs and alcohol, society is forced to confront exactly how we arrived at that situation. This requires challenging closely held ideologies outside the Overton window; that is, outside the range of ideas that is socially acceptable to talk about. We lie to ourselves when we believe criminality comes from a position of need because it's easier to believe society is bad versus the individual. If you were to believe the person is to blame for their actions, that means a pact has been broken. Judging another's shortcomings means your own shortcomings will be (rightfully) judged by others as those of an individual failing versus society's failure. If the individual robbing the liquor store isn't a victim, it harms the idea that you are a victim in need of empathy also. Moving from the idea that society is to blame to blaming individual shortcomings is a very difficult path to walk.

The "pact" I mentioned in the prior paragraph is this: I will not judge your decisions and actions if you do not judge mine (obviously, within certain parameters). Infidelity, laziness, drug use, and general promiscuity (among others) fall under this category. We fail to shame poor actions because we want to engage in other poor actions ourselves and don't want to be judged for them (we are anyway, just not publicly). This general lowering of the bar results in us not holding people to any standard, in some cases not even to legal standards. This also leads to us fabricating stories in such a way that we can blame society rather than the individual.

Criminals only steal because society has not paid them enough and makes items too expensive. The homeless are only homeless because rent is too high. People only become addicted to drugs because others led them astray. Believe what you will, but odds are whoever is reading this is not a flagrant criminal, currently has residency, and is not currently shooting up or coming down from heroin use. If you can do it, anyone can. (If you are a flagrant criminal without residency and are currently shooting up or coming down, I applaud your taste in literature; keep it up (the reading, that is)

Criminality in general is the net result of the failure of society to raise individuals with a healthy value system, but ultimately it is the individual who chooses to engage in illicit behavior or unsocial activity. In its most extreme forms, I understand some criminality fuels alcohol and drug habits that actually will kill the user if they cease using the substances associated with their addiction. Untreated heroin withdrawal can lead to death from dehydration or electrolyte imbalance from vomiting and diarrhea. Alcohol withdrawal can lead to delirium tremens that can lead to death.

In saying a criminal needs to steal to fund their habit, someone could interpret these facts as, "Yes, the user will die if they can no longer fund their habit." But this ignores reasonable alternatives. For example, if I say, "I need a mansion or I'll die," it is somewhat correct in that, without adequate shelter, an individual has a significantly increased chance of death due to exposure to the elements. That said, there are alternatives such as a house, apartment, or shelter that will also fulfill this need. To say "I need a mansion" ignores more reasonable alternatives, just like saying "a criminal needs to steal to fund their addiction" ignores more reasonable options, such as methadone, weaning someone off of alcohol over time, or medical intervention.

A close friend recently moved from a house to an apartment. While conversing about what the government should be providing, he said (or insinuated, I can't recall) the government should be providing a house to him since he needs it to live. I then told him there were both public and private shelters that would provide his need for shelter for free. He scoffed. I then asked why he needed a house specifically, to which he had no answer. Eventually, I was at least able to convince him that a studio apartment could just as easily fulfill this need for shelter, but with noticeable disappointment from my friend. Without explanation (which wasn't needed), it was apparent my friend did not want to live in a studio apartment if a house was the alternative.

While I was showing drafts of this work to others to see what they thought, a young lady took exception to the title of this chapter. In her mind, crime is born of need; that is, low-income (or no-income) people only stole so they could fund the necessities of life. No matter the item stolen (bike, car, wallet, luxury watch, thoroughbred dogs), she assumed the item would be sold to fund the thief's needs. She seemed perfectly okay with someone stealing her bike, believing whoever stole it needed it more than she did. When I asked how she knew somebody needed the bike (or money gained after selling), all I got was shrugged shoulders.

In this girl's mind, I don't believe she had ever considered that people steal for non-necessities. She was perfectly willing to believe the rich stole (out of greed) but could not ponder somebody down the socio-economic ladder doing the same. I understand why somebody would want to believe this. Within a certain worldview, people are where they are because of fate and the society around them, including the person who believed this. Assuming people are born good and are only forced into unsocial behavior, it makes sense that people would only break society's rules if they needed to in order to survive.

That said, there is no logical reason to assume thieves only steal what they need, murderers only murder if their own life is at stake, or that rapists rape because they would otherwise perish if they did not.

On top of all this, the girl I was talking with admitted without prompting that it was society's fault someone was in a position where they needed to steal; therefore, it wasn't the criminal's fault but society's. When I asked whose fault it would be if I stole her car, she said it was both me and society's. I then gestured at her and a mutual friend, asking if they would be as responsible as me if I stole their car. They responded that they are not society, so I then asked if everyone in the bar we were in would be just as culpable as me if I stole their car. After a moment of thought, they admitted that the person responsible for the theft, me, would be at fault, and everyone else in the bar (themselves included) would be innocent.

As I already had a rugged, time- and battle-tested *American vehicle, I had no need for any additional transportation, so my potential theft was left on the drawing room table.

*American in origin, not manufacturing.

Every society gets the kind of criminal it deserves.
— Robert Kennedy, US Senator for New York, 1965–1968

Chapter 4 People Are What Make Bad (or Good) Communities

What makes bad schools and neighborhoods? It's not the bricks,
mortar, or asphalt; it's the people.
— Alex (REDACTED)

There is a distinction to be made between a bad neighborhood and a
poor neighborhood. My grandfather and grandmother raised my mother
and her five siblings in a neighborhood that aged and weathered over
time, as all things do. A young relative of mine who lived with my
grandfather had a friend he wanted to come over to my grandfather's
house to play. Upon seeing the neighborhood and the house, my cousin's
friend's mother decided it was too dangerous and refused to bring her
child back to my grandfather's home. (Read it a few more times; it was
confusing to write as well.)

My cousin's friend's mother's mistake was to confuse a poor
neighborhood with a dangerous one. While there is overlap, these are not
the same. While in my grandfather's neighborhood, my car has never
been broken into, I've never been robbed, and I've never heard a gunshot
or seen unsavory characters nearby (which is not something I can claim
for my current neighborhood). My grandfather's neighborhood is
absolutely a low-income neighborhood, but it's not a bad neighborhood.

Why make the distinction between a bad neighborhood and a poor
neighborhood? Because they are not necessarily the same thing. A poor
neighborhood is one that has significantly fewer resources than the
average neighborhood for things such as upkeep, maintenance,
community walkways, and parks. A bad neighborhood is one in which
theft, violence, drug dealing, and illicit adult services run rampant outside
the apparent control of the law. While there are poor neighborhoods that
are also bad neighborhoods, there can also be rich neighborhoods that are
bad. There are parts of New York and San Francisco where multimillion-
dollar condos, apartments, and homes are on the same blocks as open-air
drug markets and all the riff-raff they attract.

What is the difference between a good poor community and a bad poor community? The people. People are who do the actions that make a community feel like either a loving home or a dystopian hell. Reporters usually describe bad neighborhoods as violent, crime-ridden, and drug-filled. Missing is the fact that people commit these acts, not the asphalt on the street or the bricks in the apartments. If the excuse is that the people living in poor communities are forced into crime (thus making bad communities), I would argue that I've been in much poorer but safer places around the world. If lack of material goods was the problem, this shouldn't have been my observation. The story of my grandfather's neighborhood exemplifies this. If poverty creates crime, my grandfather's neighborhood should not have been safe, and his home would be yet another I would not visit for my own safety.

Schools are the same way. There are well-funded schools that produce well-below-average students along with relatively poor schools that generate good, college-ready students capable of more difficult tasks. While material resources can aid in education (and all other human endeavors), the input that truly matters is the resolve of those involved in the school system.

Ponder for a moment the subject of math; how much do you think it's changed, in primary education, in the last century? I have a feeling the complexity of teaching $2 + 2 = 5$ has not changed that much over time, and as such, the materials required to educate students should be relatively inexpensive. Having a ten-year-old math book (which isn't required to teach math) doesn't present the same problems that having a ten-year-old book on computers does. Much like everything else, there is no upper limit to how much you can spend on a child's education. But with the law of diminishing returns*, the wealthier the school, the less it can actually accomplish by throwing more money at the problem. At some point, you've already purchased the newest books, the best smart boards, tablets for every student, and student-teacher ratios dreamed of by teachers' unions.

So how do you improve a school if throwing money at it no longer improves performance?

*The law of diminishing returns is such: every additional unit of input yields less and less units of output. The first $1,000 I donate to a

47

hospital will buy the most needed supplies. The last $1,000 donation, after millions have been collected and spent, might purchase slightly more comfortable linen or a subscription to Hulu for the patients' viewing pleasure (Watch It's Always Sunny in Philadelphia; even if the patients don't survive, they will have enjoyed their last several days. I would wish the same for myself.)

While attending college, I lived in inexpensive dormitories that were a single room with two occupants. My second semester, the college decided to change my roommate to someone they believed needed work on his academics. Within my dorm and year group, the previous semester, I had had the best grades, while my new roommate had the worst. The school was hoping my presence would improve his grades, and by God, it worked. His grades, over the course of living in the same dorm room as me, improved 50%, going from a 0.666 to a 0.999 GPA. My roommate was not at the college much longer.

A little background: My roommate had no real lack of material resources. His housing, schooling, food, and clothing were taken care of by his parents. He had a strong support network around him that wanted him to succeed, and a myriad of people succeeding around him that could have provided inspiration to push through and examples to follow. Instead, my roommate slept in, skipped final exams, and ignored nearly all advice and support offered. All the environmental factors were on my roommate's side, and he still failed spectacularly because of laziness. Making the story even sadder, he was not unintelligent in a way that meant he could not comprehend the materials being taught. In three different attempts at the same math-related course, he was the top scorer on the first test in our peer group. And in each of those times, by the end of the course, he failed where others succeeded. Failure was being snapped from the jaws of victory because my roommate liked watching movies more than he liked studying.

To exemplify this, one Saturday morning, I woke up and got to the business of the morning (that is, playing video games). About two hours later, at about 11 am, my dorm mate woke to a phone call, whose transcript follows: "Morning... Of course, of course... Just heading back from the library now... Thanks, mom." At this point, my dorm mate got back to his business of the morning — that is, sleeping in. Later in the semester, my roommate's family demanded he put me on the phone with them. They asked me what he was doing wrong and why he wasn't more successful. Not wanting to humiliate him, I told them I didn't know but that I would help him however I could. While I remember helping out anyone in college I could who asked (in addition to being a professional tutor), I have no memory of my roommate ever asking for help (in his defense, we weren't taking the same classes).

It's easy and entertaining to poke fun at people perceived as privileged when they fail despite having every advantage. What's more difficult is properly identifying character flaws in our impoverished citizens and noting that they have a good amount of say in the quality of their life.

In another example from my schooling, those dorm rooms were not rooms at all. In order for our upperclassmen to impress upon us our social status while freshmen, we had "holes" (as in, holes in the wall) instead of rooms. They were extremely plain, single rooms with two occupants and a sink. Amazing was the difference between two of these identical rooms. Peers of mine in an identical room had transformed this hole into something somebody would actually want to live in. The beds were always made, all clothing was either in a hamper or up in the closet, and the room smelled nice and had a generally pleasant aura. Another room of two, on the other hand, had the blinds blacked out all day, every day. Wet clothes hung from the bed or scattered the floor, and the room always had an unpleasant, musty odor. It looked and smelled, in short, like a homeless person had set up camp in the dormitory.

It's interesting to consider that these two separate groups of students had the same inputs. None had a serious job. Each had comparable college hours and were given exactly the same resource: a small dormitory to do with as they pleased. One pair flourished while the other created their own personal ghetto. What's true of these two is a microcosm of the rest of society. Even with equal inputs, some will create an Eden while others will create a living hell on Earth. If we don't recognize people's contributions to the state of their own community, we miss the main cause of why a community is thriving or failing.

As has been a theme in this book, it's easy to blame bad outcomes on things outside of oneself or one's neighborhood: not enough investment in communities, too few or too many cops (I can't seem to find which one is the actual goal), or just general government neglect. I know why this is: introspection is hard. If you find the true cause of a problem, you might not like what is at its root. For example, let's say you thought crime was too high in a neighborhood. What you discover is that there are more criminals because crime is not punished or is punished leniently. In order to solve the problem of crime, you would need to jail criminals or reduce criminal acts by those same individuals. But if you believe too many people are being jailed or that interactions with police are what create criminals, you're left looking for largely non-existent solutions because you don't like the fact that low prosecution rates lead to higher crime rates.

You may even discover that certain cultural norms create a breeding ground for unsocial and criminal activities. Again, I don't need to tell you what they are, because you know what they are, and if you don't, it won't take you long to list which cultural norms create serious problems. We ignore the root causes of many societal problems because to tackle them means passing judgment on destructive lifestyles and cultures we've decided to tolerate. Understand this is not a dog whistle to racists and bigots; I'm not advocating for not tolerating groups of people or cultures. I'm advocating that we eliminate or shame cultural norms that are destructive to those living in these cultures.

Identifying the root cause of bad schools and neighborhoods means holding individuals accountable for their bad decisions and actions rather than seeking blame elsewhere because it's easier than facing the truth.

On April 20, 2021, police responded to a 911 call involving a dispute in a Columbus neighborhood that was getting out of control. When police showed up at the scene, one of the girls (sixteen) involved shouted, "I'm gonna (sic) stab the fuck out of you, bitch," lunging at another, apparently unarmed female. One of the officers, after shouting "Get down!" four times, fired his gun, killing the attacker. (As it turns out, the fight had started over, I believe, making the bed.) Because of the races of the police officer and the sixteen-year-old girl, it made national news. The sixteen-year-old girl was living in a foster home at the time with her sister and two other unrelated foster children. She was in foster care because her mother told social services she could no longer handle the girl or her four siblings. After a short unsuccessful stay with their grandmother, the state placed the children in foster care due to the grandmother's inability to provide for all the children's needs. Prior to this, the girl's mother was raising the children on her own, as the father did not live in the same household.

After the girl's death, the girl's biological father, mother, grandmother, and aunt called a press conference, standing side by side, demanding a federal investigation and claiming the system had let their offspring down. In truth, this girl's father effectively abandoned his offspring. The mother, grandmother, and any other relatives were either unable or (more likely) unwilling to raise their descendants, requiring the county to intervene. The only time they seemed truly interested in their kin was when she was shot by police while trying to stab another individual to death over inconsequential squabbles. At that time, her mother and father seemed able to come together in order to ensure that the appropriate people were held accountable (that is, financially liable for wrongful death) for the situation that ensued. Let's hope the appropriate people were eventually identified and will be punished accordingly, though I doubt it. Ultimately, the lesson is clear: just make your bed.

Milwaukee

In 2016, Matthew Desmond, noted sociologist at Princeton University, chronicled the lives of the poor in Milwaukee's inner city and trailer parks in his book, *Eviction: Poverty and Profit in the American City*. His first-person accounts reveal lives of violence, drug use, sexual abuse of children, prostitution, and all other manner of criminal activity and squalor in the poor communities <u>he lived with</u> in his search for understanding of the plights of the poor. As I perceive his motives, his goal was to advocate for those in poverty he felt were unfairly evicted from their private apartments and mobile homes and to give voice to those at the bottom of the socio-economic ladder. Ultimately, as I interpret it, he is trying to promote a change to public policy to provide more public funding for housing for non-working individuals by increasing taxes on working families or reallocating government spending from other public causes.

51

Opposite of Desmond's goal, what he revealed through his book was self-inflicted human turmoil and chaos, the likes of which an average person would (or should) recoil at. Unemployed able-bodied individuals dependent on food stamps and welfare, unmarried women with a never-ending line of violent and abusive men fathering even more children outside marriage, and drug use to rival Hunter S. Thompson. The lives he documented were in turmoil because the individuals he followed made a lifetime of poor decisions and continued making poor decisions that, if reversed, would make their lives better (Mr. Desmond did help by driving them between courthouses and potential rental properties. I'm unsure if he decided to remain in those accommodations, but I doubt it).

To say that someone addicted to drugs can't stop ignores the fact that people have stopped doing drugs. To assert that women can't stop having children they are unprepared to raise suggests that women in general have no way to prevent unwanted pregnancies, something an untold number of women do every day, day in and day out.

Members of the Community

If you wanted a community to be better, would you sell drugs to its population, including the children? If you cared about your fellow inhabitants and the neighborhoods they occupied, would you rob them at gunpoint for the goods and valuables they have on them? Members of bad communities who engage in these activities don't care, and place their own wants above the well-being of their fellow neighbors. Bad neighborhoods are bad because they are occupied by a disproportionately high percentage of people who engage in destructive and dangerous activities. Bad schools are bad schools because they are occupied by a disproportionately high percentage of students, teachers, and parents not putting in as much effort as those at better schools. There are some reasons for this that are out of those members' control, but it largely falls on people and their individual involvement.

For those who think this language is harsh, you know that there are bad parents in this world. You also know that there are bad teachers, just like there are excellent teachers whose guidance produces individuals capable of high achievement. There are also bad students, whose only concern is exiting the educational system as quickly as possible while doing the least amount of work until then since they already know everything they need to for life. I know this because like most readers, I too went to public high school. While most of the classes I attended were filled with driven, hardworking students, I also attended classes in which the students seemed to only get pleasure from shooting each other with nail guns and picking ego-driven fights over nothing.

To deny there are bad teachers is to deny there are also good teachers. To deny there are bad parents is to deny that there are good parents. And of course, to deny there are bad students means there are no good students. If you believe that bad teachers, parents, and students are only that way because they lack the resources they need, I assure you there are bad teachers in wealthy school districts, wealthy parents whose presence is only a detriment to their offspring, and children from rich families who are also awful students, despite the privileges wealth brings. In those cases, the problem is not material wealth, but a lack of effort. And if the wealthy can choose not to put forth the required effort, so can the poor and middle classes.

Why do we not want to believe bad communities and schools are bad because of the members that make them up? Because it destroys the illusion that the problem is a deprivation of resources, and thus shifts the blame. If a community or school has serious issues, it's much easier to argue that more money would help rather than admit the problem is deeper. If the money comes in and fails to produce results, then blame will be put on the idea that it wasn't enough money, and more is needed. If no additional money is provided, the community (parents, teachers, and students) can blame the government and society for poor results. Either way, the individual members that make up the community can point outwardly instead of inwardly as to why their community is in the shape that it is.

For example, if a school had serious issues with gang violence, would newer books and laptops for students really solve that problem? What do you think would produce better results, newer gym equipment or a two-parent home? How would higher teacher pay combat hard drug use from parents and students? Would a school-issued iPad in every student's hand prevent unsafe sexual liaisons? Individual and cultural shortcomings, not lack of resources, are what create poor outcomes.

Unfortunately, addressing those shortcomings means essentially blaming people for the position they've largely put themselves in, and nobody wants to hear that. If the blame can be shifted elsewhere, anywhere, it will be, and the true problems will not be solved because they're not even being seriously addressed

We want to believe the areas communities or schools reside in are bad because people can be moved. If all that was needed was a change in location, we would only need to move people in bad communities and schools into good communities (or improve the resources allocated to those same communities) and the societal ills would disappear. Sadly, this is largely not the case. While moving a few individuals could be beneficial, it is only by exposure to better cultural norms that these individuals' lives could be made better. Simply moving every individual engaging in poor cultural norms will only shift what is considered the "good school" or the "good part of town." Problems (or success) follow people because people bring their baggage with them.

If we fail to learn and understand why schools and communities fail, we are much more likely to soon discover it much closer to home.

> *If you don't visit the bad neighborhoods, the bad neighborhoods are going to visit you.*
> — Thomas Friedman, New York Times Columnist

Chesterton's Fence

Tradition is not the worship of ashes, but the preservation of fire.
— Gustav Mahler, Austro-Bohemian romantic composer, 1860–1911
Oregon

In November 2020, Ballot Measure 110, which reclassified drug possession down to a "Class-E violation" with a maximum fine of $100, passed 58–42 in a popular vote in the State of Oregon. Drugs covered by this act include LSD, oxycodone, meth, PCP, and heroin. Included was the establishment of drug addiction treatment and recovery programs funded in part by the state's marijuana tax revenue and "state prison savings." In essence, the law decriminalized users, presenting them with a fine instead of arrest, with the intent of getting drug users treatment rather than incarceration. Violators could have the fine waived by completing a drug treatment program. Of those fined, approximately 1% completed the drug treatment program. It seems the poorly named "Drug Decriminalization and Addiction Treatment Initiative" only fulfilled half of its promised outcomes.

By 2023, OregonLive (the region's top local news and information website, associated with the Oregonian) was reporting that homelessness jumped approximately 23% in two years within the state. The U.S. national average growth in homelessness over the same period was under 1%. Incidents where a firearm was discharged and reported rose from 158 in the city of Portland in 2020 (January to April) to more than double (354) across the same months the following year (Measure 110 went into effect February 1, 2021). Shooting incidents continued increasing to 483 (Jan-Apr) in 2022, but fear not — as of 2023, the number has fallen to 347 (Jan–Apr), although a cynic might note it's still nearly double what it was over the same time period in 2020 before the ballot measure went into effect. No other state has attempted to change its drug laws so radically. Like watching someone drink mercury for their health (Note: Don't. It will kill you.), all other jurisdictions can see the obvious results and don't wish to recreate them. While many Oregon voters grew up with occasionally overzealous drug enforcement, they hadn't seen with their own eyes what happens when you remove the barriers hindering (also note, I didn't say stop) people from using drugs. What people saw prior to Measure 110 was a barrier that prevented people from using substances they enjoyed and law enforcement interactions that resulted in what was perceived as harsh punishments. The idea that those laws existed for an important reason was missed by a majority of Oregon voters, as they didn't truly understand why those laws were established in the first place. Either that, or blind optimism overwhelmed their ability to think critically and predict the fallout of hard drug legalization.

When moving from one city to another, I had relatives help me while I was out of town. There were two boxes I left for the renters who would be living in my house after I left: an internet router and a Wi-Fi router. Both boxes were needed in order for the house to be on a local Wi-Fi network. While making final preparations for the renters to move in, my relative saw the second box (Wi-Fi), didn't understand its purpose, and threw it away. When my renters arrived, they told me the equipment I had promised them was not there. Now I had a problem to resolve. When I asked my relative why she threw it out, she told me she didn't know its purpose and that since she saw me throwing away other items (whose purposes I knew), she felt right also throwing away my property.

The Fence

There's a theme that weaves so many of these understood truths together. These truths have been passed down verbally, by tradition, and instinctually through our biology. Our modern world wants so much to progress, it forgets the hard-won lessons of history, tragically learned at the cost of millions of lives and needless suffering. It screams from the past to not make the same mistakes. History may not repeat, but it does rhyme. Chesterton's Fence is a principle that reforms should not be made until the reasoning behind the existing state of affairs is known.

Imagine you have purchased a piece of land and there is an unappealing fence going right through the middle, or perhaps on the edge near the woods. Your first instinct, assuming you don't know its purpose, might be to tear it down. It spoils the view, is aged and weathered, and is an obstacle to you traversing your property. The danger is that if you tear the fence down without knowing its original purpose, you risk the consequence of no longer having it for protection. The fence could have prevented predatory animals from coming in just as easily as it could have kept livestock from escaping or going near lethal flora (flora = plants, for those who watch cable news). God forbid, it could be on the Texas-Mexico border and is the only thing keeping those gun-wielding maniacs (like myself) safely enclosed in Texas.

Our history and traditions are that fence. The world's oldest person, as I type, is Lucile Randon, born February 11, 1904, in Alès, France, who survived COVID-19 at the age of 117 and is currently 118 years and 273 days old. Of equal note, she also survived the Spanish Flu, two invasions of her native country (oddly, both at first involving an inconsequential person by the name of A. Hitler), and the Cold War. The first operational nuclear-tipped intercontinental ballistic missiles (ICBMs) didn't exist until 1959. Prior to that, missiles were intracontinental and thus a threat almost exclusively to continental Europe, where Lucile Randon lives.

Our collective memory doesn't go back further than February 11, 1904. Anything further, and we must rely on written or carved words or audio recorded on equipment such as the phonograph, which wasn't invented until 1877. At a minimum, hundreds of thousands of years of human development occurred prior to humans making markings on cave walls.

The earliest known writing was invented around 3,400 BC. Before this, painful lessons were only handed down via spoken word and trial and error. The best practices for successful offspring and the continuation of tribes, kingdoms, and then nations developed over time. This development over time created traditions that were the most advantageous in creating future offspring.

These traditions and institutions, including marriage, monogamy, and the rule of law, were developed because they worked better than other systems. If you doubt this and are determined to think these are old-fashioned ideas, go to places where marriage rates are at their lowest, where communities are not generally monogamous, and where law and order are determined arbitrarily by whoever has the most cronies on the street enforcing the will of the most powerful and tell me that's the utopia we've been striving for.

Note that a few neighborhoods in New York and LA don't count; residents there can afford their lifestyle in ways the rest of humanity can't (again, I'm looking at you, Nick Cannon). Successful practices (aka traditions) born out of trial and error (or luck) meant some groups of humans were better able to not only survive but thrive, initially against nature but later against other humans with weaker practices and/or numbers. We are the recipients of these practices, knowledge, and traditions. It is in our nature to rebel against them in our youth, I believe in order to loosen ourselves from bad ideas that have stuck around or have since become a hindrance.

But this also means we rebel against ideas that worked and would continue to work if not for our actions and reforms. We tear down fences and guardrails because, in our youth and naïveté, we don't understand their original purpose, and therefore place no value on them. We don't have the experience of knowing it can always get worse and that the arc of history doesn't always go toward justice. It doesn't always get better just because the calendar progresses. There's a reason our history books refer to parts of our past as dark ages, golden eras, and renaissances. That wall or fence in the field may in fact serve no modern purpose. It could have been built by Romans who have now left modern Britain, by Soviets who attempted to stop their population from ~~leaving~~ fleeing their country via Berlin, or by the British at the Battle of Rorke's Drift who (God knows why) found themselves outnumbered twenty-five to one in South Africa (the British won. Look it up.) in the nineteenth century.

I'm not advocating for never taking down fences, or as the metaphor goes, never making social changes. I'm saying that if we don't know where our traditions originate or what their purpose was, we should assume there was a purpose and proceed with caution. Or don't, and assume it'll all work out. What's the worst that can happen? What does any of this have to do with this work? Our ancestors were not idiots, and the ideas and traditions developed by them weren't formed by cutting the head off of a chicken and seeing where it landed.

(For those wanting to skip morbid facts, keep moving. After a chicken's head has been removed, all its nerves fire at once, giving it the appearance of flapping its wings or running. One of my aunts was traumatized by this in her youth, as a headless chicken "chased her" as a child).

Much like determining which plants were edible, how to build their homes, or how to cook meat in ways that wouldn't result in death, our traditions were born of trial and error to create functional societies. While most of our ancestors may not have understood why they did the things they did, they continued time-honored traditions because they likely had some benefit, even if those practicing these traditions didn't truly understand how this happened. Those traditions worked because they tended to solve problems. Many of the problems that these traditions solved were based on uncomfortable truths that, while accurate, identified and solved issues within the human condition we would prefer not to acknowledge. For example, we all generally agree on the tradition of not being in intimate relationships with close, blood-related family members. While many know the practical reason for why this tradition is a good idea, many have no idea what is being protected by having moral and legal rules barring such relationships. Despite this, they keep to this tradition and rightfully shame those not adhering to it.

For those unaware, there are dominant and recessive genes. Genes that are dominant override recessive genes. The physical characteristics of an individual born from their parents' genes will generally reflect the dominant genes, although the recessive genes may still exist in the individual (I know this grossly oversimplifies the subject, but genetics tends to bore me). If two closely related people have children, the recessive genes have a much greater chance of manifesting, creating offspring with far different physical characteristics (some of which are sometimes called defects) and a lower level of health than the average human born to two non-related parents or distant relatives. Some may have a close cousin or (God help us) a biological brother, sister, parent or child they are physically attracted to. To them, laws and social norms preventing the relationship are a hindrance to their perceived happiness. With nearly everyone else getting their significant other of choice, why shouldn't they get theirs?

If you really wanted to jump off the deep end, ask yourself why we have laws barring same-sex siblings from being in intimate relationships. With no chance of offspring with serious birth defects, the logical reasoning behind this seems to slip away. (Note: If anyone thinks this is advocacy for incest, they have not been paying attention). As a much less gross example, strict Muslim countries bar the consumption of alcohol and most other mind-altering drugs. Given the lethality and harm to society created by these substances (broken homes, abuse, DUIs, overdose, etc.), even if the population of these countries does not understand the potential harm, they are the beneficiaries of these traditions in ways other cultures are not. Of course, it would be easy for these countries to see the harm done, as there are numerous examples not only from the portion of the population that ignores these norms but also from nearby and distant countries and cultures that do not have this restriction. If you've been paying any attention to the personal narratives I've put forth, you'll see I don't agree with these restrictions.

Any set of traditions has consequences, some obvious and some that are only evident when the tradition is set aside. Some traditions are clearly outdated, solving problems that in the modern age have (largely) been eliminated. Other traditions, however, solve problems still persistent in the modern day, even if we collectively refuse to acknowledge them. Before dismissing old-fashioned ideas, consider that they had/have a purpose and understand there may be a cost to dismissing them.

Tradition does not mean that the living are dead, but that the dead are living.
— Gilbert K. Chesterton, English writer and philosopher, 1874-1936

Chapter 5 Money Doesn't Solve Most Problems

"If you are born poor, it's not your mistake, but if you die poor, it's your mistake."
— Bill Gates, 1955–present

On April 8, 1994, the lead singer of Nirvana, Kurt Cobain, committed suicide while on a cocktail of illegal narcotics, the most dangerous of which was heroin, by shooting himself with a shotgun in the head (a feat that, alone, takes a tad amount of planning). Prior to this, he had been attending rehab, where he escaped by scaling a perimeter wall. Three days after his escape, he strolled into a Seattle gun shop and purchased shotgun ammunition (he borrowed the shotgun from a friend, as police had previously confiscated his firearms, there being a seemingly credible threat of suicide). At the time of his death, he and his band had sold tens of millions of records around the world. Additionally, he left his spouse the estimated $50 million in assets he had accumulated over his career. By all accounts, the man had what most people would want: wealth, fame, a celebrity spouse, and (for some) enough drugs and alcohol for several lifetimes (or maybe just one). Yet, at the age of twenty-seven, his light was extinguished by his own hand, having suffered from severe depression.

Jocelyn Wildenstein (born August 5, 1940) is a Swiss-born New York "socialite" (read: partier) commonly known as Catwoman due to the extensive plastic surgery she underwent to try and maintain a youthful appearance. Given a cursory look at the black-and-white photos of her in her youth, it's clear there was a time when she was very attractive. She married into a billionaire family of art dealers and horse racers and breeders. Around the age of sixty, she caught her approximately sixty-year-old husband with a nineteen-year-old Russian model in their home, at which point Mrs. Wildenstein had a gun drawn on her by her husband for the heinous crime of seeing what was going on in her home. After divorcing, she received $2.5 billion in her settlement and $100 million per year for more than a decade. She filed for bankruptcy in May 2018, resulting in her three luxury apartments in Trump Tower being repossessed. According to Wikipedia, by her own admission, she was spending $60,000 on telephone calls and around $500,000 on food and wine per year. For those not good at math, this works out to about $456 per meal, three meals a day.

In San Antonio (my adopted hometown), there are about 3,000 people experiencing homelessness, living in either emergency shelters, transitional housing, or on the street. Of those, about 874 live "unsheltered" in areas not meant for human habitation in a city of 1.45 million as of 2023. In San Francisco, there are about 7,000–8,000 homeless, with about 4,500 of them "unsheltered," in a city of 800,000. By this metric, San Antonio has a homeless ratio of 0.6 unsheltered people per 1,000, while San Francisco has an unsheltered population of 5.625 per 1,000, around nine times the rate despite an enormous per capita wealth and income gap between these two cities. By another metric, San Antonio has 1.7 unsheltered people per square mile, while San Francisco has ninety-six unsheltered people per square mile, fifty-six times the San Antonio rate. While substantially wealthier, San Francisco is unable or unwilling to resolve its homelessness issue in the same way San Antonio has more successfully done, despite throwing significantly more money at the problem.

What can we learn from these tragic events and circumstances? Perhaps, what most of us think will solve all our problems (a bottomless bank account) might not, and may even make some problems much worse. Money can do a lot, but it is only a tool. And like any tool, if misused, it can cause much more harm than good. If money could solve all problems, Mr. Cobain would be with us today, Ms. Wildenstein wouldn't have ever needed to declare bankruptcy, and San Francisco wouldn't be the pincushion of conservative commentary daily due to the dystopian hellscape its government has created.

As an example of another often-misused tool, picture a firearm. In the right hands (take your pick of preferred military, police, or anti-fascist zealot), it has the ability to protect loved ones, maintain basic public order, or fight rampaging fascists on or off the battlefield. In the wrong hands, it can be used to rob, kill, or simply go off accidentally due to poor training or storage. The gun itself is not the problem; it is an inanimate object, the same as a rock or kitchen knife. The operator of the gun is who wields it and uses the tool for either good or evil. In the same way, money is a tool. In Mr. Cobain's hands, it was a tool used to purchase mind-damaging drugs, alcohol, and ammunition and to fuel a predictably destructive lifestyle. In someone else's hands, it could have been invested, given to charity, or spent in more wholesome ways.

On the subject of firearms and money, in 2005, while in high school, I participated in a Model UN, in which students pretended to be ambassadors from the various countries of the world. Somehow, I drew the short stick and ended up as Algeria (Note: I don't think if I were in high school today, I would have been assigned Algeria). Luckily, Algeria happened to be on the UN Security Council that year. For those not in the know, the UN Security Council, among its other duties, has the ability to establish peacekeeping operations (that is to say, they are the executive arm of the UN, capable of organizing and dispatching soldiers). We, the students, were given scenarios in which we had to act how that country's representatives actually would and "solve" real-world problems. The government in Haiti had recently been overthrown (wait, what year was this again?), and so was a modern-day problem teenagers could solve inside of a one-hour window. After explaining that Haiti was in the middle of a civil war, we were asked to come up with a solution, as the UN, to end the conflict. At the time, I was already motivated to join the military, and so I started from the perspective of "Whatever we do, we need to be able to enforce it." Providing food, aid, and safe zones sounds good, but without soldiers on the ground, anything we did would simply put more lives at risk. Luckily, the other fourteen children (the real UN Security Council has fifteen members) instantly came up with a solution (I think it took them more time to type up the resolution than it did to determine the course of action). Their reasoning was that Haiti was poor (although, I doubt half of them could have picked out Haiti on a map), and its lack of resources was fueling the conflict. Thus, their solution was simple: economic aid. They didn't require my vote to enact their well-thought-out resolution, but the other students were curious why I didn't support their solution.

Imagine any conflict in history and ask yourself, "Will more money make the situation better or worse?" My fear was that without any UN peacekeeping forces, we would have no ability to determine where the money was going. The infusion of cash could easily escalate a conflict being waged with pistols and machetes into one fought with assault rifles, armored personnel carriers, mortars, machine guns, and tanks. I envisioned an air armada of military transport aircraft, emblazoned with the United Nations seal, airdropping pallets of cash into Haiti, our group naively believing it would make its way to those starved for resources. After all the other students high-fived, having fixed the Haiti problem, we were given another prompt since we were so apt at solving the world's problems. I did manage to ask where the money for this economic aid would come from but was dismissed, the question considered a frivolous downer. If only we relied more on children to determine how to solve the world's problems.

You already know (or should) that most people's problems do not involve money but rather are a combination of other factors. For example, would winning the lottery help someone with a serious substance-abuse problem? Or is it more likely that a large infusion of cash would only make the problem more serious, increasing the odds of an overdose death? If a friend of yours was having issues with his girlfriend, wife, or in-laws, would the situation drastically improve if large amounts of cash were thrown into the mix? If a school has a problem with its students showing up or acting up while in class, would tablets, smart boards, and newer lockers really solve the problem? Or have you only invested in expensive toys and decorations that, in the wrong hands, will simply be lost, broken, or graffitied upon?

2016

During the 2016 election cycle, there was still a strong cynical belief in the golden rule (whoever has the gold makes the rules). This means it was believed that whoever raised the most campaign cash was likely to win. Jeb Bush, brother of former President George W. Bush and son of former President George H.W. Bush, was the frontrunner in terms of money raised for the Republican primary campaign. One of the only other serious challengers (as weighed by campaign contributions) was Hillary Clinton, running as a Democrat. By the end of the Republican primaries, Jeb Bush had raised somewhere in the neighborhood of $150 million for 0.92% of the primary vote. Hillary Clinton, who had raised approximately $581 million, was eventually beaten by Donald Trump, whose campaign raised $340 million ($66 million of which was donated by the candidate to his own campaign). In both the primary and general election, the candidate who had spent less than most of his rivals won the office. Even if Jeb and Hillary had another $100 million each, the result likely would have been the same, only with more donors out whatever they foolishly threw away on those candidates.

Had 2016 come down to another Bush versus another Clinton, I would have given up on American democracy. It'd be easier, cheaper, and more efficient if a random Bush and random Clinton simply marry each other and have their offspring take turns ruling the country as neo-monarchs. The winner of the 2064 election could be Bush-Clinton the IV, with the successor being Clinton-Bush the VIII for the United Democratic-Republic Party (or UDR for short). There would still be elections, but no one would need to stay up until 2 a.m. on election night to see who won.

Back to business. A lack of funds was not why Jeb and Hillary lost, and it is unlikely that more money thrown into the already well-lubricated political machines would have changed the outcome. In this particular case, the reason is that you can't just buy an election in a functioning republic; you can only try to convince voters you're the person for the job. If your message is unconvincing, no amount of advertisements, stickers, lawn signs, or paid campaign workers will make a difference, other than perhaps convincing voters you are, in fact, the wrong candidate.

We collectively seem to believe most of our problems can be solved with more money. Why? Because the alternative is depressing to think about. If a lack of resources is not the source of our problems, then we must seek out another answer as to why this or that problem exists. At the end of that tunnel is something most of us don't want to deal with or accept: we are the source of most of our own problems, and to solve them, we must look inward rather than outward.

- Why don't I have any money? I spent it all.

- Why is my house a mess? I didn't clean it.

- Why am I doing poorly in school? I'm not studying enough.

- Why am I in jail? I broke the law, and law enforcement caught me.

Each of those statements could have a scapegoat:

- Why don't I have money? Society didn't invest enough in me and underpays me.

- Why is my house a mess? The minimum wage is too low, and I can't afford a cleaner.

- Why am I doing poorly in school? The city hasn't invested enough in new books or buildings.

- Why am I in jail? I've been kept poor, so I can't afford an effective lawyer, unlike the rich.

When I was in college, I was part of a campus organization that was steeped in military tradition, preparing the graduates for military service. As part of that, during the first year, any time our upperclassmen asked us a question that began with "why," the answer required was "Sir, no excuse, sir" regardless of whether we actually had an excuse or if the answer even made sense. "Why aren't your boots shined?" "Sir, no excuse, sir." "Why did you fail that test?" "Sir, no excuse, sir." "Why is the sky blue?" "Sir, no excuse, sir."

The idea ingrained in us was that we were responsible for the outcomes of events and had an active hand in them. There was always some action on our part we could have done in order to get a more satisfactory result. In the second year, we learned that there are circumstances out of people's control that account for failure. But to effectively understand that second lesson, we had to internalize the first. There are some problems that would be temporarily fixed with money. Obviously, credit card debt, a home being foreclosed on, or a car being repossessed can be fixed with money. But people who are bad with money are seldom made better with more.

What money does is expand choices, but those choices can be for the better or worse. Instead of a starter home, cash allows somebody to purchase something well outside their means. Purchasing a million-dollar home entails property taxes, maintenance, and even a significant real estate fee just to sell. Purchasing an expensive car entails expensive upkeep, more expensive gas, and, of course, a new line of clothing and keychains so people will remember that you still have that great car. Simply by driving a new car off the lot, 10% of the purchase price is gone, with no way of getting it back. Having money will allow you larger lines of credit for purchases made with credit cards, but that money will have to be paid back someday.

Money may not solve most problems, but I will admit money buys stability… for a time. If you're about to lose your house or apartment from non-payment, of course, sufficient money will delay this. But if the underlying problem has not been solved (insufficient income, say, perhaps from a lack of a job), all you've done is delay the inevitable. Put another way, money allows you to waste time that ultimately is needed to resolve whatever is truly at the heart of the dysfunction.

Over the course of his career, singer MC Hammer amassed $70 million from album sales and other entertainment endeavors. In 1996, six years after releasing the hit song "Can't Touch This," he filed for Chapter 11 bankruptcy in Oakland, California. Today, while still impressive by average standards, his net worth is approximately $2 million. A lack of money was not his problem; it's that despite such wealth, he was living far beyond his means without any coherent plan to change course. Eventually, the cost is always paid.

How to Stay out of Poverty

I've already acknowledged that money buys stability and can temporarily stave off problems, but how do we ensure we stay out of poverty in the first place? The nonpartisan (please, hold back your laughter) Brookings Institution's research has determined three rules that, if followed, give the average person a 74% chance of ending up in the middle class

1. Graduate from high school.

2. Wait to get married until after twenty-one, and do not have children until after being married.

3. Have a full-time job.

If you feel like graduating from high school (as 84% of the adult population did in 2023), taking measures to prevent pregnancy until ready, or working forty out of 168 hours per week is too taxing, you're welcome to try and beat the odds. As one last additional carrot, only 2% of people who follow all three rules end up in poverty.

There are those (not me) who feel human weakness prevents people from doing this. Those other voices believe you can't control your sexual urges, are too undisciplined to complete high school like the other 84% of the population, and are too lazy or incompetent to commit yourself to eight hours of work five days a week. This is the soft bigotry of low expectations. You hold others to a lower standard because you feel they are incapable of meeting that norm.

People generally rise to the level of their expectations, and if nothing is expected of them, they will "rise" to meet that standard. In World War II, the average soldier of the Greatest Generation had nine years of public education. By today's standards, that would put them as having an average education to that of an eighth grader. Despite this, their character and skill were good enough to ensure democracy instead of fascism (and later communism) became the dominant force in the world and ushered in the American-led century.

Our current generation needs to be on their parents' healthcare until twenty-six because they are unable or, more likely, unwilling to handle the burden themselves, need safe spaces in case somebody says something that makes them feel bad, and scream through tears into the sky when their candidate of choice doesn't win an election. I'm not saying who has/had it harder or who is more mature. That is not the point of this chapter. The point I'm trying to make is that, in general (of course not always), poverty (or wealth) is the result of decisions we make over time.

Good decisions, generally, lead to good results. Bad decisions, generally, lead to bad results. Wealth and income are a consequence of this. Well-thought-out, planned, and executed ideas lead to a higher probability of having larger amounts of income and wealth, if that's what you want. Poorly thought-out plans (or non-existent plans) have a higher probability of leading to poverty and misery. That's not to say that a rich person made nothing but good decisions, or that a poor person made nothing but bad decisions, resulting in their current socio-economic status. Idiots win the lottery every day.

Why Doesn't Throwing Money at the Problem Work?

Wealth, and what can be purchased with it, is nothing more than an expression of human will and desire once spent. $100 to one person will buy their life-saving medication; to another, it will fund a present for their child on their birthday, and to another, it is enough to pay for twenty minutes of pleasure in a strip club or casino. It's important to note that all three of these individuals could be the same person, and that same $100 could be in competition as to where it goes. The possibilities of what money can be spent on, legal or illegal, are nearly limitless.

Money doesn't solve most problems because people spend it on what brings them value, regardless of whether or not it solves any or all of the problems in their life. The same applies to companies, organizations, and governments. These entities can (and do) spend money on things that provide value as they see it but may not necessarily solve what people agree are problems.

As I wrote this book, there was a small news broadcast from Portland, Oregon, showing homeless people purchasing packs of water (twenty-four or so bottles per pack) with food stamps (or electronic benefit transfer/EBT cards, if you prefer calling them that). Once the homeless individuals left the store, they took the bottles to a secluded area, emptied the water onto the asphalt, and then sold the empty plastic water bottles for the cash return. The amount received from "returning" the plastic water bottles was $2.40, which was spent on cheap fentanyl. Had the EBT card value been larger, even more plastic water bottles would probably have been purchased and dumped on the street to purchase either more hard drugs or higher-quality drugs. At taxpayer expense, the supposed beneficiaries were enabled and permitted to continue playing Russian roulette with their lives.

People may express values that aren't reflected in how they spend their money. For example, imagine if there was an individual who espoused nothing but left-wing ideas, but then only donated to right-leaning political campaigns. Think of what it says if an absentee father says he loves and supports his children but provides none of his time or money and instead spends it on luxuries for himself. Picture if a celebrity claimed they valued taking action on climate change, but only did so by spending vast sums of wealth taking flights to and from luxurious climate conferences at European ski resorts on gas-guzzling private jets (I have nothing against private jets; I'd like to see one with my name on the side someday).

Money, and how it's spent, better approximates what we actually value rather than what we say we value. Words are cheap, and money talks. We make spending decisions based on how we value products and services that may be destructive to ourselves. More money certainly wouldn't help a cheating spouse any more than it would help a lazy individual who wants to spend his days watching Netflix and playing video games (no knocking Netflix and video games; I've spent many an hour on both). The problems are deeper than material wealth, and addressing those problems forces us to confront ideas we don't want to confront. For most, a lack of money is a symptom, not the cause of financial hardship. We have individuals, both with six-figure salaries and others who have no real income to speak of, who spend outside their means and end up owing more than they make.

The solution is comically simple but difficult to do: spend less or make more. That may require moving, going without, changing your lifestyle, or working more. These are not easy solutions, but they are simple. There's no reason that necessary things should also be easy.

I say all this as someone who, for most of my life, has never really had issues with money. The material wants that I've had have been matched by my income, although budgeting, of course, was needed to ensure I didn't grab too much caviar and limited my visits to Brazilian steakhouses (It's cheap caviar; I bought it from Walmart until they stopped stocking it).

I've been self-sufficient since the age of twenty-two, yet I still have (like you) problems. The problems I have are not about money and would not truly be fixed with more . Additionally, these problems aren't particularly unique (although, for my privacy, I'll be keeping those largely to myself). Some far less wealthy than me do not have the assortment of problems I do. Their challenges are different from mine. Just as many know the solutions to my solvable problems, I know the solution to others' solvable problems; the difficult part is recognition and execution. If you rely on money to answer the problems in your life, you're likely destined to be disappointed.

"Don't tell me what you value, show me your budget, and I'll tell you what you value."
— Joe Biden, 46th President of the United States

Chapter 6 Words Mean Things

"Who's on First?"

— Lou Costello, of Abbott and Costello; March 24, 1938

On May 17, 2023, an adjunct art professor at CUNY (City University of New York) Hunter College by the name of Shellyne Rodriguez (forty-six) approached a student pro-life (or anti-abortion; take your pick) display. As she realized what the student's display was about, she proceeded to curse at and accost them for their exhibition (with no apparent reciprocity), according to video of the incident. After confronting the students, claiming their display was propaganda (again, define the students' activity as you please), the professor stated, "This is violent. You're triggering my students," just prior to shoving the display materials towards the students. You may believe I've left out context, or that only one side of the story is being told (or that perhaps the story is even too boring to tell), but there is video to verify all this that's but an internet search away.

As the professor's actions were being investigated by the college, a reporter and his photographer from the New York Post approached Shellyne Rodriguez's apartment door and knocked, announcing themselves as reporters requesting comments concerning the events. According to the reporters (with the backing of photos of the events), Ms. Rodriguez threatened to "chop" them up, opening the door and revealing that she had a machete in hand, which she held to the reporter's neck. As the reporter and photographer departed the complex, Ms. Rodriguez followed them outside, machete in hand, kicking the reporter in the shins as he tried to get into his car. As of this writing, Ms. Rodriguez took a plea deal for a misdemeanor charge of menacing and has been fired from Hunter College. As part of the plea deal, she was required to complete six months of behavioral therapy, part of which hopefully involves how not to hold sharpened blades against people's necks.

Of the five people involved in this incident (the professor, two students at the display table, and two employees from the New York

Post), only one of them did anything that could be considered violence if the word is to have any meaning. While anyone may be "triggered" by any action or inaction (definition of triggered: caused to feel an intense and usually negative emotional reaction), only two of the individuals have reasonable reasons to feel "triggered." I don't like having to state the obvious, but having a machete waved in your face by a person cursing and threatening bodily harm is the only reasonable reason anybody in this story should feel "triggered."

Ms. Rodriguez's loose use of language, claiming the students' display was "violent," contrasts ironically with her own choice of actions, chasing reporters down a public street wielding a machete. Declaring her own students were "triggered" (showing her concern for others' feelings and emotions) apparently had no impact on her willingness to cause reasonable anxiety (or "triggering") to others by threatening their lives and assaulting them.

In 1984, a man (at the time) by the name of Duane Owen attacked four separate women in four separate attacks, killing two. One of those killed was a fourteen-year-old babysitter, while the other was a thirty-eight-year-old, each of whom he then forced himself on, assuming "forced" is the right word at that point. More than thirty years later, he was executed by lethal injection by the State of Florida for his crimes. The American Civil Liberties Union (ACLU), wanting to capitalize on fashionable ideas, condemned Florida for not providing Mr. Owen a requested gender transition before putting him to death. Citing the Eighth Amendment to the U.S. Constitution, the ACLU tweeted that it was "cruel and unusual" to not feminize Mr. Owen (my words, not theirs, except the "cruel and unusual" portion). I admit that the above story did have extreme cruelty and unusual activity (in the literal sense of the word), but none of it was on the part of the State of Florida. Perhaps in hell, Mr. Owen will get his wish to become Ms. Owen and have done to him what he did to others.

The above story isn't included to attack the ACLU or comment on capital punishment; it is because the term "cruel and unusual" has apparently lost all meaning. If a prisoner said they needed sex for their mental well-being, I don't believe many would conclude that the state should procure adult entertainers; otherwise, it would be considered "cruel and unusual." Had the State of Florida castrated Mr. Owen without him requesting a gender transition, I would agree that would be cruel and unusual (although, in some sense, it does seem a tad fair). In one last bit of irony, the ACLU also referred to the gender-affirming care as "medically necessary"; otherwise, Mr. Owen might have… killed himself, I suppose? We'll never know.

For a correct definition of "cruel and unusual," there are documented cases in which people being interrogated had clay pots filled with rats held against their body while the opposite end was heated. The rodents, desiring not to be cooked to death, would attempt to escape into the only safe direction. The same interrogation method was also used on other orifices of men and women. I hope you cannot actually imagine what this implies. Now that is cruel and unusual in the true sense of the word.

Before getting into the serious business of this chapter, it is pertinent that you understand what the phrase "words mean things" is trying to convey. If I tell you "The sky is blue," there are preconditions that must be met for us to have a meaningful discussion about the subject. We both must (1) understand enough English to speak and comprehend the sentence, (2) understand what "sky" is, using the context of the text as a clue, and (3) understand what "blue" is, again, using the context of the text as a clue. Once we are on the same page about what we are talking about, we can now enter a debate.

This introduction isn't about whether the sky is blue; that discussion could probably go on endlessly as a futile exercise in debate. For example, the receiver may surmise the sky isn't always blue, that at night it appears black. But the original speaker asserting "the sky is blue" may take offense to this, as the unstated assumption is that at this moment the sky is blue. However, the critic of the original statement may say two people on opposite sides of the Earth could look into the sky and see different things. God help us, someone else may interpret the original sentence as saying the sky is sad, as blue is a synonym for this. Thus, all sides are right and wrong simultaneously. We've learned nothing real except that we can twist the English language (or any language) to purposefully muddle the debate rather than find meaningful truth that allows us to better understand our world and pass meaning between each other.

If we cannot agree that specific words mean specific things, we cannot have meaningful conversations with each other to communicate ideas between individuals. For example, if a pregnant female checks "male" under "sex" on a medical form at a pregnancy center, what are they trying to communicate? (Originally, I wrote "pregnant biological female" but decided this was unnecessary. Medical science has not been able to birth a child from a biological human male. No confusion can be born from this unless someone wants it because they don't like what words mean.) Given the situation, it's obvious this is a female communicating they identify as a trans man and would like to be treated as such. If the individual had previously been knighted by the king or queen of England, he prefers to be referred to as "sir" rather than "dame." So far, there are no serious issues, so long as the doctor has been told or asked if the individual is pregnant, and thus may require different medical treatment. Simply asking all patients if they are pregnant, both males and females, is a ridiculous but simple way to solve the problem of what treatment may be necessary.

Words and labels have definitions that allow us to communicate ideas between one another in a coherent way. Those words and labels may convey ideas you may or may not like, but by trying to alter definitions to meet our desires, we are making it increasingly impossible to communicate with one another (which I believe is partially the point).

As of November 13, 2022*, Tinder, a dating app, has nine sexual orientations for the user to classify as in order to identify their desired partner(s) and a search bar for genders other than male or female for self-identification. The app allowed me to select male as my gender (there is no drop-down menu for sex) and lesbian as my orientation. In addition to this, the app also allowed me to select any (or all) of the nine sexual orientations I see myself as. Thus, I can select male as my gender and my sexual orientation as lesbian, straight, and asexual (not desiring a sexual relationship) simultaneously.

Why is this important? Because other users will be matched with me based on my self-identification, even if that self-identification is insane, a paradox, or a lie. In a clichéd example, a biological male identifying as a woman with profile pictures as a woman can appear in searches presented to straight cisgender males. These males may not be able to tell whether the person they go on a date with or become intimate with is actually male or female. This doesn't even require deceit on the trans woman's part, as far as the Tinder app goes. The app only asked their gender (in contemporary conversation, this conveys whether you are more feminine or masculine) and orientation (as in, who would they like to be intimate with). We now have a problem (or at least one person does).

Between November 13, 2022, and my first edit to this book, Tinder has largely eliminated the sections requesting the gender identity and sexual orientation of its users, and now only asks what gender a user is seeking by asking them if they are looking for men or women.

If a straight woman appeared at a gay bar as a man, strictly gay men would be incensed to discover the person they've been pursuing all evening had tricked them into potential intimacy and drained their bank accounts with the purchase of drinks for their would-be partner (I can relate to that). By definition, gay males are only interested in biological men. If there was the potential otherwise, he would not be a gay man but a bisexual man, and the described events wouldn't have the same issues. I've never in my life seen or heard of a situation in which a man claiming honestly to be gay finds it pleasurable and desirable to have sex with females. Conversely, I've never seen, heard of, or come across a woman honestly claiming to be a lesbian finding it pleasurable to have sex with biological males, with a single exception (more on this to follow later). If the commonly understood meanings of the words gay, lesbian, male, and female are used, all of this makes painfully perfect sense.

For those of you who dare think the situations described at the beginning of the last paragraph could never truly happen since we all know we could identify a biological male or female with our own eyes, I give you the case of Jennifer Laude and Lance Corporal Joseph Scott Pemberton.

The pair met at a nightclub on October 11, 2014, in Olongapo, Philippines. Leaving together to book a room at a nearby motel, both entered, but only Corporal Pemberton exited the motel thirty minutes after entering. Jennifer Laude had been drowned to death by Lance Corporal Joseph Pemberton. I cannot say with absolute certainty what intimate acts occurred and in what order; all I can say is that used condoms with Corporal Pemberton's DNA inside were found after the body was discovered. Pemberton later confessed he murdered Laude after he found out she was a male. With a high degree of certainty on my part, what happened is obvious. Corporal Pemberton became intimate with Laude, believing she was a female. At some point in the evening, Pemberton realized he had been deeply intimate with a male, throwing him into a rage, resulting in Laude's murder. All of this was a completely avoidable tragedy stemming from what should have been easily communicated.

In the same way, you are communicating important messages about who you are by the pronouns you potentially request others to use (Not me. I let them guess and judge them harshly if they are wrong), your tone of voice, clothing, makeup, and general demeanor communicate important details about yourself that you want others to believe about you. As of February 24, 2021, 5.6% of the population claims to be LGBT. I use the word claim because, in our modern times, anyone can claim to be anything, seemingly without needing any proof or backing. Women who have children can claim (and have) that they are completely uninterested in men and say they are lesbian, only to marry men or have more children after the lesbian relationship doesn't work out. Men can (and have) claimed they are bisexual even if they've never dated or been intimate with a male. I'll admit, walking around my gym, my eyes have been drawn to random toned butts, but after realizing they are probably biological men, my mind subconsciously moves on, searching for more appealing eye candy (again, subconsciously. Believe it or not, I don't even realize what's happening until it does). Honest question: Does that make me bisexual? Be careful how you answer. Others more intimately associated with the LGBT community than yourself may disagree with you, perhaps even some with doctorates in gender studies.

With 5.6% of the population claiming to be gay, there is a 94.4% chance the person you would like to be intimate with is not interested in you if you are attracted to the same sex. I empathize; I really do; it's hard enough for a single person when the ratio is reversed. Do you feel it's important that a potential partner knows your sex? Better question: Do you want to know the sex of the person you would like to be intimate with? If Jennifer Loude had been punched in the face by a lesbian after discovering Loude was a biological male with male genitals, would we still feel as bad for Loude (who truly deserves our grief), or would we conclude deception was used in such a way that Loude either knew or should have known the risks of tricking people in order to have sex with them? After conversing with close female friends and relatives on the subject, I found them to be strangely troubled by the idea of men using deception in order to get women into bed. Lying about your wealth, job, marital status, and promises of a future relationship are just as important as lying,or conveniently not mentioning, about your sex. Unless, of course, lying about your biological sex is an exception we'd like to maintain now and into the future. In that case, just tear out any pages after "words mean things" at the beginning of this chapter, throw them into your municipal memory hole, and move on to the next chapter.

Believe it or not, I have seen this in its worst form in person. A trans woman at a bar asked our table not to tell anyone else she was male, since some of us knew. She appeared as a biological woman and had many would-be male partners buying her drinks, dancing, and becoming physically close. Given the overall odds that 94.4% were straight, I find it hard to believe I had stumbled upon the only gay bar in (location omitted) and that all the US Marines at this bar knew she was biologically male and were gay themselves. I do not know if she had bottom surgery (I can confirm she had spectacular top surgery), but I did have concern for her life and limb if one of those Marines found out later she was not a female.

Around 2019, Miley Cyrus, an American actress and performer, appeared on the cover of Vanity Fair and in an included interview. Prior to this, in 2015, she had claimed to be queer and pansexual (that is, capable of falling in love with people regardless of their various identities). After marrying Liam Hemsworth (a more rugged, manly, and toned male would be hard to find), brother of Chris Hemsworth, she stated, "We're redefining, to be fucking frank, what it looks like for someone that's a queer person like myself to be in a hetero relationship. A big part of my pride and my identity is being a queer person." While she has been pictured holding hands with other females or lounging on private yachts with other scantily clad women, her public dating history appears very… normal, for lack of better words. (If you don't like the word "normal," insert "average" in its place.)

I understand that, for one reason or another, homosexual individuals can and have married somebody of the opposite sex, despite not being sexually attracted to them. I also understand Ms. Cyrus may have some minor attraction to the same sex, as many females (and to a lesser extent males) do. But to claim to be queer, as I understand it, means you are an out-of-the-closet gay, lesbian, bisexual, or transgender person. If that's not the case, I can claim to be queer (as could anyone), as apparently the word has no meaning. To claim to be queer, have little to no evidence of long-term same-sex relationships, and then marry a man destroys the concept of what being queer means. If queer does not mean you are at the very least strongly attracted to the same sex (by strong, I mean you would like to pursue intimate interactions with them with regular frequency), I'll need as many queer females as possible to meet with me to explain the difference. As fair compensation, the drinks are on me.

The real reason Ms. Cyrus probably claimed to be queer is that her popularity almost exclusively rests on her sex appeal. Given that she's female, nearly all the attention dependent on her sexual appeal will come from men. There is a largely uninteresting reason men find lesbian or bisexual women sexy, but nearly all do (the sexy ones, that is). Suggesting she was a lesbian or bisexual would excite the male members of her audience and give her more attention, which usually translates into more dollars. I don't hold this against Ms. Cyrus, but many in the LGBT community would and do.

A relative of mine and I have frequent conversations about politics, current events, and occasionally religion. As long as I have known him, he has claimed to be an atheist and enjoys educating himself on the world's religions. As part of our conversations, I was curious to ask if he believed in any supernatural deity or higher power, to which his answer was that he saw no evidence in current religions but was open to the idea if more evidence materialized (such as a booming voice from the sky). Within the atheist community, I'm told, there are two types of atheists: hard atheists (who actively believe there is no god) and soft atheists (those who don't believe in a god but don't actively deny the possibility). I recognized that this "soft atheist" was, in fact, agnosticism. After that conclusion, I informed my relative he was, in fact, agnostic. An issue arose, as he did not like the label agnostic. He assured me he was an atheist. When I read the definitions (the first to pop up in Google) of atheism and agnosticism, he agreed to all the elements of agnosticism (but only some of atheism) but was adamant that he was an atheist.

To further his point, he said I was atheist to all religions except the one I (poorly) participate in. Thus, while I believe in a higher power, he insisted I was an atheist to all other religions, and could thus consider myself an atheist. This twisting of language was done so that he could logically (he is very logical) call himself an atheist. Why did he do this? In his mind, I believe he had a negative impression of those in the agnostic community. Within the atheist community, some view those claiming to be agnostic as not logical or only performing half measures to "hedge bets." From this viewpoint, the agnostics are still being irrational or unscientific. While I don't believe my cousin viewed agnostic people in this way, the atheist community at large had created such a negative connotation with the term agnostic that I believe it made an impression that left my cousin not wishing to have the label applied to himself. Regardless of what my cousin wanted to be, he was, in fact, agnostic.

In the same way, I may wish to be a different race, sex, or even species, but I cannot. I may call myself whatever I wish, but if I or others need to communicate ideas about what I am to fellow English speakers, we need to have understood words that have understood meanings. If a dog attacks me, the city may wish to put the dog down so it can't harm another human being. If a person attacks me, once the danger has passed, the city will not try to put a person down unless I am killed. If a person claiming to be a dog attacks me, the city will not treat this self-identity as true identity and put the person down. While some "otherkin" (those who identify as not entirely human) may wish to be something other than human, they are not. To treat them as such would be, by definition, inhuman (say, by spaying or neutering such people against their will or keeping them in public shelters until someone comes to adopt them).

If I told people I were a gay male but did not want to be in a relationship with biological men or have intercourse with them, they would be confused. If I told others I was Asian American but had no relative in my family tree that was Asian, they would also be perplexed. This confusion stems from the fact that, regardless of whether we like it or not, words mean things. Labels are useful for communicating ideas to one another for which we have a common understanding. If I referred to someone as a murderer, it is understood by the community at large that I'm saying someone has maliciously killed someone for an unlawful reason. To call someone a murderer who is not is considered slander, for which I could be (rightfully) sued for defamation.

You, the reader, may not like some labels applied to you or others around you. You may be rich but want to be considered middle class. You may be White but wish you could claim African American heritage. You may be grossly underweight or overweight but wish to be considered average. I'm sorry for your predicament, but reality does not care about your feelings. I say that as someone subject to these very same rules. We, collectively, need to realize what is possible to change and what is not possible to change and accept it. Fooling ourselves and others can only result in preventable conflicts.

Ask yourself, not me or anyone else, what you believe a trans woman to be. A tiny percent of the population believes this is a male who becomes a female (such as the characters in *The Hot Chick*). Nearly all of us understand that a trans woman is actually a male who, with or without cosmetic surgery, wishes they were female. Prior to the late 2010s, we already had boring, matter-of-fact descriptions of such individuals. A trans woman is (generally) a feminine male who wants to adhere to feminine stereotypes. A trans man is (again, generally) a masculine female who wants to adhere to male stereotypes. A nonbinary individual is one who doesn't wish to be associated with either of the stereotyped sexes or wishes to be able to go between them at will. Last time I checked, this is America. If a male wishes to wear makeup, skirts, and fake nails, more power to him. If a female wants a short haircut, facial hair, and masculine clothing, go crazy with it; you have (not that you need it) my endorsement.

You know the above to be accurate descriptions. If our discourse were honest, we would begin debates on public policies (including segregating sexes in sports and prison) from these simple, well-understood concepts. Instead, we have twisted language to be used against well-reasoned and grounded truths in order to have something to fight for or against. Rather than logically think through issues surrounding public policy, we have erected poorly thought-out ideologies grounded not in logic but emotion. These ideologies don't make any logical sense and fall apart with even the simplest critique.

Why do we do this? Simply put, all of us have a desired endpoint we wish society would come to. If I asked each of the 332 million Americans what they wished society to be, I would get 600 million different answers, depending on the time of day I asked each person the question. For many of us, we don't want to give the other side an inch, believing that any ground given up will only be met with a demand for more ground. So we sit, entrenched on our side, looking over into no-man's-land*, believing that if we make a move to the middle, both sides might start shooting (metaphorically... hopefully) simultaneously, one side unwilling to deal with traitors to the cause, and the other willing to take advantage of any faltering on the other side.

*In World War I, no man's land was the area in between two opposing enemy trenches. Being in this geographic area meant you were out of the safety of your own trench and were at a much greater risk of death by artillery, machine gun, mortar, and rifle fire. It was called no-man's land because, metaphorically, there were no men alive in it. Thankfully, due to the proportion of those killed in this geographic area, there is not yet a no-woman's land.

We distort language to further our aims, regardless of the confusion that results. For example, many non-violent actions (such as voicing an unpopular opinion) are called "violent" in order to elevate the level of threat and thus elicit a stronger response. In this way, the term violence is watered down to the point that rape, murder, and writing a mean tweet are all considered "violence." White supremacy used to be a term only applied to 1940s-style fascists and Southern Civil War leaders. That term has been so watered down that African American Supreme Court judges and politicians have been called White supremacists, and according to some, half the country are Nazis. The ability to identify actual White supremacists is lost as they are lumped in with a much larger group that holds none of the values of those racists.

I submit that words at any specific moment in time have specific meanings understood by the vast majority of the public. There's nothing wrong with new or changing language, so long as it aids in our communication with each other. If it fails to do that, then the language evolves into one in which meaning is obscured. We risk, at some point, becoming unable to effectively communicate with each other because our understanding of a common language has branched to the point that we cannot comprehend what each other is saying (and at its worst, don't want to).

Below is a short list of some words and concepts that have either changed drastically or lost total and complete meaning:

Family-friendly: Generally lacking adult themes such as nudity, overt or highly suggestive sexual acts, gratuitous violence, obscenity, or hard drug use.

New definition: Any event we would like children to take part in or watch.

Violence: Physical force resulting in injury, death, or serious bodily harm.

New definition: Any action taken that might make somebody else feel bad.

Safe: Free of the threat of physical force or bodily harm.

New definition: Not being offended in any way.

Racism: Prejudice, discrimination, or antagonism against a person or people on the basis of their membership in a particular ethnic or racial group.

New definition: Showing prejudice, discrimination, or antagonism against a person or people on the basis of their membership in a particular ethnic or racial group while at the same time being White while the victim is not.

Sexism: Prejudice, stereotyping, or discrimination on the basis of sex.

New definition: Prejudice, stereotyping, or discrimination on the basis of sex if you're male while the victim is female.

Problematic: Constituting or presenting a problem or difficulty.

New definition: Forbidden to believe or take part in. (For example, "It's problematic when men look at women in the gym" translates to "It's prohibited for men to look at women in the gym.")

Alternative new definition: A person needing ostracizing. (For example, "Will Smith's actions at the Oscars were problematic" translates to "Will Smith's actions at the Oscars demand he be ostracized.")

Nazi: A member of the Nazi Party or someone believing in the ideals supported by that party.
 New definition: Anyone whose actions or ideas we don't like.

Riot: A violent disturbance of the peace by a crowd.
 New definition: A mostly peaceful protest unless we don't agree with the motivation behind the riot. (Apologies for using the word in the definition of the word; you get my intent. If you don't, continue being bewildered.)

Rights: Those things that cannot be taken from you because they derive from human nature or a higher power and are therefore inherent in us.
 New definition: Anything we want to be allowed to do, regardless of any legal, ethical, or moral problems it creates.

Marginalized: A person or group treated as insignificant or peripheral.
 New definition: A group in vogue (that is, in style). Example: "Women are marginalized" used to mean this group was treated as minor or irrelevant. "Women are marginalized" now means that being female is trendy and hip, and that the alternative, being male, is not cool and is passé (French for past).

Journalist: Someone who gathers, assesses, creates, and presents news and information.
 New definition: Somebody who spends 23 seconds telling portions of a news story and 59 minutes and 37 seconds telling you their opinion on what was reported by someone else.
 New definition for those in print/online media: Somebody who spends a paragraph or less telling portions of a news story and 15 paragraphs telling you their opinion on what was observed and reported by someone else.

Debunked: Proven objectively that an idea or belief is false.

New definition: An idea said to be proven false because we don't like what it could mean if true.

In order for this book to be as accurate as possible (which is the whole point), I sought the input of friends, relatives, coworkers, and strangers to see if the ideas I put forth made sense or if they thought I was a raving lunatic needing to be rushed to an insane asylum or other state-sponsored confinement as expediently as possible. One of those strangers read the above "new and old definitions," and her only critique was that it read as if a White cisgender straight man wrote it. After assuring her that I'm the one who wrote it, I revealed to her that I was not those things she was describing. I went on to say that I was a transgender lesbian (apparently my dress, mannerisms, and physical appearance did not communicate this). After she heard this, she dropped any issues she had with the definitions I put forth (I wish I was kidding), her concerns having been resolved, and we continued chatting politely until the bar closed.

It legitimately pains me, but I will now provide the clearest example I can think of to explain why words' meanings are important. As reported by The Independent (a well-known British publication), an actor currently by the name of Elliot Page claims an A-list actor offered him sex to make him realize he wasn't gay. For most people, this statement would be interpreted to mean that an unnamed female celebrity was trying to be intimate with a male celebrity (Elliot) claiming to be gay, with Elliot refusing the offer from the A-list female actress, instead choosing to continue being intimate with men. I will not explain who Elliot Page is, because you either already know or can easily look him up to determine why I chose this as an example.

If Elliot is a man who enjoys being intimate with women, Elliot is straight. If Elliot is female (note: I said female, not woman) and enjoys being intimate with females, that would make Elliot a lesbian. If anyone finds it insulting that I would try to put a label on such a thing, then I fully acquiesce and will agree that Elliot is neither gay, straight, nor lesbian, but some type of unnamed amalgam that will baffle scientists and psychologists for millennia; a unique butterfly for whom the English language lacks the complexity to explain because of its simplicity in the face of a brave new world.

This is not meant to be insulting to Mr. Page, the purpose of this chapter is to point out that words have meaning, and that those meanings are important.

This is also not intended to be a gotcha question, but is a legitimate quandary: Is a transgender man who is attracted to females a lesbian or straight? If the label doesn't matter or has no meaning, what's wrong with literally anyone calling themselves a lesbian? At any moment, if a male calls himself a lesbian, what does this truly indicate? I am, of course, not the first to bring this up, as I'm sure the internet is full of these deep, meaningful, well-thought-out discussions (…) concerning celebrities, sexual orientations, and gender ideology. That said, I may be the first to ask you, and just you: Is Mr. Page gay?

I believe many would find it insulting if I referred to Mr. Page as a straight man, and probably just as many others would find it insulting if I referred to Mr. Page as a lesbian. How then are we supposed to respectfully converse on such matters in which labels are apparently important? If the answer is "We're not supposed to at all," then I'd like to talk to the arbiter of what concepts we can talk about and those we can't because they insult or offend somebody somewhere on the face of the planet. I'd like to add a few things verboten to consider or think about (J/K).

To put the metaphorical nail in the coffin, as of June 13, 2023, Johns Hopkins University, a private research university in Baltimore, Maryland, updated its LGBTQ glossary to define lesbians as "non-men attracted to non-men." Apparently, not only did this leave out Mr. Page, but it included inanimate objects attracted to each other via magnetic, gravitational, and electrostatic forces. Oddly, this definition even included hermaphroditic earthworms that can be said to be neither male nor female. Despite the relatively small percentage of the human population, apparently nearly all of physics and understood science (including hermaphroditic earthworms) is lesbian according to the well-known university. Who knew?

June 14, 2023 revision: Johns Hopkins has removed the previously mentioned definition, as apparently it lacked the meaning understood words are meant to convey.

In truth, there are labels that are accurate and reflect understood meaning between speaker and receiver. Some may not like those labels because they reflect a reality we may not wish to acknowledge, but they are true nonetheless. We may continue ignoring understood meaning, but again this comes at a cost. Slowly, over time, we cease being able to understand what is occurring around us because words, labels, and definitions become so vague they stop having any true meaning.

Our words have been muddled to hide the intent, to change the public's mind in one direction or the other (on a left/right basis. I accuse both sides of this deception). As we do this, our words lose meaning, and we become unable to communicate with one another about any societal problems, public policy, or even mundane topics since we can't agree on the meaning of words.

As I was cleaning my front yard, a neighbor popped her head out, and we conversed pleasantly about topics of the day, the weather, and local neighborhood events. At one point, my neighbor said it was sad there were so many homeless around us with mental-health issues. I replied, "If you mean those high and drunk out of their minds, yes, I would agree there is an issue with our "neighbors" and their mental-health issues." She did not scold or correct me because she knew what I was saying was correct. Others not as familiar with our homeless "neighbors" might have interpreted "mental-health issues" as indicating that they have developmental disorders or diseases associated with the brain. So we were all on the same page; this misunderstanding needed to be made clearer.

In 1918, US Senator Hiram Warren Johnson is purported to have said, "The first casualty of war is the truth." To summarize Carl von Clausewitz, a Prussian general and military theorist: politics is war by other means. If we combine these (accurate) ideas, we arrive at why our discourse has become so muddled and definitions so vague. Politics is war, and the truth is the first to go to attain our aims. People are not moved by the mundane, the everyday, and the common. Our discourse is moved when perceived great injustices require action. If there is not a great injustice to overcome, one needs to be made up in order to change the discourse so that contemporary societal ills can eventually be settled. We thus become willing to hide facts that don't support our side, propagandize the strong points that support our position, and slander (or libel, but I'd recommend slander as it's harder to prove in court) our opponents by purposefully misrepresenting their ideas and attacking their character.

I'll leave this chapter with this thought: Everyone I've talked to one-on-one has been far more willing to say what they truly think in private when they believe I won't abuse that trust and that their thoughts will not be known publicly. Hardline stances are replaced by nuance, and staunch opposition is swapped for thoughtful debate — not all the time, of course, but the vast majority. They intuitively know words have meaning, understand that meaning, and in most cases come to an agreement about what is actually trying to be communicated.

I personally believe we agree with each other far more than we disagree, and if we were honest with each other, we could have a more substantive public discourse based on mutual respect. The alternative is that we continue seeing "the other side" as an increasingly inhuman monster we must eventually overpower or slay. Unfortunately, if that's your solution (I can say with certainty it's not mine), I recommend getting out of real estate, gold, and silver, and instead investing in lead. Your call.

Chapter End Notes

While having this book edited, I was informed this title's chapter (Words Mean Things) could be made better by rewording or otherwise revising it. I decided to keep this title because it was what my senior instructors in the military told me time and time again. I hated that phrase because, at the time I was being corrected based on it, an act I felt was unnecessary and personally insulting. With age and maturity, I realized their goal was not necessarily to arbitrarily critique, but to develop me and others into more effective officers. It legitimately pained me to include it, but I did so because I knew that lesson also had merit. Just because things make us uncomfortable doesn't mean it's not necessary.

"It depends on what the meaning of the word 'is' is. If the — if he — if 'is' means is and never has been, that is not — that is one thing. If it

means there is none, that was a completely true statement. ...Now, if someone had asked me on that day, "Are you having any kind of sexual relations with Ms. Lewinsky?" that is, asked me a question in the present tense, I would have said no. And it would have been completely true."

— Bill Clinton, 42nd president of the United States, when asked if he was having any sexual relations with Monica Lewinsky. 1946-present

Depth

While I was working at a bar (to call myself a bartender at that job would be a huge stretch of the English language, as we essentially had nothing on draft and no liquor), I had a lot of time to listen to the background music and ponder the lyrics. For most employed people, this would be strange, as it would be assumed there would be customers to serve and work to do. This was not my experience, and I hope by the time this book is published that bar is still operating for the sole reason that I hope my former coworkers still have jobs and the regulars a place to socialize (myself included).

At first, the songs only reminded me of music I'd heard on the radio in my youth — catchy, well-known, and heard everywhere from commercials to supermarkets or just blaring out of cars for the benefit of all. But with all the time in the world, at some point, I started paying attention to the lyrics and realized there was a depth to these songs. When I asked coworkers and bar patrons if they knew what these various songs were about, they shrugged, even those who had been around when the songs were released, before I was even an idea. At first, I was surprised such things could be thought up and publicized in the way they were, seemingly without controversy or opposition given the content.

As I heard more and pondered them, I realized they came from the same human condition I was in, and it became clearer how these songs and lyrics came about. The songs themselves were crafted from fellow (more) creative human beings who had thought up such lyrics and put pen to paper. They were recorded and publicized because they were catchy or resonated with the public in such a way that people wanted to purchase the vinyls, tapes, CDs, or MP3 files. As far as I can tell, most listeners do not know the messages their beloved songs convey (but I see no issue with someone enjoying a song or movie despite not knowing what it's about).I was reminded of this notion while reviewing the previous chapter about words and their meanings.

With the tunes and rhythm being the part people paid attention to, I realized almost no one was paying attention to the words, and thus most people were ignoring or missing the point the song was trying to make (assuming it had a point and wasn't just a pop song cash-grab).One of the ideas underlying this book is that people are not thinking their way through life and instead are just reacting to events around them, unaware that they should be paying attention to what's happening. Listening to these songs, I realized many had rather interesting messages lost on the general public. While the below are just my interpretation of what the songs are about, I feel confident making the following assertions:

- Don't Stand So Close To Me, The Police: A 30–34 year old teacher falls in love with a 15–17-year-old student he teaches who shares the same feelings.

- Pumped Up Kicks, Foster the People: A child acquires his father's pistol and is about to murder another/other child(ren), probably in a mall.

- Imagine, John Lennon: A reinvocation of communism, but dressed up (no heaven, no countries, no possessions, sharing all the world). (You can still like the song, but good luck putting it into practice.)

- Born in the USA, Bruce Springsteen: Ironically, a counterculture song about the Vietnam War and a dystopian situation about working-class America. (I'll still be playing a portion of it should I ever have a campaign rally in the future.)

- Everybody Wants to Rule the World, Tears for Fears: A nuclear war occurs.

- The Thunder Rolls, Garth Brooks: A wife murders her husband after catching him cheating.

- Delilah, Tom Jones: A boyfriend murders his girlfriend after catching her cheating. He then waits for the police to break down the door to capture or kill him.

- Waterloo, ABBA: A woman acquiesces to a man's advances, comparing it to losing a war (although, oddly, she seems to enjoy it). The song was featured prominently in Mamma Mia!

- I Want Candy, The Strangeloves: A song about a man desiring a girl named Candy (not wanting a sugary treat). Given the name, a few assumptions can be made about the character of Candy.

- Centerfold, J. Geils Band: A man discovers his old high school crush is in an adult magazine and then takes action to become intimate with her, after purchasing the magazine, of course.

- Every Breath You Take, The Police: A former/potential love interest stalks their desired significant other, promising to keep watching them.

This list goes on endlessly with well-known songs and their messages that fly over most peoples' heads. The same is true of popular books, films, TV shows, and other entertainment products and artistic works. My understanding of the world and how it works was aided by having insight into others' minds via their creative works, even if their works were edgy or dark. The ideas had to come from somewhere, and since they were all created by people, each provided deeper insight into peoples' minds than they may be willing to voice in normal conversation.

In 1997, the movie Starship Troopers was released, in which young high school graduates volunteer to fight for Earth's government (known as "The Federation") against a menacing race of giant bugs known as the Arachnids. The movie, directed by Paul Verhoeven, was advertised as a violent sci-fi adventure indistinguishable from whatever other nonsense Hollywood was making at the time. Lost on nearly all moviegoers (including myself)was the satire and messaging being offered up.

Paul Verhoeven (again, the director of the movie for those whose attention spans have been destroyed by eleven-second clips of cats and people injuring themselves on the internet) was born on July 18, 1938, in Amsterdam, Netherlands. In 1943, after the Germans had invaded and conquered his home country three years prior, Mr. Verhoeven's family moved to The Hague, Germany's headquarters in the Netherlands. Here, he saw firsthand the horrors of war and Nazi occupation as a child. His experience there obviously inspired much of his future work as a director, but none as much as Starship Troopers.

His movies are some of the most violent and gory, to the amusement of moviegoers everywhere. In my youth (I was ten when the movie came out), it was the first gratuitously violent movie I saw, and (after Titanic) the second movie I saw that had female nudity (for some odd reason the male nudity didn't make the cut, unless you count the butt). Years later, I either read or heard that the movie was trying to make Nazis sexy, which at first I thought was just nonsense from those with more time and money than wisdom, endlessly picking apart contemporary cult classics for depth that may not have existed. After rewatching it in adulthood, I realized I couldn't have been more incorrect.

As I interpret it, Mr. Verhoeven was trying to make a movie showing how easily people can fall in line with fascism and can't even see that they've done so. For those that have seen the movie, this doesn't come as much of a shock, but for those that haven't, it is difficult to describe. The seemingly dumb, violent, nudity-filled motion picture was in fact not a shallow Hollywood blockbuster, but a work of fiction that had important things to say to those that were paying attention (or eventually paid attention, like me).

While I didn't have enough material to turn "most people aren't paying attention" into a whole chapter, I feel like it is a truth worth mentioning as an aside. Many films, songs, and TV shows have messages that go largely unknown by the public who watch them, despite the commercial success of such artistic endeavors. Events are happening in the news and around us on a day-to-day basis that people don't seem to understand the importance of, despite it being obvious to the point of absurdity. This is all to say there is a depth to life that seems to be missed by most people, and I find it troubling. If people aren't truly paying attention to even popular things they are drawn to, how much more are they missing? Could it also be that things that are unquestioningly true are also flying over people's heads, either because they aren't paying attention or simply don't care?

I'll leave this subchapter with this: While arriving at a job site I no longer work at, one of my coworkers greeted me by calling out, "Sup, girl?" I hadn't yet talked with my coworker about my gender fluidity and found it odd that she was greeting someone who appeared as a man in this way. Responding to her, I asked how she knew I was transitioning from man to woman. Since I appeared masculine, she became agitated and said I can't joke about such things. I then asked her how she knew I was not transitioning. She appeared taken aback as if she had just stepped on a landmine that hadn't yet gone off, but after a few moments responded with, "Well, if you are trying to be a woman, you're doing a really shitty job." The depth of that statement was lost on us both at the time.

Chapter 7 Not All College Majors Are Equal

Noah: Not that it's any of your business, but I plan to teach.
Sterling Archer: Anthropology?
Noah: What? Yes!
Rip Riley: To, uh, anthropology majors?
Sterling Archer: Thus continuing the circle of 'why bother?'
— Archer, Season 3, Episode 2

The University of Virginia (which, according to U.S. News & World Report, costs approximately $57,000 per year) has a degree program within its School of Medicine entitled Division of Perceptual Studies that, according to its own website, tries to determine whether or not "consciousness survives physical death." In short, there is a very expensive degree program to teach university students that ghosts exist (I'm not saying they don't, but for $57,000 a year for four years, I'd like to see some proof and talk to a few dead relatives — the cool ones). As I pored through op-eds advocating for this policy or that policy regarding college costs and student loans, I inevitably came across someone who has accrued hundreds of thousands of dollars in student debt (the median debt is $17,000 as of 2019; $32,000 on average). The writer discusses (or pleads) how they will never be able to pay it off at their current occupation and that it will forever be a "Sword of Damocles," menacingly always there, always threatening their well-being.

What I almost never hear is what their degree was in or what their current job is. In almost every case, they highlight how well educated they are but how poorly their job pays. The reason is simple: colleges and universities, whether public or private, will charge people whatever price they believe people will pay, just like any other organization. If the price is too high, students will stay away, unable to pay or take loans to cover the costs. If prices are too low, universities will not be able to pay for quality staff or keep the lights on.

More prestigious colleges and universities can play this game better, as the name of the university, not the quality of education, is what truly matters. Some people assume the cost of the degree is somehow related to the salary that can be commanded once they graduate from the institution. While this is true in some cases, in most it is demonstrably false and nothing more than an example of people throwing money at a problem with no foresight or future planning, instead relying on blind optimism. I have far more respect for an individual who enters a trade school than I do for an individual who studies post-colonial gender studies from an Indigenous perspective, hoping against all hope they will get a job related to their field that pays six figures to a twenty-two-year-old in their desired zip code.

Education's Value

Education is important. It grounds us in reality (for most majors) and opens our eyes to a wider world. College itself has an important, unstated purpose: to identify individuals capable of more complex tasks. Think back to your own education in grade school, high school, and college; how much of it do you actually remember? If you, like me, can't recall much, then ask yourself, what was the point? When I asked myself this question, I realized: education (generally) is not about the information learned, but about identifying individuals who can perform increasingly complex and difficult tasks.

Put yourself in the shoes of an employer. What does a high school degree signify? High school requires individuals, under close supervision by their parents (hopefully) and teachers (again, hopefully) to accomplish tasks that are generally short term. Homework is given one day and turned back in the next. Show up on time, wear appropriate clothing, and keep your violent and sexual urges to a minimum. A high school degree signifies to an employer that, under close supervision, you can accomplish tasks appropriately.

In the United States, college students generally move from their childhood home to a college or university campus and are on their own for the first time. With no parents and a largely distant instructor class, success now depends on the student's own drive. The choices of when to get up, when to study, where to eat, and whether or not to attend class fall solely on the shoulders of the student. Tasks are no longer day to day, and students may only have two tests the entire semester. Long-term planning and good judgment over the course of a minimum of four years is required to get a bachelor's degree.

From an employer's perspective, that means you can operate on your own, without direct supervision and guidance. You are viewed as likely being capable of identifying problems and solutions on your own, and thus providing more value to an employer. All that said, because there has been a large push for everyone to go to college, some majors have developed that don't require nearly as much rigorous study as others. Collectively, these obscure and largely useless majors mockingly fall under the umbrella of "underwater basket weaving." In addition, many majors serve no purpose other than to create a few college professors that teach the same course, offering little or no practical real-world use.

I know too many in these majors that may sound insulting, but it is not intended to be. Generations of college students have been given poor guidance in college and major selection, wasting untold fortunes at taxpayers and parental expense. I don't need to name these schools and majors, because you already know what they are.

Academia

This may surprise some (including many college students), but many of those instructing classes are not full professors. Those teaching courses span the academic hierarchy from teaching assistant to instructor, assistant professor, associate professor, all the way to full professor, which, ideally for the individual, comes with tenure. For a professor, achieving tenure means being given a permanent post that is difficult to be fired from. Ideally, this allows the professor to research or teach at their own discretion, without worrying nearly as much about job security or being fired for frivolous reasons. Tenured positions are coveted and take years to achieve.

Generally, this tenure process involves getting a PhD in the field, producing research, and teaching (rising through the academic hierarchy) along with some other minor field-related work. For the purposes of this book, I would like to focus on this "research." While many fields are based in fact, the scientific method, and enlightenment ideals, some are not based on any of these well-grounded and logical theories. These fields instead exist to support an idea rather than the truth, and to push beliefs instead of determining what is fact from fiction.

In the late 2010s, a group of authors, Peter Boghossian, James A. Lindsay, and Helen Pluckrose, wanted to highlight serious issues they saw in specific academic fields. Their goal was to fabricate studies and submit them for peer review to see if they would get published. The perception of what happens in peer review is that ideas must be vetted by people knowledgeable in the field, and only those ideas that hold up to scrutiny can be published in a journal.

Below are what the trio managed to get published in vetted, peer-reviewed journals:

- The Conceptual Penis as a Social Construct, Cogent Social Sciences, 2017. The paper argues that penises are not "male," but that they should be viewed and analyzed as a social construct, invented by society rather than being natural.

- Who Are They to Judge? Overcoming Anthropometry and a Framework for Fat Bodybuilding, Fat Studies, 2018. The paper advocates for creating a "fat bodybuilding" sport to compete with other bodybuilding competitions to show that fat bodies (it was in the title of the piece, not my choice of words) should be something to strive for by showing them in a positive light.

- Going in Through the Back Door: Challenging Straight Male Homohysteria and Transphobia through Receptive Penetrative Sex Toy Use, Sexuality & Culture, 2018. The paper recommends straight males insert phallic devices into themselves into places most straight males do not place phallic devices. This, oddly enough, inspires me to try and write a paper entitled, Going Through the Front Door: Heteronormative Experimentation from a Queer Perspective.

- Human Reactions to Rape Culture and Queer Performativity at Urban Dog Parks in Portland, Oregon, Gender, Place & Culture, 2018. The paper claims to be researching how pet owners react to either heterosexual or homosexual pet interactions in public parks.

- An Ethnography of Breastaurant Masculinity: Themes of Objectification, Sexual Conquest, Male Control, and Masculine Toughness in a Sexually Objectifying Restaurant, Sex Roles, 2018. I'll leave you, the reader, to look up what that last paper was communicating.

I know as you read through these fabricated pieces you have a few questions. The number one question is or should be, "What the hell am I reading?" Your second question either is or should be, "If such insanity can get published, what else can?" The answer to your question is anything, so long as the idea is in vogue. The above-published pieces passed the peer-review process because they used certain buzzwords, advocated what academia thought was important, and used long words and vague sentences to sound airy, intelligent, and refined without saying anything grounded in reality. Mountains of similar "research" and "scholarship" read exactly the same, with the exception that those authors believe what they are writing to be true and groundbreaking.

The reason for this is twofold.

1. In order to achieve tenure, would-be professors must publish a certain number of articles in specific publications.

2. Because of the shallowness of some academic fields, new (largely insane) ideas must be put forth so as to seem on par with other academic fields that actually generate scientific breakthroughs that aid humanity.

The result is "scholarship" and "research" that reinforce the idea that the field is important and merits more grant money and faculty members. Students excited by the premise (or ease) of the field of study major in these subjects not for future employment but largely because the field interests them. As an aside, I understand wanting to study subjects that interest oneself without future employment in mind. Thinking back to my own studies, I wish I had had more time to take courses that interested me. Sadly, at the time, I was on the clock, and every semester spent at college meant more expenses and an essentially non-existent source of revenue. Those funding my studies (that is, the U.S. government) also had a keen interest in me graduating as soon as possible so I could get to the business they needed me to get to.

There's nothing wrong with majoring in fields that interest you, but like all things, understand that this comes at a cost. Eighteenth-century French literature or anthropological studies of queer Indigenous peoples of the world may interest you, but the commercial viability of such studies is very questionable. The world only needs so many curators of libraries catering to French literature and experts in languages and customs used by exceptionally small numbers of humans.

I'm not telling you to avoid these fields, but that entering them forces you to sacrifice other goals, like everything in this world. Note: If you or your family is exceptionally wealthy, ignore the previous paragraph and study whatever you please; the result will largely be the same. Back to business. Studies relating to sex, race, ethnicity, and sexual orientation are simply self-reinforcing. At no point will research within one of these fields have results diminishing the need for that field of study or countering the narratives put forth.

Rather, as more ideas within the field are disproven, even more insane ideas are put forth to answer questions that are obvious. For example, women's studies address (among other things) why there is inequality between male and female income. At no point will a serious paper within the field make the determination that the inequality present has reasons that are reasonable and justifiable (such as women wanting more fulfilling versus higher-paying jobs). Rather, as systemic obstacles to equality between the sexes are removed, what is true simply becomes more and more obvious. Within these fields, the goal is not to further our understanding of the world; rather, it is to further "the cause," whatever the cost.

The Cause

In the wake of police shootings in the early 2010s, the Washington Post began coalescing police department statistics to generate a database of police-involved homicides. The goal was to highlight perceived (whether true or not, perceived is an accurate term) rampant police use of lethal force, especially as it is used against minority groups. In 2019, according to their database, eleven unarmed African-American men were killed by police (Keep in mind, unarmed doesn't necessarily mean not dangerous; cops have had their weapons taken off them or been killed by unarmed attackers).

At the same time, 2,574 homicides took place in which both the offender and victim were African-American, according to the FBI. Unfortunately, I've been unable to find data indicating if either of the parties were armed for the 2,574 killed. Any death is a tragedy, but a sense of scale must accompany this so we can try to prevent that which we don't want to occur. If our goal is to save as many lives from preventable violent deaths as we can, we need to focus our efforts where we can save the most lives.

One of the statistics noted above will be parroted, seen on every cable news network and debated ad nauseam, while the other will be ignored. I'll leave you to determine which is which. There is only one reason this is the case, and that's because of "the cause." There is a story (and story is the right word) developed through which all raw news, information, and statistics are filtered. If it helps the cause, it makes it through. If not, it is discarded as inconvenient at best and outright denied at worst. There is not just a single cause, but multiple causes that compete for attention. Different members of the population subscribe to different causes, and many support multiple causes. That said, each individual has a hierarchy of these causes, and if there is ever a conflict between two or more, the cause higher up the pyramid wins out. For example, if you are a feminist and supporter of the LGBT community, you must pick a side when a trans woman wants to be put into a female prison. You can either support the feminist idea that women must be protected and have access to female-only spaces, or you can support the LGBT advocacy for mixed-sex prisons for trans men and women, but you can't do both.

What the Hell Are We Talking About?

It may seem like a departure from talking about academia and college majors to talk about police shootings and some nebulous idea referred to as "the cause," but these are all linked. Specific academic fields don't actually care about finding out the truth if it comes at the expense of the cause, that is, supporting a set of ideas that cannot be questioned. For example, imagine if a women's studies professor held in their hands proof that men and women naturally develop differently and want different things, free of socially constructed gender roles.

Because this flies in the face of the field they have dedicated their life to, they will likely bury the study rather than further our understanding of ourselves. If a gender studies academic determines there is no rational basis for the idea of a person being nonbinary, they will not likely be rushing off to publish their proof in Biology of Sex Differences, a leading academic journal related to gender, unless perhaps they are tired of their job and wish to be fired and ostracized in the most expedient way possible.

To identify why "the cause" is so powerful, imagine living in Vienna in 1907. Assume that you could prevent the deaths of 50 million people lost in World War II by killing an eighteen-year-old Adolf Hitler. Under our current understanding of justice, this person hasn't done anything wrong and killing someone is generally agreed to be immoral unless it's justifiable. I personally would send the teen dictator-in-training to meet his creator a little early with extreme prejudice, but that's not the point of this exercise.

Preventing World War II would, for most, overwhelm all other ethics and morals, including not executing a teenager who hasn't done anything wrong (yet). Avoiding lying, cheating, stealing, and killing would all fall second to ensuring the horrors of the Second World War don't occur.

Now take that example and apply it to any modern radical activist's ideas, and you can understand why "the cause" is so important, and why nefarious means of getting to that goal are acceptable. The cost of failure is thought of as so high and so intolerable that any means necessary (and I do not use that term lightly) must be used to ensure that "the cause" is successful. In modern times, this translates into steelmanning your side while strawmanning the other.

Steelmanning means presenting your own side's best ideas and arguments, while straw manning means presenting the other side's weakest arguments from an individual that either doesn't exist or isn't part of the mainstream conversation. If I wanted to steelman an argument that an American-led world is better for everybody, I would highlight the precipitous drop in war-related deaths after America rose following World War II. If I wanted to strawman the same point, I would say some people believe the American race is superior, and that with the master race running things, everything has been better since. While such an individual may exist, they are not part of the mainstream conversation. If victory at all costs is the goal, there is no sense in conceding any ground to your opponent, indicating they have good points, or that they are even a person worthy of respect.

In some academic fields, this means that if there is a debatable set of ideas, there is not actually a debatable set of ideas. There is the correct set of ideas and values, and anything outside of that is ignorant, stupid, and backward, regardless of the evidence presented in support of it. For example, there are mainstream academics who believe the founding of the United States was not in fact in 1776, but in 1619, despite all evidence to the contrary. No amount of documents and evidence to the contrary will convince some of these academics and "intellectuals," because they are not in fact trying to be academic or intellectual; they are trying to convince people their particular cause and goal is just. Anything in the way of that goal must be attacked, regardless of its accuracy.

Five Decades

Imagine dedicating your entire life to a set of ideas, and then one day in some dark flash of inspiration discovering they are objectively false. Picture yourself having had four to eight years of college education in a field in which you dedicated all your mental and physical energy, having gained and maintained employment in the field, having devoted decades to a set of ideas, only to discover or have someone present information to you negating everything you know and everything you've done, and are probably still doing. You may even feel the ideas are justified in pursuit of a better world, even if the data backing them up crumbles before you.

Are you (A) going to publicly renounce everything you've known and "accomplished" or (B) remain stubborn about your ideas still being accurate, relevant, and just?

In 1968, an academic, Paul Ralph Ehrlich wrote the book, The Population Bomb. Ehrlich himself holds a PhD in… I'm not entirely sure. The biographies I can find seem to identify his bachelor's program (zoology) but not the program of his PhD. It seems he had an interest in butterflies, so I imagine his actual degree is either in zoology, biology, or something around that field. The book he wrote originally predicted hundreds of millions of people would die in the 1970s due to shortages of food.

When this failed to materialize, he amended his prediction that this would occur in the 1980s. The book sold over two million copies (although this sounds like a challenge to me). Currently, Ehrlich is the president of the Center for Conservation Biology at Stanford University, along with positions in the American Association for the Advancement of Science, the American Academy of Arts and Sciences, the American

Philosophical Society, and the United States National Academy of Sciences.

As of 2015, when asked about his apocalyptic overpopulation predictions made in 1968, his response was, "I do not think my language was too apocalyptic in The Population Bomb. My language would be even more apocalyptic today." His book continues to sell, and he continues to stand by it, despite falling rates of hunger and starvation over the course of the last five decades.

Today, deaths from hunger are nearly all man-made, mostly due to war. Despite being wrong for five decades, his name is still the name in the overpopulation debate, and will probably remain that way until the world population dips ever so slightly. As far as I can research, he has never had a serious job outside academia. His books and papers are required reading at various institutions of higher education, despite him being wrong longer than most people reading this book have been alive. Being wrong hasn't stopped him from participating in organizations advocating "lower consumption of resources" in high-income countries.

Translation: You reading this book have it too good. You eat too much, drive too far, have too large of a house, and consume more than you should. All you have to do to save the world is not do those things, and Dr. Ehrlich will pat you on the back and call you a good person.

Had an engineer been wrong for five decades, designing buildings and roads that crumble, they'd likely be in jail with their credentials stripped. If a nuclear scientist designed reactors that leaked radiation over half a century, there is little-to-no chance they'd be given another crack at the bat. If a pilot couldn't predict on which day their plane would have to land to refuel, whatever school or organization trained the pilot would be shut down for producing dangerously incompetent aviators.

All that said, apparently making apocalyptic predictions that never materialize over half a century is rewarded in some fields, since that is what makes the field interesting. Why someone who specialized in butterflies feels competent telling every person on Earth how many children they should have and what the cap on their material use should be is beyond me, but that has not stopped him. Perhaps as long as he keeps revising his predictions into the next decade or century, he'll never have to admit he was ever wrong (and I suppose his books will continue to sell, but that can't possibly be the motivation).

Why Aren't All College Majors Equal?

This question has two answers that I was unable to combine in a way that made sense. Unlike the rest of the book, I'll start with the more controversial reason first and then move to the less controversial one.

Number one: Not all college majors are equal because they require different amounts of work and intelligence to earn. An engineering major, which typically takes five years to earn and requires much higher-level math and science than the average major, is more rigorous than my own majors, construction science, and a master's of business administration. You may not agree with the idea that I've ranked majors, but I can guarantee that you don't view all bachelor's of science and bachelor's of arts and the majors that make them up as equal. You have your own hierarchy of how difficult you believe different college majors are, and that's perfectly fine.

My point is not to arbitrarily rank majors according to my values; it is simply to say that not all majors are equally valued by people and society at large. How do we measure societal value? You can approach it in at least two ways: one which I ascribe to and one I do not. 1) You can poll people and ask them how much they value each profession or major and plot them on a graph against one another. 2) You can look at the average income of a graduate in a particular profession and with a particular major and compare it to other majors and professions.

Predictably, you will not get the same results from these two methods. While many do not approve of workers involved in the fossil fuel industry, society rewards those with relatively large salaries since nearly everyone purchases and places value in fossil fuels and their derivatives in their day-to-day spending.

Number two: Supply and demand dictate that if there is a large supply of people who want a specific job (and therefore a specific degree requiring it), all things being equal, the job will pay less. If there are not a lot of people who want a specific job or not a lot who can meet the job requirements, the pay will be higher. There are many people with art-related degrees (music, drawing, photography, acting) because many people want to be professional singers, musicians, artists, or actors.

Unfortunately, because so many people want these highly coveted jobs, there is an oversupply of people going into these fields compared to what society wants.

How do I know there is an oversupply? Because I have met many starving artists and known nearly none that can support themselves and a family with the income generated; I have yet to meet a starving engineer, doctor, lawyer, or pilot. I, for example, occasionally enjoy live music while I eat dinner on the weekends, but for all other times, I don't need armies of musicians for my entertainment.

Additionally, I only have so many walls for art, and if a single piece of art can take some artist a year or more to make, that means that in order to get a square of my wall covered, I may need to be able to fund the artist's expenses over the course of an entire year. This critique is not specific to art-related degrees; it just came to mind first. Many people want jobs that align with their hobbies and interests, rather than treating a job like a job.

I would love if someone paid me to play video games and catch up on blockbuster movies, but unless I'm going through the painstaking process of testing video games or become a critic and must watch all movies of note, I'm out of luck. As it turns out, society only needs so many video game testers and movie critics and will only reward someone commensurate to their contributions.

Why We Want to Believe All College Majors Are Equal

No matter what we admit to ourselves or others, we will be compared against our fellow human beings. You are wealthier than some, and poorer than others. I'm better looking than some and uglier than (many) others. After our education, our value to the economy is measured in income, and many do not like that their value (income) is lower than others. Those who perceive themselves as intelligent hate that there are those wealthier and with higher incomes than themselves who they perceive as dumber, believing they themselves are the ones society owes due to their contributions.

The high income of another indicates society has placed a higher value on some professions, and not as much on others. Income and wealth create a hierarchy of achievement, and many don't want to believe others they don't respect are more valued than themselves. Great achievement creates great jealousy, and the green-eyed monster has certainly not disappeared going into the twenty-first century.

No one wants to hear that their interest in women's studies, photography, or French poetry is going to be valued less by society than a business major whose very simple goal is to attain as much wealth as possible. Nor do they want to see people in professions they don't respect making more than themselves. One of the most obvious examples of this is teachers versus male professional athletes. Since I began paying attention, the debate has always revolved around the argument that those educating our kids shouldn't be paid less than those playing a game played mostly by children (in terms of raw numbers).

I'm sure it causes untold amounts of hatred that the highest-paid public employees in each state are generally college football coaches. Professional athletes and management are only paid what they are because ads and tickets can be sold to watch their performance, and they can influence others to buy specific products that they endorse in ways an average teacher cannot. We want to believe there is equality between all academic pursuits because it allows us to believe all pursuits have equal merit and equal value, to include the one we are interested in. I know for a fact my own pursuits were on a hierarchy, and that mine weren't at the top of that hierarchy. Even when I made those decisions, I knew the consequences and accepted them. We have far too many making decisions with obvious consequences and then being unsatisfied with the result, blaming forces outside themselves.

Chapter End Notes

This chapter has been critical of portions of academia for good reason. There are fields that try to answer simple questions in the most ludicrous way imaginable because answering the question isn't enough; the answer must reflect certain values and ideas that cannot be questioned. If it is impermissible to ask certain questions and answer those forbidden questions with the truth, the fields in question are not in fact academic, but dogmatic.

I saw more stupid people in graduate school and three decades in academia than I ever did who ran a hundred acres without going broke.

— Victor Davis Hanson, American classicist, military historian, farmer, and political commentator, 1953–present

Chapter 8 Not All Cultures Produce Equal Results

You say that it is your custom to burn widows. Very well. We also have a custom: when men burn a woman alive, we tie a rope around their necks and hang them. Build your funeral pyre; beside it, my carpenters will build a gallows. You may follow your custom. And then we will follow ours."

— Sir Charles Napier, British governor of Sindh, India, 1843–1847, on the Indian custom of suttee (burning the widow on the same funeral pyre as her deceased husband)

In Afghanistan, after the US pullout in 2021, women were barred from secondary schooling and nearly all industries outside healthcare and education. In accordance with the customs of the culture, the legal minimum age for marriage was set at sixteen.

In some cases, the groom's family essentially buys the female from the bride's family (the payment being compensation for the original cost to raise the daughter). The personal desires of the bride are the last things considered, if at all. By decree of the de facto government, the only portion of a female body that can be visible is the eyes. Women cannot legally travel more than forty miles from their home without a male relative or spouse present. With the average number of children per female being 5.33, you can imagine what they occupy their lives with.

In 1983, Grand Ayatollah Khomeini, leader of Iran, passed a fatwa allowing gender reassignment operations as a cure for "diagnosed transsexuals" (his translated words, not mine). After Thailand, today Iran has the greatest number of gender reassignments in the world. The reason for this? It is permissible in Sharia Law (as interpreted by Mr. Khomeini) for a man to become a woman. It is impermissible to be homosexual, the penalty for which is death. If young Iranians begin showing signs of same-sex attraction, the alternatives are gender reassignment or execution by the state.

Given the option for you or your offspring, which sounds like a better option: removal of the genitals (and a quick name change) or death by hanging (they do it from motorized cranes now, so at least it's modern)?

Note: In 2007, Mahmoud Ahmadinejad, then President of Iran, gave a speech at Columbia University in which he asserted there were no homosexuals in Iran, at which point he received laughter and boos from the crowd. In one sense, he was accurate. If there were any LGB members, they would either be "fixed" or killed, thus bringing the official count back to zero.

It is some type of cosmic irony that the contentious nature of the trans discussion is so hotly debated in the West, while one of the most socially repressive nations on Earth has not only been tolerant but supportive of the trans community for decades. If laws get too oppressive in America, there's always the Persian Gulf…

In China, 12.8 million Muslim Uyghurs live in the same country as approximately 1.3 billion Han Chinese (about 90% of the country). According to Amnesty International, the People's Republic of China has imprisoned hundreds of thousands of Uyghurs while also sending hundreds of thousands more, perhaps a million, to ~~internment~~ reeducation camps. Included in the atrocities are allegations of forced sterilization and forced labor for being of a different race or ethnicity from the dominant culture.

In 2021, NPR (National Public Radio) host Rachel Martin reported on a recent development within the French government. Prior to 2021, if an adult had sex with someone under the age of fifteen, they could be prosecuted for breaking the law, assuming the act was not consensual, which had to be proven for the perpetrator to be punished. If the act was consensual, the older participant could not be prosecuted, as prior to 2021 there was not an age of consent in France. The French government enacted legislation to create a minimum age of consent, which was set at fifteen after significant condemnation at the lack of one. Please do not use this information to plan your next vacation.

On April 13, 1975, New York Times journalist Sydney Schanberg wrote a piece entitled Indochina without Americans: For Most, A Better Life; Communist Rule Is at Least Uncertain; Napalm Is Not. This was in reference to the communist Khmer Rouge takeover of Cambodia and the subsequent US pullout. Within less than half a decade, somewhere around 25% of the population of Cambodia had been killed or died due to the actions of Pol Pot's communist government, popularized in the Oscar-winning film The Killing Fields. Entire urban areas were cleared of educated middle-class citizens, who were forced into rural Cambodia to perform work they were demonstrably unequipped for. At least there was no napalm. Why bring these up? Because it is obvious these cultures, scattered across the globe and across time, do not have the same values you, the reader, have (unless you're in these cultures, in which case everything seems on the level). You would rightfully recognize these other cultures as truly systemically sexist, homophobic, racist, and homicidal, and would probably sneer at the people who run and guide such societies. These are obvious examples of nations and cultures where change would be desired, but there are unfortunately others closer to home. Before going further, it is important to define what multiculturalism is. Imagine all people, nations, tribes, sects, clans, and other such subdivisions of humanity. These various groups have different (or no) gods, traditions, holidays, coming-of-age ceremonies, architectural styles, chosen food, calendars, and preferred adult beverages (or "booze" to those with a worldview crafted from watching late-night comedy). If you believe these various cultures can live peacefully side by side without any conflict arising, you are a multiculturalist (and also deeply incorrect).

In 2015, those living in the city of Hamtramck, Michigan (a small town of about 30,000 surrounded by Detroit) became the first in the US to elect a Muslim-majority city council. 2020 census data suggests approximately half of the citizens are Muslim, with large numbers with Yemeni and Bangladeshi backgrounds. Within Wayne County, where both Detroit and Hamtramck are located, approximately 70% of the population votes Democrat during presidential elections. Eight years later, in June 2023, during Pride Month, the majority-Muslim city council voted to ban Pride flags from any flagpole on city property (In the city council's defense, they banned all flags promoting any particular religion, ethnicity, race, or political party from city-owned property, declaring it a "neutrality" ordinance.) Normally, these two groups, supporters of the

LGBT and Muslim communities, vote in lockstep with one another to fight common opponents. Once those opponents were gone, however, new opponents formed, and a schism occurred due to mutually exclusive goals. The question is a fairly benign one: Should the municipal government celebrate same-sex and transgender activity or not? You either have to tell the Muslim community to celebrate and endorse something that is against their religion or (as happened) you have to tell the gay community that government advocacy and celebration will not occur, but you cannot have both simultaneously.

Multiculturalism insists that multiple cultures can live side by side without losing social cohesion and that ultimately there is great benefit. But would you, the reader, wish to live next door to someone who wanted to sell or have sex with very young women, castrate gay boys against their will, or intern racial groups because they did not conform to the majority's ethnic, cultural, and religious beliefs? If you're a live-and-let-live type, you might (and might be right now). I, on the other hand, having seen scores of different cultures with my own two eyes, know that not all cultures are equally desirable and good. Many have cultural practices that would horrify even the most tolerant and accepting New York Times or Washington Post reader and would send them running back to their gated communities. The fear from multiculturalists is that if it is determined that not all cultures are equally desirable and generate good results, a cultural hierarchy will be created (it already exists but is too taboo to bring up). Thus, it's easier to pretend all cultures are equal in merit rather than to go through the cringeworthy exercise of weighing cultures against one another to determine which practices and values generate the best results.

"Best results" may be subjective, but there are common benchmarks that can be used as a guide — life expectancy, income, education level, amount of violent crime, etc.

Mutually Exclusive

For those not in the know, things are mutually exclusive if they cannot exist at the same time. In a Venn diagram, this is represented by two circles that do not overlap. An example of this might be atheists and Catholics. You cannot logically believe Jesus is the son of God and also believe that God never existed.

Simultaneously, you cannot rationally believe that everyone is racist while thinking at the same time that you are not. In both cases above, it's one or the other, not both. Now that we've gotten past that little lesson, we can move on to why it's important. Cultures are all different in some form or fashion and have values associated with those differences. Some value order over freedom, tradition over novel ideas, or equity over merit. Those differences manifest in how society will be run, dependent on which culture has the most influence. If a group becomes influential enough, it will be able to change the rules governing society. In a multicultural society, there will always be a dominant culture. It is an inescapable truth, and the only true question is this: Which culture will be the most influential?

If one culture believes polygamy is fair game, it is incompatible with monogamous societies. A culture advocating death for homosexuals cannot coexist within a nation supporting and celebrating LGBT individuals. Only one of those values can be reflected in the law of the land if the laws are to remain sane and enforceable. All this is to say, even in a multicultural society, there will always be a dominant culture. That culture will set the rules and enforce them with varying levels of success. The dominant culture is not always good, and certainly not always bad, if the words good and bad have any actual meaning today.

Culture from Alex's Perspective

Personally, I have great respect for the cultural contributions America has been the beneficiary of.Generally, the best ideas have been taken and improved by those who have found their way to our shores and those whose ancestors assimilated into the broader American culture, both foreign and native. We found ways to improve Italian pizza by inserting cheese into the crust (Pizza Hut, 1995), enhanced German rockets to get to the moon instead of blowing up in the United Kingdom (Operation Paperclip, 1945) and created entire entertainment empires from cultural stories from around the globe (Disney, among others, 1923–present). While two out of the three above may sound like a joke, I offer them in complete seriousness.

Throngs of the best and brightest seek out employment, education, and residency in the United States specifically because of the culture of the US (I choose the definition of culture as "the customs, arts, social institutions, and achievements of a particular nation, people, or other social group"). You may not believe it, but according to Gallup, as of 2018, the most desired country to migrate to was the US (Canada was second). 155 million people wanted to live in an intolerant, bigoted, inequitable, and racist country above all other countries, including the one they were living in. It would be easy for me to convince you, regardless of your political background, that the title of this chapter is accurate.

As a simple exercise, imagine I ask you, "Is American culture the best in the world?" Some would answer yes, others no, but I have a strong feeling nearly no one would answer "American culture is equal to all cultures on the planet." Thus, we've created a question in which people admit, one way or the other, "American culture" is one of many on a hierarchy, in which America may be at the top, in the middle, or dead last, depending on how you define American culture and how you weigh that against your own personal values. Hopefully now that we've all admitted there are more and less desirable cultures, I can explain why we deny this truth. History is long, and the generally more interesting parts that people pay attention to are wars, atrocities, and injustices.

Many of these injustices had, at their heart, a belief that one group or culture was better than the other. Different groups defined this differently over time, including separating people into "clean and dirty," "civilized and uncivilized," and even "racially superior and inferior." Distinctions between people allowed animosity to build until, at the breaking point, conflict erupted. The solution to this was to develop the idea that all peoples and cultures are equal, none being better and none being worse than the other. If an Aryan was no better than a Slav, a Sunni no worse than a Shiite, and native culture no different than immigrant culture, then there is no reason their arbitrary differences should result in bloodshed, conflict, and injustice. What develops from this assumption, however, is an observable, objective paradox.

Assuming that all cultures are equal in merit conflicts with what we can see with our eyes and hear with our ears. Some cultures have stellar, enviable outcomes, while others, to say the least, do not. This begs the question, if all cultures are equal in merit, why do some have extraordinary, consistent success, while other cultures have consistent, awful failure?

If we rely on the flawed assumption that all cultures should produce equal results, we inevitably go searching for explanations outside the obvious, looking for farther flung and more improbable explanations that allow us to avoid the unfortunate truth that not all cultural practices result in equal outcomes because some cultures are actually harmful to those people falling under them.

In our minds, a decision has to be made: we either ignore what we can see or we change our mind to reflect reality. This is generally a subconscious decision. Who, after all, would willfully believe falsehoods in order to maintain a fake worldview? What are examples of poor cultural practices? Those activities that predictably lead to bad results — a general tolerance of alcohol and drug abuse, acceptance of activities leading to broken families and child abandonment, and allowing criminality to go unimpeded by those sympathizing more with lawbreakers than their victims.

If there are those that disagree, I suppose their utopia would have either the same or more substance abusers, single parents, and crime (It's a bold strategy, Cotton. Let's see if it pays off for 'em). The list of other poor cultural habits could itself fill an entire book. Take note, this is not specific to only a single sex, race, sexual orientation, nationality, or gender identity. Different groupings of humanity create their own distinct culture that may revolve around one or more of these identifiers, but each creates its own culture that, again, can be for the betterment or detriment of the members that make up those groups.

As an example of poor cultural practices, I would like to bring up the case of the Pine Ridge Indian Reservation (as a Native American, I have unique insight into this problem and studied the issue in college). According to The Guardian, about two-thirds of the 20,000 residents live with alcoholism, one out of every four children is born with fetal alcohol syndrome, and the life expectancy is around a decade less than the rest of the United States. Unemployment is about 80%, and the suicide rate is four times the American average. This culture, to put it mildly, is broken. No human being walking the face of the Earth would look at this culture (regardless of how it got there or continues) and consider it on par with all others.

If you disagree, I'll be happy to discuss arrangements for you to visit the area so you can experience the "culture" yourself. Prepare yourself, though — it's a dry reservation; that is, it's illegal to possess or sell alcohol. I would like it noted that I genuinely believe all peoples and cultures have something positive to contribute. It may sound "problematic" and laughable, but even Nazis managed to build pretty decent highways (I did drive on one, so if you disagree, I'm going to need data to back it up).

We should not dismiss people or cultures out of hand and should recognize that different people have different ways of doing things. What works in one nation or community may not work elsewhere. For example, many Middle Eastern countries largely eliminated male jealousy by fully covering the bodies of females in clothing, in the same way you can stop a dog from barking at other dogs by obstructing its line of sight of those other dogs *(I've seen it done in person, both with dogs and people)*. Does this solution come at a high cost? Of course it does, as now women are burdened with specific, legally defined outfits unjustly distinct from their male counterparts. After all, there are no solutions, only tradeoffs.

If anyone believes this is Islamophobic, I can assure you it is not. If anything, it is anti-male, comparing them to animals acting on their most basic of instincts.

If you believe you know how everyone on Earth should act and what values they should hold, know that you join a specific demographic called everyone. Even if you tolerate those among you not conforming to how you would like them to live, this idea still requires enforcing by you or others conforming to the same worldview. One of the strongest arguments against colonialism was that one group should not be able to impose its values on another, instead allowing for self-rule and enabling the enforcement of local values.

I will not try to define for you what the cultural hierarchy is because it will be different for everybody. To some, a culture that doesn't allow you to marry more than one woman is not only backward but antithetical to their religious beliefs. In other cultures, you can be put in jail and fined for killing or eating the meat of cows. There are even some cultures where, if you are famous enough, normal laws don't apply to you. That being said, with every man, woman, and child's input across the globe, you will get an understanding of which cultures are desirable and which ones aren't.

Why We Want to View Cultures Equally

In 1939, Germany invaded Poland because German leadership believed its own population and culture were superior to that of its neighbors (and everyone), beginning World War II. Following this, about twenty other countries were either invaded or capitulated to German military forces because, according to the Nazi leadership, their cultures were also subservient to the "Aryan" race and civilization and therefore deserved to be conquered.

The fear of this same type of racist and nationalistic upheaval led to a modern desired belief that there is no superior culture and certainly no superior race. Biologically, it seems insane to me to try and identify a "superior race." Even if one were to try and perform such an odd exercise, it would require someone to identify what the best qualities are of a person and attempt to determine which genes support these end goals. Some genes produce taller or shorter people, and others produce larger or smaller genitalia (both male and female; let's not discriminate), which is either desirable or undesirable (believe it or not, this argument has historical context, hence all the Roman statues with small male members). Some genes produce offspring better acclimated to the tropics, others to the Arctic, and there are even genes dictating the number of fingers on a human hand.

It seems just as ridiculous to me to argue for a superior race as it does to argue that blue eyes are any better than dark skin or six fingers, but perhaps there are those that disagree. Human characteristics that at one point in time seemed to provide more desirable traits in other places and times were equally undesirable. Large, statuesque men at one point would have been ideal soldiers, able to wield heavier weapons and use them with greater strength against their enemies. In World War I, all this would have done is provide a larger silhouette for the enemy's snipers and machine guns to hone in on, with almost no benefit from the larger frame. Time had made one "superior" gene inferior while making other qualities superior in terms of survival.

All that said, there are obviously cultures that produce better and worse results. The fear is that if it were accepted that cultures are ranked differently, individuals from those cultures would be treated as members of those groups, not as individuals. For example, if we thought of the "redneck" culture as backwards and stupid, then an individual from a rural family would have the stereotypes of a redneck applied to them without anyone even trying to understand the individual to determine if they conformed to the stereotype. Oddly, I've never come across someone conforming to redneck stereotypes who actually had a red neck.

History — horrors based on ethnic, national, and cultural violence — drove modern thinkers to adopt the idea that all cultures are equal so that no sub-grouping of humanity would believe they were superior or inferior to another group and begin conflict with them for this reason. As has been said time and time again, the road to hell is paved with good intentions. A tolerance of poor cultural practices has transformed into a celebration of nearly all cultures, regardless of how good or bad that culture's results are.

You may think this is a positive, but I don't believe it will take too much creativity for you to imagine a culture you would not prefer to celebrate (or… gasp… live in). If you think otherwise, give me the option of airdropping you into the location of my choice and we'll see how well you appreciate your new surroundings. (This actually sounds like a good setup for a reality show.)

At the beginning of this chapter, I listed cultures that are antithetical to Western liberalism and ones you can hopefully identify as backwards and morally reprehensible. If you cannot, I suggest your spine is made of some type of boiled pasta (perhaps linguini) and that you could be convinced to go along with anything so long as others around you thought the same thing. If so, please try to surround yourself with more intelligent people than yourself so that at least you'll blindly follow their lead instead of the lead of whatever idiots just happen to be in your vicinity.

King Sharaman: In all my travels, I have never looked upon a more beautiful city…
Princess Tamina: You should have seen it before your horde of camel-riding illiterates descended upon it.
— Prince of Persia, Sands of Time, Disney, 2010

(following the battle between King Sharaman's forces and the city the princess resides in)

Note: Inclusivity

We hold these truths to be self-evident, that all men are created equal, that they are endowed by their Creator with certain unalienable Rights, that among these are Life, Liberty, and the pursuit of Happiness.
— Declaration of Independence, July 4, 1776

Scheduled to take place on October 22, 2022, the University of Massachusetts Amherst hosted an event titled BIPOC LGBTQ+ & DISABLED Women in STEM Conference, whose original invitation can still be found by googling it (although, perhaps not for that much longer). It encouraged attendees to "Engage with diverse speakers from across the country and enjoy a locally catered meal" and to "Come enjoy a safe space to meet and embrace identity with fellow women in STEM."

That said, if I understood the headline of the flyer, White women were specifically excluded unless they were disabled, gay, bisexual, trans, had native African heritage, or Indigenous American (Indigenous Europeans don't count). I'm not saying straight, able-bodied cisgender White women didn't attend the event. I'm saying the flyer seemed to exclude them (along with 50% of the population, including gay, Indigenous, Black, Asian, and disabled males unless they were trans women). A NASCAR event would be considered more inclusive than this by all but the blind (that is, willfully ignorant, not disabled).

Although not stated in the flyer, I believe those who created and attended the event would have considered it "inclusive" and "diverse." That said, by including a list of those welcome and excluding those not, this event was the opposite of inclusive and diverse, as it excluded people whom the conference was not intended for. Despite the flyer encouraging its attendees to "embrace identity," many identities were left out, or excluded, if you will. If the organizers of the event didn't intend for it to be inclusive, their point was well made. Hopefully, the drinking fountains and bathrooms weren't as discriminatory.

As an aside, I have no problem with group-identity events (such as a STEM conference for women) so long as the opposite can be held without ridicule. If there can be an event for Indigenous STEM students, there must be an acceptable event for Italian STEM students. If it is permitted that an event can be exclusive to lesbian theater arts majors, it must be permissible to have the same event exclusive to straight theater arts majors (for the dozen or so that exist). Either discriminatory events (whether by rules or implied) are okay, or they are not. To permit one group privileges that other groups cannot be permitted to have strikes at the heart of American ideals of equality.

If you believe some groups deserve privileges others don't, there's a long list of historical figures who would be giving you high-fives right now, welcoming you to the club. Most of them will be sporting symbols and salutes you probably won't be a big fan of...

In October of 2023, there was a tech conference called The Grace Hopper Celebration of Women in Computing in Orlando, Florida. To be more inclusive, the event was claimed to be for women and nonbinary individuals wanting jobs with tech companies such as Amazon, Apple, and Google. As it turns out, larger numbers of males attended than would be expected at a "Women in Computing" gathering, with large numbers of those men claiming to be nonbinary so that prestigious companies in attendance would interview them.

This so incensed some of the organizers and attendees that the "chief impact officer" of AnitaB.org (the event organizers) got on stage and chastised those male attendees he claimed were not nonbinary but were in fact cisgender men trying to invade female spaces. This particular story could fit in about three other numbered chapters, given the themes, but here we see where the path to inclusivity leads — segregated events in which some people are welcomed as full participants, while others are second-class attendees at the discretion of the organizers. Don't worry, though. Male allies were welcome so long as they "celebrate women... and want to work with, and for women." (I don't know about you, but I don't want to work with or for any men, women, or any other gender. I want them to work for me!)

As this story was being reported, I asked myself: What trumps what; is self-identity in regard to gender and orientation to be regarded as true, or are others' interpretations of what you are more important? Even if there was a cisgender male who showed up, claiming to be nonbinary, who gets to say whether they are or not? If we get to define ourselves, the events that took place shouldn't have been an issue. For a male, the moment he checks a box or calls himself (or themselves now) nonbinary, he becomes nonbinary. If this is not the case, and others get to define (accurately) what we are and what we are not, our debate into gender and sexual orientation takes a swift turn in a direction I don't think the "chief impact officer" intended.

Inclusivity, to its supporters, does not mean inclusivity as the word implies. The word inclusivity alone means to include the most amount of people possible into events and society. On the contrary, in the modern context, inclusivity means some privileged groups are included and others are not. "Inclusive" does not mean inclusive of everybody; it means inclusive to groups we approve of. In some instances, however, groups desiring to be as inclusive as possible eventually are put into a position in which "in vogue" groups become at odds with one another.

Around 2018, a trans woman who had not undergone gender reassignment surgery (that is, they had the genitals they were assigned at birth) approached several aesthetician businesses in Canada requesting a Brazilian wax. For those not in the know, a Brazilian wax is the removal of all or nearly all pubic hair by waxing; a service nearly exclusively requested by females. The owner of one of these facilities was male, with only one female worker who could perform the service. The woman was a devout Muslim and had a stance of refraining from physical contact with males unless they were married or related. Apparently, this prudish custom also included a prohibition of touching male genitals for anyone but their husband.

Which seems more inclusive, telling the trans woman to seek the wax elsewhere, or forcing your employee to perform services that were not anticipated over the course of employment in that particular field? In this situation, there were two mutually exclusive outcomes, and someone had to be told to move along. As the story goes, the owner did not make his female employee perform the service, and the trans woman sued the business, along with at least fifteen other equally transphobic businesses across Canada. Unfortunately, the drive for this particular brand of inclusivity hasn't stayed north of the border. Small battles occur every day across America on this front, some with odd outcomes.

A former coworker of mine in the military had worked hard, demonstrated great competence, and rose through the ranks to attain a high military position. He told me that one day he was walking on his base when he saw a bald male wearing a bright pink, shoulder-length wig with their uniform. A US military hairstyle must meet certain requirements, including length and color. A military member's hair is permitted to be dyed only if it could be construed as a "natural" hair color. My friend walked over to the service member's commander and asked him why a male was in uniform with a bright pink wig. The other commander replied something to the effect of "He identifies as a woman." My friend then asked him why a woman was in uniform with a bright pink wig. The other commander then realized that, regardless of gender identity, the service member wearing the brightly colored wig was not "in regs" (within regulation). The service member's commander was trying to be so inclusive that he allowed members working under him to openly flaunt the rules everyone else had to obey. I believe the outcome was that the pink wig stayed at home.

What does being inclusive mean? Common sense tells us it is the opposite of being exclusive and, therefore, must only mean that we are trying to incorporate the most diverse number of groups we can. In reality, the drive only includes some groups while actively excluding others. At no point would it be thought of as inclusive to have a straight man lead GLAAD (Gay & Lesbian Alliance Against Defamation). Similarly, it would not be considered inclusive to have a Black Republican representative in the Congressional Black Caucus; a group of Congressional African Americans in the US Congress which is made entirely of Democrats (not for a lack of trying; the group will not allow Republicans to join). There are even some "inclusive" events such as gay pride parades that actively exclude gay, lesbian, bisexual, or transgender police. Thus, "inclusive events" tend to actively exclude more than they include. If we're admitting it's fashionable to exclude, then I'll say I miss the '90s.

121

Chapter 9 Choices Have Consequences

There's a lot of flat squirrels out there.
— unnamed USAF pre-deployment training instructor on why we
should pay attention to his experience-based wisdom, 2021.
Scheduled deployment to Africa, T-minus 23 days.

Courage means taking action in the face of obvious danger. Stupidity is
the same.
— Alex B.

On February 11, 2018, a Colorado couple, tired of working for the
Man, purchased a twenty-eight-foot sailboat. To fund it, they sold their
SUV, furniture, and any other items not deemed necessary for their goal
of sailing the world, all the while documenting their journey via social
media for others to view and appreciate. The couple, by their own
admission, were "new to sailing." A day after departing to tour the
Caribbean, the boat sunk by their own hands about twenty-five miles
from where they started. Luckily, they'd stayed near the coast the whole
time, and they and their dog survived. Had they been any more
incompetent, they would have gotten too far for help to arrive in time.

On July 31, 2018, a separate couple, from Washington, DC, were run
over by a car in Tajikistan. The Islamic State claimed responsibility for
running over the group of seven bicyclists, stabbing four of them to death
(if they weren't already deceased), leaving three survivors to tell the tale,
none of whom were the couple from DC. The DC couple's education and
worldview had led them to believe that people were generally good and
that they would be able to deal with any culture and people they came
across on their enriching travels around the world. To this day, the State
Department travel advisory has a country profile whose first line reads,
"Exercise increased caution in Tajikistan due to terrorism" (for those bad
at geography like me, Tajikistan borders Afghanistan).

On November 14, 2022, a mother of five, Nicole (thirty-eight),
decided the best way to keep a fire pit going was to pour gasoline on it.
The gas ignited and caused an explosion in the container she was holding.

She died three days later after suffering burns that covered 100% of her body. In the process, she also burned her eleven-year-old son, who required twelve days of hospitalization. In late 2022, I witnessed a seventeen-year-old teenager pour gasoline on a fire pit to relight it. After warning him I had just heard of someone being killed doing exactly the same thing, he continued applying copious amounts of gas to the ash heap, which still had a few smoldering embers. Luckily, the relatively full five-gallon plastic gas can did not explode in his hands, and he lit the gas-soaked timber without incident.

In 2017, I was working overseas in the military. There was a temporary satellite dish that was set up with a rope barrier around it and a rotating red light, cautioning people to stay away from the dish. While working around it, my coworker wished to transit through the area because, for the job we were performing, it was easier to go through rather than around. I grabbed the nearest twenty-year-old I could, who operated the dish, to explain to my friend (a major — a much higher rank than the twenty-year-old and myself) how dangerous it was to pass in front of the satellite dish. As his eyes went wide, the twenty-year-old explained that if the major had walked in front of the satellite while it transmitted, his head would be "cooked." The twenty-year-old was not clear on whether it would kill him or simply cause brain damage.

Recently, while undergoing a construction job safety orientation, my instructor, who worked at the same site, told me a true story about a mid-level concrete worker on a scissor lift operating a gas-powered concrete saw, cutting into a concrete slab above him. His apprentice, a new construction worker, informed the journeyman from the ground that his concrete saw was leaking gas. The journeyman waved off the caution with some four-letter words I choose not to repeat. The journeyman hit a metal reinforcing bar in the concrete, creating sparks and igniting the journeyman in hellfire since he had become soaked in gasoline. The journeyman was able to jump off the scissor lift but was held up above the ground by his fall-arrest system, essentially a rope to prevent falls, which prevented intervening workers from putting out the flames in time. The journeyman soon passed away.

This list could go on endlessly (and does) in tabloid papers and news websites all over the world. The above are only a small subset of the most recent that come to mind as I type these words. Every person reading this has similar stories of short-sightedness, stupidity, and laziness either in themselves or, most likely, in others, causing pain, costing money, and resulting in catastrophe. While hindsight is 20/20, you also know that with just a little forethought, much of this pain and anguish could have been avoided. The real question is, how do we avoid it?

Who ultimately is responsible for the decisions we make and the fallout? In each of the lethal situations above, warnings were so numerous it would be comical to say "we" as a society should have done more. Every gas can I've ever seen sold has warnings from top to bottom. Roped-off areas with flashing red lights are clearly communicating danger that a person would have to ignore at their own peril. Hours of construction safety orientation classes and equipment instruction manuals clearly state the dangers of operating in unsafe conditions. Willful ignorance on the part of individuals is what resulted in the above tragedies. Is this victim blaming? Yes, it is. The victims listed above (and in innumerable similar circumstances) are mostly to blame for the tragedies that befell them. Simply because they are the victims of their actions does not mean we shouldn't understand they were key in causing their own outcomes.

If you believe more should have been done by society at large, ask yourself if you would have done the same thing. If the answer is yes, ask yourself why. If you can't come up with an answer you can learn from, I recommend purchasing life insurance and updating your will. For many, there seems to be a disconnect between the actions we take on a day-to-day basis and the consequences that ensue. This doesn't even leave out major businesses, governments, and organizations, whose day-to-day choices can be just as short-sighted and suspect as many of those of individuals around them. So shortsighted and optimistic about predicted future outcomes, these individuals and organizations are seemingly (but not actually) incapable of linking past decisions to current outcomes. Why? Because linking prior decisions and choices to current circumstances means confronting the reality that poor decisions we made led to poor outcomes instead of bad luck or the actions of others. We find it easy to identify these qualities in others or organizations we don't like but don't use that same omnipotent lens inwardly.

In January of 2019, a razor company advertised its products during the Super Bowl, seemingly indicating that men weren't good in general but could be better by buying this company's razor and grooming products. Prior to this ad, they had maintained a 65–70% market share, which dropped to 60% in the wake of the ad. Apparently, no one at this company thought insulting half their customers would do any harm and would instead, to the contrary, increase sales. Why anyone would think like this is beyond me, but I bet they had great credentials and went to "great" universities. Not only did this particular company not offer any apology to its customers it called bullies, harassers, and assaulters, but other companies have similarly insulted their own customer base in order to seem more hip and with the times. Pro tip: If your goal is to try and sell as many widgets or widget-related services, try not to insult those who buy them. (Unless, of course, your customers are idiots or masochists, in which case, insult away.)

That doesn't mean I don't have empathy for those who make decisions that ruin not only their own lives, but the lives of their friends, family, and coworkers. They are each individual people with hopes, dreams, something to contribute, and, most importantly, a spark of the divine. They are my fellow human beings, who are on both similar and dissimilar journeys as myself. I see my success in their successes, and my problems as problems they have or will at some point face. In short, I see a reflection of myself, but at a different time and in a different body, having different circumstances and different but similar problems across our lifetimes.

That also means I hold my fellow man to the standard I hold myself. I don't drive drunk and then curse the car going through the same intersection without checking for anyone running the red light. I don't rob a convenience store only to blame bad luck for being caught as I sit in prison because my partner shot a bystander who refused to give up his car keys. I don't blame society for contracting a sexually transmitted infection, having taken no precautions whatsoever to prevent the spread of easily understood diseases, as is communicated to every child before the age they begin having sex. Choices have consequences, and we must understand that bad decisions over time generally lead to bad outcomes.

I recently read an article about Crystal Hefner, who was sixty years younger than her husband, Hugh Hefner while he was alive. The article was concerning her soon-to-be-published memoir, Only Say Good Things. As I perceive the article, Ms. Hefner complained about a 6 pm curfew and her husband tapping her on the head to indicate her roots were showing, and was embarrassed to participate in what she described as "group sex," what most people would call orgies, with her nonagenarian husband. She was twenty-one when they met. They "dated" for five years and then were married for the last five years of Hugh Hefner's life before he died in 2017. If you think she may have had a hand in her own perceived suffering, you're not alone and definitely not crazy. I doubt anyone going to the Playboy Mansion had any illusions about what activities took place there or the type of man Hugh Hefner was. After the parties were over, and Mr. Hefner, being dead, could generate no more money, Ms. Hefner decided to disparage her controlling deceased husband and explain how hard she'd had it.

Are all outcomes dependent on our individual choices? Of course not. Planes crash because a bird just happened to get sucked into one of the engines. Even the best-trained soldiers are subject to the cruel randomness of war and may be killed without firing a shot, seeing the enemy, or even knowing danger had been lying under the ground he or she was walking on. Life is random and chaotic, but if you start and end your understanding of life from there, you neglect the significant influence you have over outcomes.

Take, for example, the following real-life events of a court martial (military jury trial) I sat on as a juror involving exceedingly bad judgment mixed with bad luck. For our purposes, I'll call the involved parties John and Jane. A male military member, John, had been accused of raping a sixteen-year-old family friend, Jane, during a sleepover (John was in his mid-twenties, I believe). Here are the uncontested facts: 1) John, his wife, his two children, a niece, and Jane were watching TV one evening. 2) After John's wife, his children, niece, and Jane went to their separate rooms to sleep, John entered the room where his two children, niece, and Jane were sleeping. 3) While his children and niece were sleeping (supposedly — I have serious doubts), John had sex with Jane.

What were we as a jury to determine? Whether or not the sex was consensual (an unfortunate little-known fact: sixteen is the age of consent on a federal military base). The evidence of the case could probably fill an entire book, but that's a tale for another time. The facts as determined by the jury were that the girl had lied, likely to conceal a separate sexual relationship with her at-the-time boyfriend. She was trying out for the girls' basketball team but needed a doctor's examination to be sure she was fit to play. She and her boyfriend, in their teenage brilliance, believed the doctor would determine she was in fact not a virgin. Needing an explanation that maintained her moral innocence, she accused the family friend of rape before the doctor could (not) determine she was not a virgin and, of course, communicate this to her parents. The jury (myself included) voted to acquit.

I do not know the exact fallout from this, as I don't remember any of the names. When I tried to search for the events, Google was helpless. That said, I can predict the fallout. Even after having been found not guilty, John would never be promoted again. His wife, if she had any sense, would have left him and taken the kids. None of John's friends or coworkers would have invited him to family get-togethers or socialized with him, lest they be accused of associating with a perceived pedophile or letting him around their kids (or, God help us, teenagers). Simultaneously, Jane's reputation and integrity have been ruined at a critical stage of her development (you know, for the fake rape allegation). What I do know is that these events occurred because of the incredibly poor judgment of two separate individuals brought on by the bad luck of needing a physical for a sports team.

Technically, a pedophile is someone attracted to a prepubescent child (that is, they haven't gone through puberty, for those who believe reality TV is real). The accuser, in this case, had most definitely gone through puberty.

Point being, while bad luck played a role, the above events could only have happened because of the actions of two separate individuals each making painfully poor decisions. There was no racism, homophobia, socio-economic factors, or other such commonly blamed causes. There wasn't even alcohol or drug use, to my great shock.

Why do we find it so difficult to hold people accountable for the bad decisions they make? Because an implicit deal has been made: don't hold me accountable for my bad decisions, and I won't hold you accountable for yours. We know, or should know, the recipe for desirable outcomes but don't wish to seem judgmental when we see people veer, sometimes wildly, off this course. In its most extreme, we have open-air drug markets and people overdosing in the street because we fail to hold people to any kind of standard, lest we be judged for our own actions. The net result is that we are all collectively worse, with nearly no standard whatsoever being held over anybody. The recipe for success, while known, is treated as if it were only one way to live, equal to all other ways of living. To those that believe this, I would urge them to take a walk around my neighborhood and see if they believe what they see is equal to all other ways of living. I'd recommend bringing at least some mace. Bear mace.

There's a lot of flat squirrels out there.

I started this chapter with a quote that needs some clarity. The skills my air force deployment instructors were teaching me involved hand-to-hand combat, what I'll call "military driving" concepts, land navigation, and other skills potentially needed for our survival while deployed overseas. While the training was interesting and unique, the teaching still required getting twenty- to twenty-five-year-olds to pay attention. How was this attention gained? By our instructors offering up stories from their own experiences in which the skills they were teaching us saved either their own or other people's lives. They needed us to want to learn in order for us to gain as much knowledge as possible. In essence, we were the squirrels. Untold numbers of squirrels, ignorant of the danger around them, dash frantically into roads all across America to meet their untimely end. If, on the other hand, we learned about these dangers beforehand, perhaps one of our fellow Americans wouldn't be scraping us off the road, and instead, we'd later be sipping mai tais in Vegas, impressing young women (or men) with our stories of heroism and bravery.

You are in that same position I was in. There are decisions, today, that will lead to your (and others') premature death or serious injury. Glancing at that text while driving on the highway. Consuming illicit narcotics that "definitely" don't have a lethal amount of fentanyl. Taking a selfie near the edge of a cliff. The boring decisions you make day to day have the potential to kill you and others around you.

On June 26, 2017, Monalisa Perez was asked by her boyfriend to shoot a Desert Eagle, one of the most powerful handguns sold, at him while he held a book in front of himself against his chest while thirty people watched on. The couple were trying to be internet stars by creating "content" people wanted to see. It was their first video. The bullet pierced the book, killing Ms. Perez's boyfriend, leaving her child fatherless, with one more child on the way (as Ms. Perez was pregnant with her now deceased boyfriend's child).

Ideally, people would learn from this and not engage in suicidally stupid ideas based on others' errors, but for many, this will not be the case. Thus, the squirrels will continue being flattened, requiring the rest of society to pick up the pieces (sometimes, literally). At the very least, some will learn, and thus even those squished will serve a purpose: showing others what not to do. It is up to you to determine whether you'll be the person who learns or the person others learn from.

Why do we want to believe choices don't have consequences? Because by believing our actions don't have consequences, we don't have to hold ourselves accountable when bad things happen, instead blaming society, fate, or luck. The role of being a victim is simple: you tell others how bad you have it, blame your condition on something outside yourself, elicit sympathy, and move on to the next awful set of choices and continue making things worse. Nothing is learned, no problem is solved, and no one is to blame except "the system." This chapter isn't merely to tell others to own up to the choices they've made; it's something I must do myself. There's been many a time when I stayed up too late playing video games to the detriment of my alertness the next day. The good people at my bank know when I've gone out to a casino or poker room because the money seems to only flow out of the ATM and never back in to deposit the next day. Writing this very work is something whose consequences I will have to deal with, for better or worse, and live with that decision whether I like it or not.

Unintended Consequences

On November 19, 2014, Rolling Stone, a monthly magazine that focuses on music, politics, and popular culture (or so claimed by

Wikipedia), published a piece by Sabrina Rubin Erdely titled A Rape on Campus. The well-credentialed writer had graduated from the University of Pennsylvania and had her work appear in Men's Health, Mother Jones, the New Yorker, and GQ, among other publications. Her piece concerned a (at the time) woman named "Jackie" (the piece gives no last name), who claimed she had been taken advantage of at a frat party by a group of young men belonging to a particular fraternity (whose name at this point isn't important, but if you're curious, nothing is stopping you from looking it up). According to the piece, not only had she been severely attacked in a very intimate way, but afterwards, her friends discouraged her from reporting the incident or seeking medical care for fear their social lives or aspirations to be in other sororities/fraternities would be at risk. The story ends by saying "Jackie's" academic performance declined, she became socially withdrawn, and that the university she attended was not doing anything meaningful to bring her attackers to justice.

The initial response from the university in question after the article was published was to suspend all fraternity and sorority organizations for a set amount of time (a few months, I believe). The fraternity "involved" was graffitied with phrases such as "UVA Center for Rape Studies" and "stop raping people" after it had suspended all chapter activities. The story confirmed what many wanted to believe occurred day in and day out: rich male fraternity members taking advantage of young, vulnerable women because their privilege allowed them to do so without consequence. The fraternity responded to the piece by saying no such party had taken place — and it hadn't. Numerous university, government, and media representatives investigated the Rolling Stone piece, given its cultural significance, only to discover that not only was the article fabricated from start to finish, but that the writer didn't even bother asking any of those accused of rape any questions whatsoever. Apparently, the writer learned from whatever journalism school she attended to "believe whatever someone tells you, and for God's sake don't ask questions, unless it helps the story."

I'm going to lose some points here, but I feel it's important that you understand my two rapid reactions to the story. I was originally amused knowing that "Jackie" and the writer had so damaged their credibilities that neither were likely to meaningfully recover it. I take no joy in the random suffering of others, but if someone has done something wildly immoral or illegal, for me, there is a sense of justice when such things are discovered, and people get their just rewards. If there are those that think this stance is harsh, know that there was the very real possibility of more than half a dozen innocent young men going to jail for decades on a fabricated story. As of this writing, I can find no real information about what happened to "Jackie," other than that she was never incarcerated or sued for falsely accusing her academic peers. The writer of the piece was fired, and numerous defamation lawsuits against Rolling Stone and the writer ended this sad tale. The writer failed to properly investigate her own story, probably because she wanted to believe it was true, the paper failed to effectively question the piece before publishing, and the American public was told a string of lies to push a narrative.

What is that narrative? Privileged men attack women with no consequences, requiring a societal correction. Is this narrative true? On some level, it is. In the same way, as has been demonstrated, it is also true that people will lie about vicious crimes that didn't occur for attention or other easily understood motives. This leads me to my more sobering, second reaction. While I was glad "Jackie" had not been attacked by a group of young men, I knew what the real fallout would be: the next time such an event occurred, people would be less likely to believe the accuser. What was supposed to further the cause of achieving justice against violent sexual deviants would in fact have the opposite effect.

A lot of space was dedicated to that story, and while it may not at first seem related to the chapter, it in fact provides a perfect capstone. A young woman lied for attention (I leave it to you to determine why she made up the story, though I will in a moment describe the probable motivation), resulting in her integrity forever being in question. Had the story held, numerous innocent young people would have been cast into the criminal justice system. The writer of the piece, probably wanting the story to be true, neglected well-understood principles of investigation in order to get a deeply flawed message out. Not only was she fired, but I don't believe she wrote again for a national newspaper or magazine I would recognize.

At the end of the day, obvious lies and incompetency reinforced the idea that perhaps not every story of sexual assault is true. Knowing these

131

attacks happen on college campuses, city streets, and in Americans' homes every day, it is unfortunate that this should be what people take away from the story, but I know that's what occurred. If there is a silver lining, perhaps it is that would-be liars will think twice before fabricating salacious, manufactured stories.

Now, unfortunately, I must cover the inciting incident and final consequence. The story "Jackie" told Rolling Stone started when she was infatuated with a boy that was not giving her attention. To try to entice him, she made up a story in which she was a victim in need of saving (she probably had not taken Feminism 101 yet and didn't understand she didn't need a man to save her or to be happy). Sadly, the story ends by derailing an effort to reform military sexual assault procedures. Proposed congressional legislation at the time, entitled The Military Justice Improvement Act, would have set up a justice system separate from the chain of command, ideally putting indictments and trials in the hands of legal professionals rather than military commanders (at the time, a service member's military commander had to initiate a military trial instead of legal professionals). Because the rape story was debunked, the public in general was much more wary of reforms regarding sexual assault. Whether or not you believe the legislation was a good idea isn't the point. The point is that one person's infatuation with a classmate led the nation down a different path than it may otherwise have, and had choices been different, perhaps the consequences of those choices would have been more favorable.

At points, I mentioned that some of the participants in the above story likely wanted the story to be true. How do I know this? Because the story was published without it being thoroughly investigated by any of those involved. The facts sought out and reported all went in the same direction, with no skepticism whatsoever until after the piece was published. The writer herself had made a career of writing about women and children being taken advantage of by men in power. She wanted the story to be true because it gave her a villain to fight (more on that later) and victims to save.

Every corpse on Mount Everest was once an extremely motivated person.

— unknown author, unknown date

Chapter 10 Most People's Main Obstacle Is Themselves

Insanity is doing the same thing, over and over again, but expecting a different result.
— Contested Origin

Sam Brinton, a nuclear engineer, worked at the US Department of Energy managing spent nuclear waste disposal. Because this male identified as nonbinary (as neither a man nor a woman), dressed in women's clothing, wore lipstick, was bald, and sported a rather well-put-together mustache, he was held up as an example of inclusivity during the Biden administration, 2021–2025. He was caught on camera in two separate incidents stealing bags from airport baggage claim on days he was not flying and was subsequently fired by the Department of Energy.

After losing his job and being arrested for felony theft (ultimately requiring him to pay approximately $3,500 for the theft of the items, perform community service, and enter an "adult diversion" program), he was again caught stealing luggage from baggage claim at Reagan National Airport. There are some who surmise that he enjoyed sporting these stolen goods on television, social networks, and press opportunities for reasons only Sam knows. Given that we don't have an itemized list of everything he stole over the course of his life or what he wore during every instance he was filmed or photographed, we'll never know.

While any criminal activity is an employer's concern, Sam Brinton's employer also relied on the individual maintaining a US government security clearance. These clearances are to ensure that an individual has the character to perform the job and cannot be blackmailed into revealing sensitive government information. To obtain these security clearances, individuals are required to disclose their current and former residency, current and former employment, credit score, criminal associates, foreign associates, criminal history, debt obligations, and foreign assets. If someone selected for a security clearance has a change in the above, there is a strong likelihood of losing that clearance since they can no longer be trusted. Mx. Brinton knew this and pursued his thieving ways despite the risk.

I chose to describe Sam Brinton with male descriptors to indicate that he is of the male sex, not to indicate that I am attempting to disrespect the kleptomaniac's gender identity. I had pondered using they/their as his gender pronouns but did not want the previous paragraphs to be unreadable. For example, if using they/their, a sentence from the above would read: "They were caught on camera in two separate incidents stealing bags from airport baggage claim." While some may read context clues leading up to this sentence, others not as gifted in the English language may feel this sentence refers to two separate people and would be confused about who else I was talking about. As I wanted to be as inclusive as possible to those perhaps with English as a second language (ESL), I chose language that was as clear as possible to the greatest number of people. You're welcome.

It is not inaccurate or insulting to say that Sam Brinton is a male nonbinary individual, which is distinct from a female nonbinary individual. If I said Sam Brinton is a man who is nonbinary, this would be nonsensical, as this is two separate gender identities. Since I too am nonbinary at times, I don't feel this is inappropriate. It may even aid in understanding, such as when a female nonbinary individual is looking for other female nonbinary individuals as intimate partners but doesn't wish to be with male nonbinary individuals. If there are no nonbinary individuals to whom the distinction is important, I will withdraw the previous idea and acquiesce to the new fact that every nonbinary individual doesn't care if their potential partners are male or female.

Mx. Brinton is like many others of our time: not understanding that they are creating the problems most detrimental to their own lives. How could Mx. Brinton have avoided the scandal stated above? By (1) not stealing and (2) not continuing to steal after being caught. There is no transphobia or homophobia that resulted in the man's downfall; rather, it was a direct result of a lack of character. It is easily identifiable and simple to understand (for the most part). He, like the rest of us, was his number-one obstacle. He didn't need nefarious religious zealots, redneck truck-driving hicks, or pearl-clutching WASPs to bring him down, as he was able to do this perfectly well on his own.

While perusing the news one day, I saw a video of some visitors to Yellowstone National Park. Some had spotted a black bear and her two cubs. Naturally, their first instinct was to exit their car and race towards the wild animals as quickly as they could to either get pictures or just bask in nature with all of Gaia's children. Don't worry though; the children weren't left out; of those racing towards the 175-pound wild animal, one clutched a toddler in his arms. Luckily, the animals had more sense than the people and raced away from them before the number of either humans or black bears ticked down ever so slightly.

Lori Lightfoot was the fifty-sixth mayor of Chicago from 2019 until 2023. She was the first openly (self-identified) lesbian Black woman to serve as mayor of a major city in the United States. Upon losing her election in early 2023, she blamed the citizens of Chicago (whom she led and was elected by) for being too sexist, homophobic, and racist to re-elect her. Why this group of deplorables elected her in the first place (or chose to replace her with another African American) is a mystery, but perhaps during her initial campaign in 2019, her constituents were too ignorant to notice she had been married to a woman back in 2014 and didn't understand that she was an African American female. Once her voters woke up, they quickly sent her packing because of these attributes, and not due to any of her policies over the course of the past four years. Of course, the previous conclusion was nonsense. Mrs. Lightfoot lost her election because, on her watch, crime in Chicago became much worse. She openly fought her city's law enforcement because it was fashionable at the time, and her city suffered because of that. In a city that is 30% African American and 51% female, she only received 17% of the votes, suggesting disapproval even within her demographic groups.

It was easier for her to think racism, sexism, and homophobia resulted in her loss rather than people not liking the consequences of her leadership. Tying this back to the chapter's theme, there was no self-recognition that her policies on crime led to more crime, and thus eventually led to lawbreaking being a political issue she had no way out of. Rather than learn from her mistakes and backtrack in meaningful ways, she decided to blame forces and attitudes outside herself. You see, she wasn't a victim of her own disastrous decisions, but rather a victim of rampant sexism, homophobia, and racism in one of the most left-leaning cities in America.

In Cook County, where Chicago is located, 75% of the vote went to Democrat nominee Joe Biden in the 2020 election, leaving 24% voting for Republican Donald Trump. A close friend of mine who had never owned a dog decided to purchase one on a whim. Whenever I visited, I would be sure if I brought anything I would store it outside the reach of her dog; whereas, my friend did not (although I did warn her). After a few days of ownership, the dog tore apart a pair of her shoes. My friend was angry and scolded the dog, at which point I told her again not to keep her shoes where the dog could reach. A week or so later, the process repeated, with her dog eating another pair of shoes. Again, she scolded the dog and was mad at it. I informed her again that the dog is going to do what the dog is going to do, but you can change the outcome by keeping valued items out of his reach. Inside of a week, the process repeated. Oddly enough, at some point, the dog simply got tired of chewing through shoes, and the problem miraculously resolved itself.

While I agree you can train dogs to act better, the problem was not with her dog. The problem was that my friend was not learning from her mistakes and decided to point her frustration at an animal incapable of thinking at the same level as (most) human beings. This wasn't even a failure to plan ahead; it was a failure to learn from one's mistakes even though the same undesirable outcome occurred over and over again. It's easy to see it in others, but it's much more difficult to see it in ourselves.

This isn't simply a problem for my friend and her dog; this is a far larger problem spanning our entire culture. We've entered an era in which individual responsibility is ignored for the sake of the individual's feelings. We, collectively, don't want to make a person feel bad for the situations they've largely gotten themselves into, so we invent guilty parties and institutions outside of that person to blame the failure on. It's not your fault you're unemployed; it's the economy. It's not your fault you're addicted to drugs; society led you astray. It's not your fault you failed the class; the school system failed you (although showing up may have helped). I understand how judgmental this sounds (because it is), but you know this to largely be true. Whatever your own particular vice(s) is/are, you know your continued participation is your fault, not someone else's. Your (and my) past and present choices are what largely define where you are and where you will be in the future. Bad things happen, but much worse things happen if you don't think your way through life.

I thought I would have to do a deep dive to find stories related to this chapter. Sadly, as I went about my day-to-day business, humanity's stupidity hit me in the face as I scrolled through my various news feeds. Around New Year's 2023, a Massachusetts mother of three was reported missing from work. Over the course of the search for her, police determined the husband's internet history contained "how to dispose of a 115-pound woman's body" along with "how to dismember a corpse," according to law enforcement. It could be that the husband was simply curious, such as when someone asks Apple's Siri where to hide a body (it used to direct you to iron foundries; I think they ditched that feature), but the "115-pound" part was a bit specific. While under home confinement for an unrelated fraud conviction, he made numerous trips to a hardware store without prior notification to authorities. Prosecutors allege he spent $450 on cleaning supplies, including buckets, tarps, and mops, the week of his wife's disappearance.

This now gets a tad darker, but I feel the question is appropriate: If you were trying to figure out how to kill someone, would you search how to do it on the internet for anyone to find? Would you, while under home confinement, attempt to covertly purchase "The Jeffrey Dahmer Package" from a major box store? This genuinely evil individual's true opponents were not the police, family of his wife, or any other potential witnesses. The downfall of this person (thank God) was his own laziness, stupidity, and shortsightedness. It did not require a Sherlock Holmes, Nancy Drew, or Hercule Poirot (Death on the Orient Express) to bring him down — just a lazy search on a computer and public trips to chain stores that could be easily traced back to him.

On a lighter note, in 2020, I had a neighbor in my gentrifying (not gentrified) neighborhood that did not feel safe walking around on her own (a good assessment, given the neighborhood). Since I needed to walk my dog, my late-fifties neighbor liked to tag along, and I honestly enjoyed the company and conversation. She expressed to me that she felt unsafe in her home and walking around the local area. I informed her that with my dog, firearms, and bedroom on the third floor (it's a really narrow house),

I'd never felt safer in my life. Because she rented versus owned, she could not have a dog. More concerning to me, she did not believe in firearms.

Knowing not all people feel safe around guns, I suggested she keep pepper spray. Her remark to that? "But what if the crook gets ahold of it?" (I thought, Well... then I suppose you'll be robbed or killed, and it will be very sad. Additionally, somebody will have to find me a new neighbor.) I only had one other thought that thankfully I didn't voice. I was going to suggest she buy a whistle to blow if she felt in danger. At that point, an adult would come and solve her problem (hopefully). Less than two weeks later, I saw her walking around the neighborhood. She asked me if I "noticed anything different about her" (a dangerous question concerning females) and motioned to her hip. As I looked down, I saw she was now carrying pepper spray attached to her waist. Curious if my advice helped, I asked how she felt. She responded, "I've never felt safer in my entire life."

My neighbor (until my slight intervention) had a problem that she had largely created herself. She chose a house (not a cheap one) in a particular neighborhood, desired to exercise in that exact same neighborhood, refused any type of self-defense items, and then wondered why she felt unsafe. The difficulties created were nearly all self-imposed, yet there was no recognition of this. Worse yet, the solutions suggested to these self-imposed problems were almost entirely disregarded because they didn't fit the model of where she felt safety should originate from. She didn't want a gun or pepper spray because she either thought ownership of these items caused more problems than they solved or that she would not be able to use them effectively. The only rational explanation for her lack of concern for her own safety is that she believed it came from elsewhere, namely the police.

I have nothing but respect for law enforcement, truly. They have a dangerous job and are currently far less respected than they should be. I feel nothing but pride in my city and state government as I see them go by (as I drive slightly slower than they do), knowing they are the front line to ensure civility remains (if you doubt that, venture into the areas where they are absent). That said, when seconds count, help is minutes away. I assume that if I'm being robbed, attacked, raped, tortured, or otherwise maimed, the police will show up just in time to draw my chalk outline and file a very detailed report on how it happened. On the right day, they might even get the guy (or girl) who did it.

Why do we blame others rather than ourselves for our various problems? Because it is easy and requires no work or introspection. Self-responsibility has been replaced by an endless list of grievances and victimhood that elevate that individual higher than any real accomplishment. Simply the act of "being" has replaced merit. With any identified problem, there exist two sources, although most of the time it is a mix of the two: (1) something outside the individual has created a problem, or (2) something within the individual has created a problem. For example, if someone has become addicted to drugs, the primary reason is that the person at some point chose to try them (I know there are some physically forced to take drugs, but that is the exception not the rule). That said, the only way the individual would have the ability to try legal or illicit drugs is if society has tolerated drug use to the point that it is not difficult or expensive to feed this addiction. For those individuals addicted to drugs (and their "allies"), it's easier to blame everything except the individual. If it's someone else's fault, there's nothing you as an individual can do. If it's your fault, the only things holding you back are your own willpower and choices.

Speaking of choices and willpower, while I was bartending, there was an individual who came by on a Sunday afternoon I only ever saw once (as opposed to the regulars I saw with almost daily frequency). Over the next few hours, he explained his situation to anyone and everyone that would listen to his troubles while covering the drinks of everyone at the bar. Luckily for this individual, it was a Sunday afternoon, so "everyone" amounted to about five people over the course of three hours. As it turns out, the individual, in his mid-twenties, was getting a divorce from his husband and currently living in a men's shelter. I believe he had all his possessions in a small, clear backpack with him at the bar. As he bought everyone else's drinks, he told everyone present he planned on spending $250 that day on alcohol to help him forget his troubles. With the prices at the bar I was working at, this would be enough to kill him several times over. At around 2 p.m., he wandered away from my bar by himself, off to another (more expensive and classier) bar elsewhere. If I had sat down with this individual and quizzed him about a fictional person committing the same acts prior to him doing them, I believe he'd easily be able to not only identify the serious issues presented, but also identify more effective ways to deal with the problems. I truly hope he didn't spend all his money on the way back to the men's shelter, but given his problem-solving abilities leading up to this, I doubt it.

Resolution

I have a strong feeling that when you hear other people describing their problems, your mind races towards solutions, easily identifiable and within the reach of the average person. That said, you may not express these solutions knowing the receiving party doesn't actually want solutions; what they actually want is an empathetic ear and perhaps a shoulder to cry on. By providing solutions, you're telling the other person there is something they can do, but it will take time, effort, and thought. The receiver generally already knows this but has already made up their mind that they don't want to actually do it.

For example, I got a summer job in high school making and delivering pizzas for a chain restaurant. A high school friend of mine also wanted extra money and told me he was looking for a summer job also. When I asked a few weeks later how the search was going, he told me an electronic entertainment store didn't want to hire him, so he stopped looking. When I told him what I had done — gone up and down the street applying at every business available — he said he didn't want to work at any of those places, so he abandoned the idea of a summer job. You see, it's not that my friend couldn't find work; it's that he couldn't find work that was acceptable to him, so he gave up. His problem was not a tight job market. My guess is that he thought it was beneath him to work at any number of fast-food chains or other establishments employing teenagers.

A friend of a friend of a friend (we'll call her Rachel) told me she was in a bad mood for the evening. Apparently, her male friend (who we'll call Brent) had stopped texting her after a "miscommunication" about their relationship. You see, even though Rachel and Brent socialized frequently and had been intimate, they had not yet had conversations about their relationship or monogamy. So, Brent continued to see other women, which Rachel was okay with so long as she was "the number-one woman in Brent's life." Despite this requirement, during one of Brent's dates with another woman, Rachel texted Brent telling him she would be getting on a dating app. Brent got jealous and stopped texting Rachel.

It was apparent to me that this Brent was not the "monogamous" type, and that Rachel was in an actual relationship with Brent. Rachel did not want to admit this to herself or others, because while it's easy to explain that someone hooked up with their friend, it's harder to explain to others that the reason their boyfriend isn't around is because he's on a date with another girl (or boy). My friend's friend's friend's problem was that she was trying to square the idea of an intimate relationship with her partner not being as invested as her. It was obvious as I heard this story that she was strongly infatuated with this person, but that this person wasn't willing to reciprocate in a method that indicated true desire and effort. What should have been obvious to her was obvious to me (and would be to nearly everyone), but willful blindness prevented her from determining the truth. Admitting that she wanted a deeper relationship with Brent would mean pursuing a man with no intent of a monogamous relationship and having to explain that to others openly (or I suppose conceal it).

A separate acquaintance of mine has described numerous physical and mental ailments, including stomach pain, loss of eyesight, cancer, and numerous other issues to include suicidal thoughts. Wanting to help, I told him to see a doctor or specialist to help resolve his issues that, to me, seemed largely absent, at which point he became agitated at me. He thought I was talking down to him by telling him to do... basically what anyone would do, as if he could not figure that out for himself. He expressed that what he wanted was empathy and understanding, not obvious solutions. As far as I know, my acquaintance hasn't ever taken my advice about seeing professionals, and I suspect in the near future a new ailment will appear. Concerning for me is that he may have a serious issue that needs to be dealt with, but his search for empathy overshadows his desire for a resolution. The solutions to the problems are obvious, but the steps required take work; it's labor many do not wish to undertake, because it doesn't get them what they actually want and may, in fact, hinder it. After all, if there's no problem, or if the problems are all resolved, there's no reason for anybody to be empathetic for non-existent issues.

Speaking of empathy, I'm now inundated with grievances from every direction from people wishing me to feel bad for their situation and work towards a solution that is... usually quite unreasonable. Originally, I planned on naming the "influencers" (that is, people wanting to be famous by making videos of themselves on the internet) but decided there were so many of these, it didn't make sense to single any out for ridicule. A number of their grievances concerned a lack of facilities specifically geared towards those who weigh significantly more than average. Their complaints surround planes, hotel bathrooms and towels, and clothing not accommodating their large frames. The fact that roomy airplanes, large hotel rooms, and obscenely large towels exist makes no difference, as they usually cost more or aren't provided by default.

There are two ways of looking at this "problem." One is to assume that society in general is fatphobic and unwilling to accommodate everybody. This is the easy route, as it paints the person with the grievance as a victim completely unable to operate in society the way everybody else does. From this point of view, the rest of us need to design every building, car, scale, dress, airplane, and bulletproof vest for every body type, including the abnormally tall, short, thin, or large.

The other way is to encourage the individual to lose weight. Sitting at my computer by myself, I can already hear the screams of those opposing such a simple idea. They can't. We're unable. It's too hard. Critics of this idea believe it's easier for everyone else to change rather than the individual. I will admit it is difficult, as I've struggled with my own weight going up and down depending on the year and my drive. But losing weight has been done, is being done, and will be done in the future by others.

Recently, a coworker imparted to me that he would like to lose weight, but because he was working, married, and had children, that it wasn't possible. I then told him that there was a way to lose weight without any commitment of time or money: stop eating (which I then switched to eat less or eat healthier). He told me he couldn't. I then asked him if I were to pay him $10,000,000 to lose 5 pounds in a month if he would be able to. He then very quickly answered yes. He then realized the point that I was trying to make; it is possible under his exact circumstances, but that it was an issue of motivation and self-control. The excuses previously provided faded, as he recognized they were being used as a crutch rather than a true limitation that couldn't be overcome. Three months after our conversation, I needed to contact him over the phone for work related reasons. During the call, he informed me he had lost 25 pounds since our conversation.

Here, I would normally ask who's responsible for our health, but you already know the answer. For the influencers wanting larger plane aisles and towels in hotel rooms, you can probably guess it will not, for the most part, happen. Thus, those influencers will continue suffering needlessly, without any public recognition that the problem is largely of their own making. You know it, I know it, and the majority of those this issue afflicts know it. You can still feel bad that a person must deal with these problems, but when the solution is identified and ignored, there's only so much we can do.

If there are those that believe weight loss (or gain) is impossible, give me full authority (think boot camp or prison) over an individual, and I'll show you what is and isn't possible. This may be hard to hear, but the truth hurts. Odds are, no one is oppressing you or me. Your (and my) life circumstances are largely dictated by the choices we make and the way we choose to live our lives. The price of freedom is the consequence of our choices. You may choose to live in oppressive conditions, but you need to understand you hold the key to the exit. If you're living beyond your means, the solution is simple.

If you're working somewhere that's making you miserable, the solution is also simple. I don't need to tell you the answers because you already know them but may be unwilling to pay the cost. Life is compromise and trade-offs; there is no paradise where you get it all. If the cost of living in your city is too high, change cities. If you hate your boss, there are plenty of other bosses (or none if you choose self-employment) out there that you may hate slightly less. If your intimate partner is lazy, abusive, or has serious substance abuse problems, I'd recommend seeking out other partners if you can't tolerate their faults. Does that involve risk? Lower pay? Moving? It might. You may have painted yourself into such a corner that you refuse to consider alternatives at a subconscious level, but alternatives are always there. Being a victim is easy; identifying that you are the victim of yourself is hard.

Antebellum

Between 1937 and 1938, the Soviet Union engaged in the so-called Great Purge, in which large numbers of people were arrested, jailed, exiled, or killed in order to consolidate power around the dictator, Joseph Stalin. High-ranking leaders in the army, air force, and navy were removed from their positions or executed for fear their loyalty was in question. All of this would have been generally inconsequential, unless, of course, a war started in which the most experienced and knowledgeable weren't able to run the war...

To hit this point home, I've copied and pasted this straight from Wikipedia: *During Joseph Stalin's Great Purge in the late 1930s, which had not ended by the time of the German invasion on June 22, 1941, much of the officer corps of the Red Army was executed or imprisoned. Many of their replacements, appointed by Stalin for political reasons, lacked military competence. Of the five Marshals (read: four-star generals) of the Soviet Union appointed in 1935, only Kliment Voroshilov and Semyon Budyonny survived Stalin's purge... Fifteen of sixteen army commanders (read: three-star generals), fifty of the fifty-seven corps commanders, 154 of the 186 divisional commanders, and 401 of 456 colonels were killed, and many other officers were dismissed. In total, about 30,000 Red Army personnel were executed.*

When Operation Barbarossa (the surprise German invasion of the Soviet Union on June 22, 1941) was executed, the Soviet Union started being turned into East Deutschland with alarming speed, with Nazi Germany getting within fifty miles of Moscow. The purge mentioned in the last paragraph meant the country was unable to resist rapid German advances, which nearly toppled the communist government.

Was all this predictable? Of course. Were there serious consequences? Even more so, yes. Look up the casualty rates by country in World War II, and you tell me who screwed the pooch the worst (not literally, you perverts). Hitler didn't need to execute the Soviet Union's generals prior to the war or make Stalin completely unprepared for the invasion. The Soviet Union managed to do this all on its own, with Stalin's citizens and soldiers ultimately paying the price.

145

Chapter End Notes

There will always be an opposing force creating problems for you. What is preventing you from overcoming those obstacles is largely yourself. If you, against all evidence to the contrary, believe you are simply a victim with no way out of your own circumstances, continue believing that. A fate worse than death will occur; nothing will change. But don't worry, others will feel bad about you and your situation. At the end of the day, isn't that what we're all looking for?

Did I ever tell you the definition of insanity?
— Vaas, Farcry 3, Ubisoft, 2012

Chapter 11 Not All New Ideas Are Good

"Not one step back!"
— Joseph Stalin, July 28, 1942, order No. 227 to all Soviet citizens
and members of the Red Army

In 2015, Harvey Weinstein, a successful Hollywood producer, was questioned by police after a twenty-two-year-old woman accused him of touching her inappropriately. After this, a deluge (that's a flood, for those in Rio Linda, California) of women and aspiring (or actual) actresses piled on the original accusation, and Mr. Weinstein could not escape the sheer numbers of those accusing him. Following this and numerous court trials, Weinstein, seventy, was given a prison sentence he is unlikely to ever complete while still vertical. And thus, within the public view, the #MeToo movement was born.

I must point out for older readers or listeners that you are meant to read "#" as "hashtag," not "pound." Reading it incorrectly could lead you to believe the #MeToo movement is a tad less socially progressive and more suggestive of some type of kink. I didn't invent the hashtag, pound sign, or movement, so don't come after me for the name. That blame lies elsewhere.

At its heart, the goal of #MeToo was to usher in the idea that we as a society should "believe all women." That is, when women publicly accuse men of harassing or attacking them, we as a society should believe, without any proof, that the harassment or attack did occur, and that we should jail or banish the accused individual from respectable society. The idea of innocent until proven guilty was set aside for a new standard of justice: guilty until proven innocent, if accused by a female. While the movement did take down some truly despicable people who abused their wealth and power, it came at the cost of our justice system and traditional American values.

In the days leading up to the 2020 presidential election, Tara Reid (no, not the actress) accused then-Democratic nominee Joe Biden of sexually assaulting her in 1993 by pushing her against a wall, kissing her, and inserting his fingers into her by reaching up her skirt. At this point, while the #MeToo movement was at its peak, it now had a devastating choice to make: either #MeToo could survive, or Joe Biden, destined to beat then-President Trump, could survive — not both. To believe all women would mean Mrs. Reid's accusation would need to be acted on, criminally investigating the nominee on the eve of the election, or at the very least removing Mr. Biden as the nominee and replacing him with another member who may not have been able to beat Mr. Trump. Believe all women, within intellectual circles, was dead.

Mrs. Reid has since fled to Russia, claiming she is not safe in the United States. Given her support for democratic socialist Bernie Sanders, it seems odd that she fled to the same country Bernie Sanders supported and honeymooned in when the Soviet Union still existed. There are some who speculate she may have been a Russian asset, which may call into question supporters of "Democratic Socialists"

Two years later, a defamation trial between movie stars Johnny Depp and Amber Heard took place in Fairfax County, Virginia. Ms. Heard had published a piece in the Washington Post in 2018 that all but named Depp as a domestic abuser. This effectively blacklisted him from filmmaking. Over the course of the trial, a jury of Ms. Heard's peers determined she was a serial liar and awarded Depp the majority of the money that changed hands. More important than the inconsequential nature of the squabbles of divorced celebrity millionaires was that people saw a long, drawn-out trial in which a well-known actress lied about abuse and was herself an abuser.

The public at large rightfully concluded that women are just as capable of lying as men, and that perhaps "believe all women" was, like communism, good on paper but a nightmare in practice. The pendulum swung back the other way, and "innocent until proven guilty" became the standard again in most people's minds. Only those blissfully unaware or willfully ignorant still think believing all women all the time is a good idea.

So I've covered all my bases: believing all men all the time is equally as moronic of an idea for a justice system or society to operate from. This chapter is not about #MeToo; it's about how simply because an idea is new doesn't mean it's a good idea. This is not to outright disparage ideas simply because they are new, but to advocate skepticism whenever something new arrives to replace something that is currently working. Many of us have not lived long enough to see bad ideas tried and failed, and for those of us who have, we seemingly have short memories or are willfully oblivious for fear of what accepting the truth will do to our own worldview.

While we have historical archives and access to all of it in the palm of our hands, we seem stuck in the ever-present now. We don't draw wisdom from the past; rather, we regard it as something to view with disdain since it doesn't fit with our current values and morality. Bad ideas and assumptions lead to bad conclusions, and those bad conclusions lead to the execution of disastrous actions, making the current situation worse. New ideas may promise to make things better but rely on fundamental beliefs that may be wrong.

For example, let's say you were led to believe your race was the "master race" and that members of that race were smarter and stronger than all others, ensuring its eventual ruling of the entire world. At one point, national socialism was a new idea, replacing others that had fallen out of fashion before it. After decades of this belief, you look around at your smoldering capital and see Russians, French, Americans, and British imposing their will on you and those you believed to be racially superior, as the Nazis did in 1945.

How could morally and racially weaker enemies win? How could it actually happen? You would find yourself at a crossroads: they did win... So, if the laws of nature dictate that the strongest will prevail... perhaps we aren't the master race... Of course, even getting to that conclusion relies on so many false assumptions and bad ideas that that person is already fairly lost. Belief in racial superiority and the subjugation of those not like you were and are bad ideas, relying on theories that are not true.

But we don't have to go back more than seven decades to find catastrophically bad ideas. Following the death of George Floyd at the hands of police, a wave of anti-cop sentiment filled US cities, resulting in protests and riots demanding police reforms. In the Capitol Hill neighborhood of Seattle, police evacuated the East Precinct building on June 8, 2020, leaving it to be taken over by protestors. Thus, the Capitol Hill Occupied Protest (or CHOP, later to be renamed the Capitol Hill Autonomous Zone, or CHAZ) was born.

The law enforcement-free area only covered a couple of intersections. At its core, the "defund the police" movement was intended to make the enforcement of laws more difficult. The following assumptions are central to the defund-the-police movement: (1) Society is structurally racist; (2) laws are not enforced equally, with marginalized groups punished more harshly for the same crime; and (3) people are inherently good, only being made criminals by an unjust society.

If law enforcement officers and the justice system are irreparably racist, then the best that could be done would be to take away the tools with which police departments perform their racist work. Less money means less equipment, more money for social services, and, most importantly, fewer cops. If people are inherently good and only made criminals by a racist society with police officers on the front lines, then if we remove those law enforcement officers, people's better nature will take over, and a more just society will emerge.

What emerged in CHOP/CHAZ was chaos, violence, and a regression to survival of the strongest. Masked men with military-style rifles patrolled the streets, enforcing rules as they pleased. There were four shootings in ten days, leaving two teenagers dead. It is unknown if the shootings were related to the demonstration, but it is known that first responders were delayed from arriving at the scene by the protest. An area covering only a few intersections had descended into chaos, yet the structurally racist elements (aka the police) had been removed.

The American public saw what a city (or tiny portion of a large city) becomes without law enforcement. The power vacuum left when police evacuated was filled with warlords and gang-style violence. What should have been learned was that without any law enforcement, communities fall to anarchy and bloodshed. People's better natures don't take over; people take over. And the masked, rifle-wielding enforcer may not be as willing to take your concerns into account over an elected city council or mayor.

There's nothing stopping you from defunding the police, but what rises in its place will be far worse than you imagine. By early July, the city leadership had had enough; the area was cleared, and the Capitol Hill Autonomous Zone was no more. If the experiment had worked, Seattle would have expanded the area in which no police or law enforcement officers of any kind would be allowed. Seattle would have become a utopian bastion, free from structural racism and arbitrary terror police inflict on marginalized groups. Rather, the experiment showed how bad a situation can get and how quickly it can get that way.

Not everyone learned this lesson, as over the next few years, other jurisdictions tried lowering police budgets to conform to the fashion of the time. More natural experiments were created, with entirely predictable results. Those areas where police budgets were lowered or law enforcement was prevented from enforcing societally agreed-upon laws descended into urban hellscapes citizens fled from (those who could).

To some, the increased violence and crime were acceptable prices to pay, as long as it led to more equity regarding who was arrested and jailed. Here's an interesting question related to equity and incarceration: Do all groups of people commit crimes in equal proportion? If I were to insinuate that Māori (Indigenous Polynesian people of mainland New Zealand) commit crimes at a higher proportion than Americans, is it racist (I actually don't know if that's true or not; I believe this is a taboo topic in Australia and New Zealand)?

What if I insinuated that males in general commit crimes in much greater proportion than their female counterparts? Should we incarcerate males and females in numbers proportionate to the population, or should we instead jail them when we discover they have done something wrong? There is a belief that some groups are overrepresented in the prison population, but if I suggested we should incarcerate more females or free significant numbers of violent male offenders for equity's sake, I would likely find myself with few allies.

Add this to the list of bad ideas contemporary society has not yet shed to the dustbin of history. Speaking of equity and bad ideas, in 2023, California's Board of Education approved new recommendations to the state's school districts. In order to combat different students from either excelling or falling behind in math courses, the board recommended eliminating advanced courses to those gifted (my words, not theirs) in mathematics. Even that does not go far enough to explain why education professionals wanted to hold their own students back.

The truth was that the board and its supporters did not like that some groups of students tended to succeed in math, and others did not. For a more equitable result, their idea was that all students should proceed in their education at the same (slower) pace, even if that ultimately meant some students would learn less. The ultimate goal? That all subdivisions of humanity have equal mathematical abilities — no more, and no less. The idea that different people have different gifts and drives, oddly, made no difference.

In another public sector, health, we get this: On September 10, 2023, the Associated Press published a "news piece" (read: opinion piece) titled *Patients need doctors who look like them. Can medicine diversify without affirmative action?* in the wake of the US Supreme Court overturning affirmative action in higher education. The writer of the piece advocates that affirmative action was needed to generate more African American doctors to treat African American patients.

That is not where my mind went to when I read the headline. My mind raced towards where this logic takes us, and it isn't forward but backward. Imagine a racist in need of medical care refusing treatment from anyone unless they were a White male. Even if this interaction weren't hostile, imagine a Hispanic male requesting another doctor because the one treating them at the hospital happened to be a Black female and thus did not look like them. If this idea were taken seriously, we would quickly careen into a new era of sanctioned segregation.

If you happen to be a patient in need of medical care, I highly doubt your primary concern is that when you hold your arm against the doctor and/or nurses, the hues of skin match. I imagine instead you would like the doctor that had the most satisfied (and alive) patients, perhaps with some reasonable concerns about the cost of treatment. At the end of the day, the question is this: Do you want the most qualified person treating you, or the most qualified who just so happens to match your race, sex, or ethnicity? If it's the former, congratulations, you have excellent survival instincts. If it's the latter, congratulations, your obituary will confirm how socially progressive you were and how well you supported your own race's or sex's medical staff.

*Within the last few years, I was driving down the highway when my left leg and arm started going numb. My heart started racing, and I believed I was having a heart attack. I raced towards the hospital four miles away, trying desperately to convince myself I was fine and could make it without pulling over and calling for an ambulance. After throwing my car into the ambulance bay, I rushed inside to figure out what was wrong with me. The nurse who began treating me was clearly a gay male Hispanic, given the bracelets and pins he was wearing. The doctor who arrived later, a White cisgender woman, explained I had had a panic attack, apparently from consuming too much caffeine. Until typing this paragraph, I hadn't even considered the identities of those treating me important whatsoever, as they both did an excellent job and aided and comforted me throughout my ordeal. At no point did I concern myself with who they were, as I only cared whether or not they could keep me above room temperature.

Historical Context

Between 1931 and 1933, the Soviet Union, at the time led by dictator Joseph Stalin, had about 125,000 workers (the vast majority of whom were forced laborers, what some may call slaves) construct the White Sea-Baltic Canal in modern-day northern Russia. As part of the first five-year plan (communists of that era seemed to love five-year plans), it was dictated that construction would take twenty months using methods that wouldn't have seemed different than in the fifteenth century, using minimal modern materials, equipment, or motorized vehicles to cut costs.

All the materials, vehicles, and equipment either had to be locally produced, or limited capital (read: money) had to be used to purchase these items from foreign countries. Due to the speed and limited cost demanded of the project, which was completely disconnected from any realistic capability, given the inputs, the project ultimately was "completed" within the timeframe demanded but was almost wholly unusable for its original intent. The depth, originally proposed to be eighteen feet deep to accommodate oceangoing vessels of the time, instead had a depth of 11.5 feet at various points to speed up construction. Its economic use limited, there was and is minimal traffic on it to this day.

It exists more as a reminder of the stupidity of central planners, far disconnected from the reality on the ground. Modern historians estimate 25,000 laborers died creating a canal of almost no use. At the time, it was believed in that part of the world that central planning could not only create a more equitable society but that this would not come at the cost of industrial output.

153

Five-year plans were created to focus economic activity in a direction that furthered a defined state goal, but they were so grand and expansive as to be physically impossible to complete. It was believed that without capitalists sloshing away funds (as profit), all projects could be completed less expensively and more fairly in regard to the pay of the average Soviet citizen (for those who were actually paid). Grand projects such as this were made to highlight to the country and the world at large that, under communism, "big projects" could be accomplished as a sign of Soviet power and the superiority of its economic system.

What history actually reveals is that corruption, incompetence, and a criminally flagrant disregard for human life are all that result from this mode of thinking. While there are many modern thinkers who still cling to the ideals of communism and socialism, it is only by closing one's eyes and covering one's ears to history that these ideas still seem worth pursuing.

What ideas propped up the above anecdote? A belief in the superiority of state ownership over the means of production. Nationalization of all industry (that is, ownership of all businesses by the national government). Economic planning organized not by individuals but by central planners in faraway capitals. There is a reason almost no country on Earth organizes itself like this to this day: It inefficiently uses both natural and human resources and empowers the most corrupt and incompetent to make decisions for all others.

Like fascism, the above was at one point a new idea, proven in the blood and suffering of countless victims to in fact be an awful way of trying to organize society, no matter how good the intentions were at the offset (if in fact there were actually any good intentions). Why do we continuously fall for bad ideas? We want the ideas to work and to have better lives. Anything or anyone opposed to the proposed idea is perceived as a hindrance and only makes that desired outcome more difficult.

We confuse action with progress and are far more optimistic about the outcomes of ideas put into action than sanity should allow. In a similar fashion, when we perceive problems around us, we determine that something must be done. A nuclear plant melts down in the Soviet Union? Work to remove all nuclear power plants. A man is shot by police?

Remove the police. There are people living on the street? Give them houses. The knee-jerk reaction to do something (and something probably not well thought-out) drives us from one ill-conceived set of actions to the next, ignoring history and entirely predictable results.

Optimism that this "new" idea will get us closer to utopia will nearly always clash with reality. Here's an interesting new idea: Can a man become a dog? By December of 2022, a Japanese man by the name of Toco spent the equivalent of $15,000 on a dog costume that gave him the appearance of a collie. He shares videos of himself online in which he is eating "dog food" (that is, food he changed the appearance of to resemble dog food) from a bowl, lounging in front of windowsills, and performing tricks he somehow taught himself.

In an interview with the *Daily Mirror* (a British newspaper), he claimed his "…friends and family seemed very surprised to learn I became an animal." Reading the article, I didn't come across any language where Toco said he was acting like a dog, or enjoyed dressing like a dog (or not dressing?) but instead had actually become a dog. For my part, this only creates new questions.

If this person has become a collie, can he legally become intimate with other dogs? Which laws should apply—those that apply to animals or those that apply to humans? If he bites somebody, should he be arrested or put to sleep? Can he travel in the cargo hold of an aircraft with the other pets, or will he be required to purchase a ticket? While this is comical to think about (the story itself was only published to show the absurdity people find themselves in these days), what if this same man started getting surgeries instead of a suit to look like a dog?

What if he demanded the right to urinate on fire hydrants and defecate on neighborhood lawns (San Francisco doesn't count; you can already do that without a dog suit or surgeries)? Odder still, what if he began competing in and dominating dog shows? Reality being what it is, this is in fact not a dog but an adult man wishing to either be a dog or have the appearance of one. Laws applicable to people should be what govern him, regardless of how he dresses or what surgeries he may have undergone to give himself the appearance of being a dog.

The idea that a man can become a dog is absurdly false and relies on assumptions and ideas that are themselves untrue. It is so obvious; anyone believing Toco is a dog should probably not bear children, for fear that the stupidity of the parent will spread downward, thus creating the actual inevitability of an Idiocracy situation (2006 movie in which everyone is dumb in the future due to the stupidest among us procreating in larger numbers than the intelligent).

If a person wants to dress and act like a dog, go right ahead; I have no issues with this. If a person wants to get on all fours naked in the street, peeing on light posts and humping strangers' legs, I now have a problem with that. Freedom may mean allowing people to do what you don't want them to, but there needs to be mutually agreed-upon lines in which some activities are permissible, and others are not. If we should only be subject to rules based on our whims in that moment, then there are in fact no rules, and everyone should be allowed to do whatever they wish at any moment they wish to.

I could describe what horror this would create, but you already know, so there's no point. Here's another interesting new(ish) idea: Should doctors and other healthcare professionals kill or maim their patients? While normally, a healthcare professional is expected to heal a patient, what if a patient wants to die or be harmed (say, by the removal of a limb or appendage)? Certainly, someone who knows how to end someone's life skillfully and painlessly, or remove a working limb or eye, is the best person to do this job, but is it a good idea to?

If I believed drilling a hole all the way through my head would make me smarter or more whole (hole?), should a healthcare professional be legally and morally excused if they are paid to perform that "operation" (I would call it an execution, but as previously covered, apparently some words no longer have meaning)?

Even if we were more permitting of euthanasia (that is, the practice of ending the life of a patient to limit the patient's suffering, and who in this world is not suffering?), I don't really see the need to have someone in medical school for a decade to learn this "skill."

We have individuals without a high school diploma who seem perfectly (and sometimes expertly) capable of painlessly ending another person's life without the need for a doctor's office, hospital room, administrative staff, insurance, or involving government funding for the procedure. Perhaps with a healthcare professional's note, indicating an individual no longer wishes to live, a trade professional could economically "terminate the suffering" at a fraction of the cost at a time and location more convenient to the "patient," rather than having to wait for an appointment with a doctor or nurse.

At the very least, this would allow healthcare professionals to continue to work within the confines of the Hippocratic oath, to "do no harm." We could even work those incarcerated for murder into this scheme by having some type of work-release program, lowering the prison population and ensuring those rehabilitated have employment once released (perhaps taking an oath to only do harm — the Dahmer oath?). If anybody takes any of these suggestions seriously, please do not run for political office. If you are currently in office, feel free to pass these ideas off as your own to your constituents as quickly as possible.

Progressive Vs. Conservative

The two above-named ideas are naturally hostile to one another and have followers in different places who have different ideas about what these words mean. Progress in one person's eyes could be a regression in another's, and following traditional values can be seen as progress to different individuals. What does it mean to progress? If that means bucking the status quo, then allowing one man to marry multiple wives of "diverse" ages could in fact be considered progressive, assuming it was replacing tired, archaic, and prudish customs.

What does it mean to be conservative? If it means going back to earlier laws and traditions, it could mean a backtrack to legally segregated communities and voting restrictions on large numbers of the adult population. Why bring these terms up? Generally, "new" ideas fall under the category of progressive, while "old" or "traditional" ideas tend to be held by those calling themselves conservative. Given the title of the chapter, I leave it to you to determine where I may or may not fall.

These two concepts work as yin and yang, requiring each other in order to arrive at an ideal state. I have been very hostile to new ideas in this chapter, and I want to close by acknowledging that not all new ideas are bad ideas. There has been a generally slow and steady progression of humanity over the millennia, and it is only through new ideas that older, worse ideas were discarded to the ash heap of history.

There is a need to have an opposing force, both to new and old ideas, to arrive at the optimal state in which these ideas are in balance. Moving too quickly results in untested and poorly thought-out new ideas that end up doing more harm than good. On the other hand, stagnation results from strict adherence to traditional ideas to the detriment of those living under those ideas.

Somewhere out there is someone currently typing "Not all traditional ideas are good ideas," and I am supportive of this framework. I leave it to that someone to make a better case for discarding traditional viewpoints, as this is not where my mind skews (although, if there's money to be made, I'm sure my neurons will fire in rapid succession to also make this point in a convincing manner).

Closing Notes

Fashionable ideas are just that, only seeming important in the moment. The clothing that seems hip and cool in the present will be looked upon with ridicule in short order. The fact that we ever adhered to such outlandish outfits as overly baggy jeans, ridiculously puffy shoulder pads, or cargo shorts can be seen in tandem with the ideas that have fallen out of favor. For some, only in hindsight do they realize what was silly and not that well thought through. Many others can see it when it's happening but unfortunately must battle uphill as the unpopular naysayer.

We have enough sheep parroting whatever they hear some celebrity or faraway news commentator saying; I urge you not to join the mob.

"The fire wants not for justice, the fire wants not for reason, the fire desires only to be fed!"
— Jessica Biel's character, Season Four, Episode Seven, *BoJack Horseman*, just after killing Zach Braff by setting him on fire.

Note: Inequality

"I wrote a best-selling book. If you write a best-selling book, you can be a millionaire, too." — Bernie Sanders, democratic socialist

Life's not fair. Through accident of birth, some of us are born more intelligent, better looking, stronger, or healthier than our fellow human beings. There is no way around this; it's simply a fact of life. This alone, absent of any societal norms, rules, or inheritance, creates inequality. Random events of chance (disease, winning the lottery, losing a close loved one) can't really be controlled either.

I do not pass judgment on those who, through no fault of their own, have found themselves in an unenviable position. In a just society, we owe it to our fellow citizens to help when life's roulette wheel simply gave them a zero. Pretending people's lives are determined solely by fate, however, denies the monumental differences personal choices make.

Assuming you still work, on a near daily basis you choose to get out of bed, wear acceptable clothes, transport yourself to your place of employment, and perform acceptable work. At any moment, you could choose to go to a disreputable side of town, find an adult entertainer and some heroin, and pass the hours in temporary pleasure. Sure, you'd probably be fired, your significant other might leave you, and you would have started down a path of dependency and ruin, but what's stopping you?

Is it that fate has deemed you worthy to live a worthwhile life, or is it that you understand the consequences of making the wrong choice? And if you understand the consequences of your actions, why can't others? Do you contain some special gift others don't, or do you simply hold others to a lower bar than yourself?

Really ask yourself why you hold others to a lower standard than yourself and those close to you. If you're of that mindset, the real answer is that you think others are incapable of doing what you can. Rather than hold people up to the same yardstick, you've determined there are classes of people simply unable to accomplish what you, lucky you, are able to achieve.

We may not all have been dealt the same hand, but we can control what we do with those cards. You have two choices open to you: (1) complain that the game isn't fair and resign yourself to fate, or (2) use what you have been given to get what you want. Inequality will always be with us. Even if we are all one day equal, there would still be those who are more beautiful, taller, smarter, and stronger, making their lives relatively easier (in some ways, and more difficult in others).

Most of us see and understand what creates most inequality, and it's not fate. We make choices, and by necessity, we live and die by those choices. If it's a contest between equal misery or unequal prosperity, the choice should be clear. If the 400 richest Americans redistributed all their wealth (somewhere in the 3–4 trillion dollar range), every American would be given a one-time check of around $11,000. Where I live, this is about five months of rent, a third of the original cost of my vehicle, and with my current spending, it could sustain me for a little under two months.

Unfortunately, we can only pilfer from the wealthy once, as after that they will be in the same boat as everyone else. If we redistributed the wealth the top 1% of Americans hold, every American would get a check for approximately $100,000. For most, this is less than one-third the cost of a modest home in suburbia, two average new cars, or five roundtrip first-class tickets from LA to Tokyo. Would your life be easier with a $100,000 check? Of course. Is it life-changing? Not for long (even shorter if those employing you could no longer pay you, their wealth having been confiscated).

From my personal experience, income and wealth generally seem to flow to those willing to work hard to get it. I already know the arguments against this worldview, and I can already hear the same tired opinions, over and over, against this idea. The conversations are so timeless and clichéd, I can accurately predict the debate from start to finish, with nothing new added and nothing accomplished.

This isn't intended to be a debate; this is me revealing the truth, and you can either accept it or deny reality to your own detriment. I've been careful through my writing to use the word "generally" because, of course, there are exceptions. I'm not writing this to point out exceptions; I'm writing this to point out general truths that are, or should be, obvious.

Crossing the Rubicon

The die is cast.

— contested origin, antiquity

In early January, 49 BC (before Christ, or if you prefer, before the common era), Julius Caesar, citizen of the Roman Republic, crossed a shallow waterway called the Rubicon with a single legion (about 2,500 men) on his way to conquer Rome. Strangely, 13 was Caesar's lucky number, as that was the designation of the legion that followed him into Rome.

In doing so, he became an enemy of the Roman Republic by bringing his army into Italy, an action that declared war on his own government (later to become his government). Today, "crossing the Rubicon" means a point of no return. Had Caesar never crossed the river, he likely would have been forced from his post, not served as emperor of the newly created Roman Empire (by himself), and would have been less than a footnote in history.

His crossing was an act that represented one he could not come back from. After that point, it was either victory or death (he extended meeting his creator by five years by winning after crossing). Although the subject matter in the previous chapters has been controversial, the following remaining chapters will go beyond what many in our age believe can be tolerated.

As such, for me, this is the crossing of the Rubicon. I cannot take back words I've said or written, so I'll live and die by those words. The subject matter is too important to go unsaid, and for me, this is the hill to die on. The chapters deal pointedly with matters of race that I have written with the utmost thoroughness and nuance I know.

Understand that not every conversation concerning race is racist, and not every idea voiced concerning sex is sexist. When we reduce every thought and action to racism, sexism, homophobia, and transphobia, we neglect to see and think about any other factors that may exist. When we don't consider all the factors, we neglect what is probably at the root of many societal problems or outcomes. I believe this is done purposefully because what is at the root of many societal problems is too taboo to consider.

To ease into this, I'll start in the reverse with something easy. Asians, generally, are good at math. That sentence is accurate, in the context that it is being said in the United States about Asian Americans. By any objective measure you choose (highest level of math reached, SAT scores, competitions, etc.), this is true. In other places with other groups collectively called Asians, this may be inaccurate.

While there are subsets of groups considered Asian that as a group are poor (or poorer) at math than average, Asian Americans as a group are better at math than the average American. In our current world, thoughts instantly race to biology or income inequality for an explanation but neglect a huge (and what I believe to be key) factor: culture. Generally, Asian American culture values education in the hard sciences (math, chemistry, physics, etc.) more than the general American population.

As students, they study more hours than their peers in subjects relying on math as a base. Additionally, Asian American families generally hold their offspring to higher academic standards than their non-Asian peers. Why is this taboo? Because to accept that there is a culture that produces good, desirable outcomes requires you to admit that there are cultures that produce bad, undesirable outcomes not determined by wealth or biology.

If I were to say all Asians are good at math, that would be racist and inaccurate. If I only asked Asians to help me solve math problems, that additionally would be racist (and stupid on my part). But to say something true about groups of people is not necessarily racist. Germans are good at brewing beer. Mexicans make good tacos (I've tried Japanese-made tacos in Japan; trust me, they were awful). Men are bad at housework. Not all Germans make good beer (or tanks), and certainly not all men are bad at housework.

But to admit something that is true that involves groupings of people is not necessarily said in ignorance and bigotry. When everything is reduced to groupings of people, the individual is not held accountable for decisions and actions they make. There is nothing about holding children to higher standards or studying more hours that can't be done by anybody or any grouping of people.

A Black, White, Hispanic, gay, or albino parent can also hold their children to high academic standards. A disabled, poor, transgender, or Native American student can also study just as many hours as an average Asian American. But you have to "do the work," as is commonly said about other subjects.

I would challenge anyone disagreeing with me on this subject to find out for themselves the number of hours studied by any sub-grouping of humanity and determine that hours studied are not linked to higher mathematical achievement. I predict once this is determined that the difference between high achievers and low achievers is an order of magnitude different in hours studied.

As another easy, laughable example concerning race, imagine looking at situations not about race only through a racial lens. Is it racism that explains why the NFL and NBA have a disproportionately low number of White players? Is there systemic racism baked into the American system that excludes lighter-skinned individuals from reaching the pinnacle of these high-paying professional sports? Is this disparate outcome due to privileges White players lack, or perhaps due to wealth inequality?

Can communities that are nearly all White not hire better coaches and buy better equipment? Actual racists or White supremacists may have conspiratorial, race-based explanations for this, but in truth, there are simply (mostly) cultural reasons to explain this outcome. No one (minus the above-stated racists) actually cares about the lack of Caucasian members in these sports because what people really want from their sports teams is for them to win and show the other SOBs their team stinks.

Sports are an escape that allows us to have local and regional pride and fully invest our emotions. Nearly no one in San Antonio cares that the Spurs' players don't "look like their community"; they want those professionals to crush the other team with extreme prejudice (and I look forward to the day they can do this again).

A coworker of mine was trying to demonstrate what constituted a sexist statement while discussing acceptable and unacceptable attitudes. Another of our coworkers, "Emilia," was a military pilot; although, at the time, all of us essentially had desk jobs. My coworker's example of an unacceptable sexist comment was "Emilia is a bad pilot."

My response: 1) She could in fact be a bad pilot. I don't know; I've never flown with her. In all fact, knowing her professionalism at her current job, she's probably better than average. 2) Calling someone who happens to be female a bad pilot doesn't necessarily make you sexist. 3) If you were consistent in only calling females bad pilots or have never flown with Emilia or other female pilots, there is a large likelihood you are bigoted against females and their ability to fly planes.

If I made the statement "President Obama was a bad president," me not being Black but criticizing someone who is does not make me racist. I may be mad he didn't take enough steps towards a worker's paradise by implementing more communist-oriented policies. I may be angry he didn't invade Slovenia, ensuring a stronger US presence in the Adriatic Sea. I could also be furious the seas didn't lower over the course of his administration as he promised they would. But what I'm not doing by stating "Obama was a bad president" is implying "he can't be a good president because he has too much melanin."

You probably don't truly know me or my character; only a few hundred people do. You have no way of knowing what's racing through my head or whether I really am racist, sexist, homophobic, or transphobic any more than I know you. It's the same with nearly every person you come across. If I had advice, it would be to assume those strangers you don't know (me included) are not harboring bigoted ideologies. Some or all may be, but until words or actions demonstrate this clearly, we will all be better off if we assume those strangers are not the bigots they could potentially be. Our values, in addition to our laws, hold that treating people as innocent until proven guilty should be the goal (even if by many measures we are not there). In the same way, assuming people are not bigots until they demonstrate prejudiced words and actions should be the aspiration Americans (and I guess everyone else) hold. If we start from the notion that people are bigots until proven innocent, those strangers you come across day to day will find you guilty until you demonstrate innocence; an innocence that has a bar set so high it is impossible to reach (unless of course, you are super racist, in which case, don't worry about it).

Whether or not by the end of this book you determine that I am in fact bigoted, I urge you to start from the assumption that I am not. I know for a fact there is no accepted defense for being labelled racist, sexist, homophobic, or transphobic. It is simply a charge leveled against someone who must accept it and, like death or taxes, take it as an unstoppable inevitability. Attempting to highlight close friends, coworkers, or a slew of diverse intimate partners adds nothing and would simply be seen as proof of more racism by trying to use those relations as a shield to the charge. I will not attempt such a futile exercise.

"The only way out is through."
— Robert Frost, poet, 1874-1963

Chapter 12 Equity Is Not Fair

You today, me tomorrow.
— Aleksandr Solzhenitsyn, "The Gulag Archipelago", 1974

A coworker and I who frequently drove together often got to talking about politics and events of the day. My friend believed both that (1) people should get what they need, and (2) each should provide what they can*. I easily understood this set of ideas, even if my friend didn't, but I was curious. "What if someone refuses to work?" I asked him. After all, a person, even if they refuse to work, has needs such as housing, food, and clothing. The car ride was loud, and elements of the conversation were missed, but his answer ultimately was, "I guess we won't shoot them."

How do we define equity in the modern era? Equity means people reaching the same outcome. That means the number of doctors, presidents, prison inmates, CEOs, etc., are perfectly represented in proportion to the population. If a city is 65% Black, that means 65% of the police officers must be Black in order for equity to be reached. If a county is 51% female, then 51% of businesses must be female-run. If Asians make up 4% of the population, in order for society to be equitable, 4% of the prison population must be Asian. If these (and many other) goals have not been reached, then societal equity has not been met. If some of the above ideas about an equitable society sound crazy, please continue reading.

In 1848, Karl Marx and Friedrich Engels (Why is it always the Germans? typed the writer with German ancestry) published "The Communist Manifesto", advocating for a revolutionary (revolutionary: involving or causing a complete or dramatic transformation) change to government and society. This change involved dissolving the ownership of capital (read: private businesses) by individuals in order to further equity among all people. The ultimate goal was an equal, classless, stateless society. At the cost of around 100,000,000 lives lost from manmade famines, purges, executions, and forced labor, most of the world learned communism doesn't work. Communism as an idea is dead, but not the concepts that propped it up. Those concepts linger, and only their names have changed. In the same way that a rose by any other name would smell as sweet, simply renaming disastrously bad ideas results in the same nightmarish outcome.

The phrase "each from his ability, each to his need" was popularized by the two individuals named in the last paragraph in describing how communism should work, and where I gathered my understanding of my friend's unrecognized ideology. The idea is so simple, a child could comprehend it; unfortunately, only the most mature children understand how destructive it is.

Equality of opportunity used to be the American standard for what society should strive for. With equal access to education and jobs, those best qualified will get into the best schools and get the best positions. Under this meritocracy, your drive, intelligence, and hard work are what let you achieve success rather than simply being politically connected or of the correct lineage. By putting the most talented and most driven in important jobs, society as a whole benefits, as those most capable of making complicated decisions have greater odds of making the right calls. I completely understand we have nowhere near equal opportunity, but I also understand that this should be the goal to strive for.

There are factors that would be nearly impossible for a government to control in order to achieve equality of opportunity. For example, one of the predictors of a child's success is having a two-parent household. If you're the government, how do you "fix" this situation in order to have parity between a single-parent household and a two-parent household? If you believe providing money to the single-parent household will bridge this gap, you've just replayed what has already been done over decades with devastating results. There is no substituting the advantage of a two-parent household, and the "fix" has simply created more single-parent households, to the detriment of all.

Slowly but surely, the word equality has been replaced by equity without much fanfare but with huge implications. The goal of a society striving for equality is one reaching for equal treatment of all individuals. The goal of a society striving for equity is a society striving for equal outcomes. If you don't believe me, Google image search equity, and you'll see a variety of comically childish illustrations depicting why the goal should be equity over equality.

If you're thinking, "Equality of outcomes… Where have I heard this before?" you're not crazy. It is communism disguised as racial and social justice, but the goal is the same: a classless society in which equality of outcome has been reached.

What is the problem with trying to reach equality of outcomes? There is not equality of effort. If some put in more effort than others but get the same outcome, why bother? Imagine a situation in which you're working sixty hours a week but getting the same reward as someone who sits in their apartment watching Netflix all day. Do you think you'd be motivated to work sixty hours next week? Or do you believe you'd join the apartment-dwelling Netflix viewer? If everybody makes the same rational choices, we quickly reach a point at which no one is working, but everyone expects the fruits of society's labor, which no longer exists. It is only at that point that equality of outcomes has been reached, as now everyone is equally poor. Equity having been achieved, everyone was happy and sailed off into the sunset.

Communism, and thus equity, ultimately fails because people need motivation to work harder. Regardless of whether we live in a capitalist or communist society, we are in competition with one another. This competition is over residences, cars, potential partners, etc. We can't all have penthouse suites in Manhattan and be married to Mila Kunis (although if we do perfect cloning, I have a recommendation for who to start with). In capitalism, hard work is encouraged by higher pay. If you find this laughable, ask yourself this simple question: Are you paid more for ten hours of work or forty hours of work at the same job? In communism, because higher pay is not ideologically possible, competition for powerful positions replaces money as the marker of success. Who gets to date the supermodel and live at the beachside villa? In capitalism, probably the rich guy, and in communism, probably the well-positioned government crony.

Interestingly, the only real difference between capitalism and communism is this very simple question: What is something worth? To a capitalist, something is worth what its purchaser will pay for it. If some idiot spends $100,000 on a shiny rock for their nineteen-year-old girlfriend, then the diamond is worth $100,000 at the moment of sale. In communism, something is valued at what it costs to produce (in theory).

If it costs $1,000 to get that same shiny rock out of the ground, then it is worth $1,000 instead of $100,000.

Here we see the other main problem of communism over capitalism: surplus and shortage. If jewelry stores sold the same diamond for $1,000, the high demand for the sparkly pebble would mean there would be more people willing to purchase it at $1,000, and there would immediately be a shortage (after all, who doesn't want to impress their nineteen-year-old girlfriend?). On the other hand, if it cost $10 million to produce that same diamond, there would be a surplus produced, as there would be plenty of suppliers willing to mine for diamonds, but not many consumers willing and able to pay. This is an oversimplification of supply and demand and competing economic systems, but for those interested, myriad works go into great detail on this.

The writing is already on the wall for where a drive for equity will take us. Equality of outcomes will never be reached because it cannot be reached. Even if for a moment in time all people had exactly the same wealth, education, and inputs (such as a two-parent household), in the next second, this equity would be broken. Some would choose to invest their money, others would spend it on luxuries, and others on drugs. Time takes on the same dimension. Some would choose to further educate themselves in careers that ultimately pay better, others would be content and take whatever job they could get at the moment. Others would refuse to work, choosing a life on the streets instead. Because equity can never be reached, there will be an endless fight to achieve it, until it's at last realized that the cost of striving for equity has destroyed society.

If the goal of equity is equal outcomes, why should I personally do anything? (If the answer is "for the good of all," I'll provide a PO box so you can send me my slice.) If you told most people they would be paid regardless of how many hours they worked, the vast majority of people would not work at all. They would take up hobbies, watch whatever is put in front of them, and otherwise commit themselves to leisure activities. The net result of this would be that society would crumble, as no one would work but demand work from others. Who would choose to serve coffee? Who takes the night shift at the factory? Who would willingly work 70 hours a week (as many do in my current industry, construction). Reward is what drives people to take up less desirable jobs, work more hours, and ultimately grow themselves. When people grow, we all reap the rewards.

Even though we are all in competition against one another, that competition grows the pie. For example, while running in a competition in the Air Force, another member was roughly as fast as me. Normally, I ran at a leisurely pace and could take a break whenever I wanted. In this competition, I knew the other member was always right behind me, always just about to pass me. He knew he was always right on my heels and strived to pass me. As a result, we both ran the fastest we had since early college. Only one of us could win against the other (unless we somehow tied), but the competitive drive inspired both of us to achieve something we probably would not have on our own. Who benefited? All of us, as we now had more fit soldiers, should war be necessary. If we were all rewarded and praised no matter what place we came in, most would probably just walk the course, or not even compete.

For those who believe equity should be the goal, ask yourself how far you're prepared to go. Do you want every American to have equal income? What about equal wealth? If all wealth were equalized, would we need to repeat that process constantly? What happens if one person spends all their wealth, and somebody else invests it? How do we pay a brain surgeon the same as someone who simply refuses to work? Taken to its logical conclusion, do we need worldwide equity? If equity should be done in America because it's the right thing to do, why not expand this idea to the entire world? The answer is simple. No one outside of true believers would sign off on programs that would redistribute wealth directly from themselves to the rest of the world until, collectively, we were all equal. The profound unfairness of this is obvious, and policies whose goal is equity would destroy innovation and hard work. If there is no incentive to achieve because anything earned will be sent elsewhere, people will simply not want to achieve. Why go to medical school? Why work long hours? Why bother saving, clipping coupons, or acting financially prudent?

What Equity Would Actually Look Like

As I perused data about the highest-earning "content creators" on OnlyFans (a website that has become a hub for adult-oriented material), I noticed something odd. The top content creators were nearly all attractive young women. On a "Top 15 OnlyFans Content Creators" list, twelve of the fifteen were female, nearly all wearing what most would call provocative outfits or in tantalizing poses (I might add, I have no problem with this; everyone has to make a living).

An interesting thought: Should we as a society move in a direction where men and women have equitable incomes and representation on OnlyFans? It is clear from my thirteen-second search that young cisgender (as far as I can tell) women dominate the site, both in terms of numbers and earnings, leaving behind more than half the population that could also generate income from showcasing their... natural talents. But is that a desirable societal outcome? In short, do we desire a society in which there is equal representation on OnlyFans between males and females? That question could be asked across numerous industries, jobs, and side hustles.

Within the construction industry, for every female, there are about ten males. In my own prior profession in the US military, it was about 85% male and, sadly for me, only 15% female. Within the tech industry, Asians make up 14% of the workforce but only 6% of the US population. Despite representing approximately 6.5% of the US population, three out of five of the highest-paid athletes in the United States are male African Americans, with the remaining two appearing to be White males (I don't follow sports much; I just looked at the photos). None were female, Asian, LGBT+ (again, as far as I can tell), handicapped, or belonging to any other marginalized community on my radar.

If we attempted to be as equitable and inclusive as possible, we would build professional sports teams not with the best players available but with the best available that also happen to match the demographic breakdown of their fan base. Comically, following an equitable makeup of professional athletes would mean that in each sport, about 60% would need to be non-Hispanic White, 20% would need to be ethnically Hispanic or Latino (or Latinx if you unfortunately prefer; I do not for my own ethnicity), 12% would be Black, 6% Asian, <1% Native American, and <1% Hawaiian or other Pacific Islander in order to match the demographic makeup of the US. Additionally, assuming there were sports that didn't bring in the same revenue as others (such as women's soccer, professional cornhole, or dressage (horse dancing)), equity would also mean money would have to be diverted from more popular sports to less popular sports. Why funds should be diverted from baseball and volleyball to bowling and fencing is a mystery to me, but at least all professional sports participants would receive equitable pay. I know at the very least that male gymnasts would probably enjoy equity of airtime between themselves and female gymnasts. One might even get name recognition, assuming someone doesn't switch the channel (and if you don't know why that's the case, reread Chapter 2 until it dawns on you).

Those Desiring Equity

Bernie Sanders, as of this writing, is an "independent" senator and two-time presidential contender. As a self-described democratic socialist, he has supported universal healthcare, tuition-free early education, raising the minimum wage, canceling student debt, expanding social security, funding large public-works programs, and taxing the rich at a higher rate to pay for these policies. In effect, he supports a redistribution of wealth in order to, in his words, reduce the "outrageous level of inequality that exists in America today."

Over the course of the 2010s, he and his wife earned approximately $5 million from salaries, pensions, and book sales, far more than the average American family. As quoted earlier, when he was asked how he could square his income and wealth with his public stance combating income and wealth inequality, he responded, "I wrote a best-selling book. If you write a best-selling book, you can be a millionaire, too."

To this day, he has the power to create a more equitable society at the touch of a button. With an estimated net worth of $3 million (versus the American household average of $122,000), he could donate $2,878,000 to twenty-three Americans who have no wealth whatsoever and bring them up (and him down) to the US average.

Even most of those advocating equity don't really want it. While in military training, my peers and I lived in a new apartment complex that was quite nicer than the surrounding area. One of my fellow trainees suggested society needed a more equitable distribution of wealth and income, as he didn't like the sight of what he perceived as poverty and squalor in the surrounding community. When I suggested to him he move into a less expensive apartment or home and donate the money saved, he scoffed, dropped the subject, and continued living in the more upscale apartment complex.

It's easy to advocate for equity if you believe that either (A) you will financially benefit from a redistribution of wealth or (B) you are left out of the redistribution game altogether. In the same way, it's easy to advocate for policies you will financially benefit from at the cost of someone else. Student debt forgiveness sounds like a great idea if you have student debt, but not so much if you're an individual who never went to college but now must fund the forgiveness of others through taxes.

What type of equity do I think is just? (If you don't care what I think, feel free to stop reading. The hardcover, paperback, or audiobook has already been purchased, so my personal concern is now largely absent.) I stick to the simplest, most easily understood and communicated version of equity: the quality of being fair and impartial.

In my view, equity is achieved when equality of opportunity is achieved. A just form of equity would mean people's outcomes, good or bad, are dependent on their actions rather than immutable characteristics of birth such as race, ethnicity, sex, or upbringing into a well-connected or wealthy family. If there is a lying, cheating, lazy White male, a just society would treat this individual the same way as a lazy, cheating, and lying nonbinary Japanese individual. Simply because the Japanese individual may have had ancestors treated unjustly or is not a member of the majority does not justify treating these two individuals differently. The equality I described will still create inequality, but inequality that is based in a just system.

For example, you wouldn't want a murdering rapist to have reached "equity" with a hardworking single parent who follows the rules. Unless you're a true believer, you shouldn't want these two individuals to reach equity because they have not done equal things. One has flaunted nearly all rules of a humane society while the other has not. One of these two groups deserves scorn and jail (if not more), while the other deserves to be treated equally among law-abiding citizens.

In the same way, a person who refuses to work because they simply don't wish to should not be rewarded in the same way as those who provide products and services we all collectively need and want. If you believe this not to be the case, how do you justify driving by someone poorer or less well off than you and not giving them your wealth (and I don't mean the $20 in your pocket; I mean half your 401k)? You don't deserve your income and wealth any more than that individual you speed past does, and it would ultimately be unjust not to give them what you worked hard for.

But I already know the thoughts running through your head because they are the thoughts of any sane adult. You work hard for your money, you sacrifice, you plan, you went without, and you did what was necessary to achieve what you have. Why should you give up what you have to help someone who did not do those things? There are others, those wealthier, who should foot this bill since they didn't really earn their money or have more than they need, you tell yourself.

Well, in many people's eyes, regardless of your socioeconomic status, you are that wealthy individual. Some who are not as wealthy as you believe you have too much, that you didn't really earn what you have, and thus have a moral responsibility to forfeit some (or most... or all) of it to support those who don't have as much. Why do we want to believe equity is just? Because it seems simple, fair, and doesn't require us to do any deep dives into why people end up in the places they do. Most in this camp believe something has been taken from them that they are due, and we as a society should try and fix this gross injustice. Under this ideology, the homeless unemployed heroin addicts should have access to the same resources as Jeff Bezos (Amazon founder), regardless of the fact that Mr. Bezos founded a company providing nearly limitless value to society, versus a person who doesn't want to answer to anyone or do anything useful to anybody.

In an absurd example of how society could be made more equitable, imagine if somebody wanted society to reach equity between the number of abortions that men and women get. There are only two ways this could be accomplished: make abortion illegal, or encourage trans men to get pregnant and abort their potential offspring. (Technically, there are three solutions, but the last is even darker and more absurd. I'll leave you to ponder what that might be.) If you think this example silly and/or insulting, it's no more strange than other policies advocating equality of outcome with unequal effort.

To close, I urge you to investigate what happened to nations whose goal was equality of outcome and how people reacted and acted in such societies. There still exist countries today that notionally strive for equality of outcome, and each is in tatters. Their citizens flee to countries that are less equal, knowing that even if they aren't as well off as their new neighbors, they're at least better off than they were in their country of origin. Our most strident anti-communists immigrated from countries whose goal was equity, and their voices are the strongest, warning us of the consequences of going down such a path.

Before you go down the path of believing equity should be the goal, search out those voices and see why they are so adamant the West not go down the same rabbit hole. Or don't. Ignore those marginalized voices and assume you've got it all figured out. They just didn't have the right people in charge. We'll do it right next time. Just let me know when you're going to implement your utopian plan so I can pack up the gold and get the last flight out of town.

"How do you tell a Communist? Well, it's someone who reads Marx and Lenin. And how do you tell an anti-Communist? It's someone who understands Marx and Lenin."
— Ronald Reagan, 40th president of the United States

Chapter 13 You Are Not Responsible for Racism and Bigotry You Didn't Commit

"I have a dream that my four little children will one day live in a nation where they will not be judged by the color of their skin but by the content of their character."
— Martin Luther King Jr., August 28, 1963

In 1977, the ABC miniseries "Roots" became a nationally watched historic epic chronicling the story of enslaved Africans and their descendants across generations. It portrayed the evils of slavery and the resiliency of the now African Americans to endure what most Americans today could not. There was a catch to this, however. As depicted, the protagonist enslaved in Africa was captured by a group of Black men in Western clothing with whips and chains being led by what appears to be a sneering White British man. While such events probably occurred, this would have been a true rarity. In truth, slaves captured in Africa to be later sold in the Atlantic slave trade destined for the Americas and elsewhere were captured and sold almost exclusively by their fellow Africans.

Europeans in that era had an ominous reason for needing African slaves to be transported to the Americas. Agricultural plantations in the New World had a tendency to kill the European workforce with tropical diseases. At the time, it was thought that African populations were more adaptable and could survive (which they did) the harsh conditions that would more easily kill European settlers (I'm sure there was also the small factor of not having to pay them or requiring their consent). This is exactly why Europeans couldn't colonize Africa until the "Scramble for Africa" in the late nineteenth century; disease (or locals) would likely kill any European stupid enough to travel into the interior. In order for the Atlantic slave trade to develop, African kingdoms and tribes had to capture their fellow Africans, bring them to the coast, and sell them to Europeans for firearms, clothing, and other manufactured goods. Not until the development of medicines for tropical diseases such as quinine (for malaria) in the mid-nineteenth century could Europeans enter the interior of Africa and eventually colonize it.

What point am I trying to make with all this? If slavery is evil (and I agree it is), then we need to hold all historical people, cultures, nations, and kingdoms to the same yardstick. If it was evil for South Carolinians to own slaves, then it should be equally evil for the West African kingdom of Dahomey to have captured and sold slaves. If we judge the British, French, and other European nations responsible for buying and selling their fellow humans, then we should also judge Middle Easterners, Indigenous Americans, and Asians for the same. We should hold up for ridicule those waving away atrocities particular groups participated in because they had a more diverse set of skin tones, religions, or cultures that weren't European. More to the point, you (the reader) are not responsible for racism and bigotry you did not commit.

We should no more hold African Americans today responsible because other Africans of a different era sold slaves than we should hold accountable the European descendant Americans for the fact that slavery existed in America. Would you hold accountable Japanese Americans because the Empire of Japan attacked Pearl Harbor more than eight decades ago? Would you hold all Muslims accountable for the terrorist attacks on 9/11? Of course not. One of the cornerstones of America is that you must be judged as an individual for your actions, your bigotries, and your own personal views. Then why do we hold up the descendants of Europeans as collectively being guilty for slavery?

In the census of 1860, the US counted 395,216 slaveholders out of a free population of 27,500,000 Americans. That means about 1.4% of the free American population owned slaves and 98.6% did not. If we're going to judge entire peoples for what less than 2% of them historically engaged in, no one will be judged innocent, and we're all equally guilty of being oppressors (unless you're Ben Affleck, in which case you are more guilty because his family did own slaves, which was hilariously revealed on PBS).

If you don't feel like an oppressor, guess what? Nobody else does either. I can assure you, there are no innocent groups in history, and there were certainly no historical figures or people who would pass the impossible standards that modern America imposes on itself (and for some reason, only itself). How would you feel if somebody judged you for something not done to them by somebody that is not you? If we are to punish any modern Americans for the sins of their fathers, or worse, those that simply looked similar to those who committed atrocities, where does that logic take us? Every group that has ever had historical injustice done to them (which is everybody) would demand the same level of restitution for awful things they personally did not suffer. Where does this lead us except endlessly pointing fingers at each other for things we not only didn't do, but don't support. The list of historical grievances is inexhaustible, a bottomless pit that nothing good can come from.

This is not to say past discrimination, both personal and state-sanctioned, did not lead us directly to where we are in the present, with all the inequalities of the modern day. Nor am I saying there is no racism, sexism, or homophobia today that directly harms the progress of all people, including women, racial minorities, and LGBT individuals. There also exists current racism and sexism which harms males, straight individuals, and descendants of Europeans. Laugh if you will, but I know I'll be checking the Hispanic and Native American boxes on college applications if I ever need to compete for the limited number of slots available again (we'll ignore whatever I put on every single job application that for some reason needed to know my race. It was probably accurate, whatever I put).

In 2022, there were jobs that otherwise qualified individuals did not get because of immutable characteristics they have no control over. In 2020, United Airlines announced that over the next decade they plan for at least 50% of their trainee pilots for its new flight school to be women or minorities. If every individual person was equally qualified for every job and wished to work at said job, this would be fair and equitable. But every individual person is not equally qualified for all jobs (or desires said jobs), and you know it. I don't want my homeless, heroin-addicted "neighbors" to be flying the plane I'm on, regardless of their other identity groups and choice of intimate partners.

Additionally, everyone isn't equally drawn to want to be airline pilots, no matter how much we want them to be. The result of wanting complete equity in all jobs no matter how elite or menial will mean some of the better qualified for any job will be excluded to the detriment of us all. I don't know about you, but I'm more concerned that the most qualified person is flying the plane me and my fellow Americans are flying in rather than the most qualified who has the right skin tone and/or genitals. I wouldn't care if the pilot was a female cross-dressing bisexual Somali Buddhist, so long as that individual is the most qualified to fly the plane. If I have a choice, for my own safety, I'll be selecting an airline that hires the most qualified pilots instead of the group most in vogue in the ever-present now. If you think differently, good luck up there.

A woman who went by the name Rachel Dolezal* was elected president of the Spokane, Washington chapter of the NAACP (National Association for the Advancement of Colored People) in 2014. During an interview with a local ABC reporter, it was revealed that both her parents had been White, while a picture from her childhood appeared to show her as... very Caucasian. You may be asking yourself why such an issue should come up, but apparently, this was national news important.

As it turns out, Mrs. Dolezal had curated her appearance and passed herself off as African American, probably by tanning to slightly darken her skin and keeping a hairstyle associated with the Black community. Soon after, she was forced from her NAACP post due to the fact that she was not African American. Why a woman who voluntarily joined a marginalized community and thus became the target of systemic racism can't run a civil rights organization is unknown to me, but others felt differently. Her racial identity as White disqualified her from leading an NAACP chapter, regardless of her accomplishments to reach that station.

*Mrs. Dolezal eventually changed her name in 2016 to Nkechi Amare Diallo, which translates to "what God has given/gift of God" in the Igbo language of Nigeria, a country I don't believe she's ever visited and a language I don't believe she speaks (although, if she has both visited Nigeria and speaks the language, I give her my personal accolades for so committing to her identity).

If, as Ibram X. Kendi (born Ibram Henry Rogers) asserts, "The only remedy to past discrimination is present discrimination. The only remedy to present discrimination is future discrimination," then we are lost. We will forever be punishing one racial minority (or majority), group, or sex (or some other subset of people) endlessly for all of time, focusing on attributes we should strive to push to irrelevancy. Today's racial and gender preferences will be someone else's future discrimination they lived through. Do you want colleges to offer more college scholarships to males than females? Would you like the male sex to have a leg up in college selection because, as of 2019, there were only seventy-four men receiving bachelor's degrees for every 100 women? Do you want the most qualified with the best chance of graduating college to be accepted, or do you want the most qualified that happen to have the correct organs between their legs?

If we are to hold people up today as either victims or oppressors based on their lineage, where does that stop? In the Middle Ages, Vikings rampaged what we now know as the British Isles, killing locals, raping women (and probably no small number of men), and stealing individuals to become thralls (slaves). Given that many of the inhabitants of the United States descend from those same British Isles, are we Americans entitled to reparations from the Scandinavian countries of Norway, Denmark, and Sweden? Should we sneer at Swedes for what their ancestors did a millennia ago? Should we demand apologies from people who took no part in the atrocities of the past? What would an apology even mean to people who were not killed, raped, or enslaved?

In truth, as suggested by conservative British intellectual Douglas Murray, the only people truly capable of righting wrongs are those who committed the acts. In the same way, in my personal opinion, you are only rightfully owed restitution if you are the one that was wronged. For example, imagine if a Native American killed their neighbor but was never prosecuted, and he later died of old age. Would it be right for the neighbor's children to demand money from the Native American's children? Do the Native American's children have a duty to apologize for the murder? At its heart, the question is this: Are we responsible for what our ancestors did, and if our ancestors suffered, are we owed something for that ancestor's suffering? If the answer is yes, I'll set up a mailbox. Send me your name, and I'll determine whether or not your family ever oppressed any of mine, and determine what the proper restitution looks like.

On the Fourth of July, 2023, ice cream company Ben and Jerry's Twitter account announced, "...it's high time we recognize that the US exists on stolen Indigenous land and commit to returning it." Since modern times are insane, apparently people took the call from a dessert company seriously, and it became national news. Evidently, founders Ben Cohen and Jerry Greenfield believed Mount Rushmore needed to be returned to the Lakota Indians, the most recent Indigenous Americans to hold the land prior to the United States.

In response, Don Stevens, chief of the Nulhegan Band of the Coosuk Abenaki Nation, informed the press that his Indigenous group would like their land back from Mr. Cohen and Mr. Greenfield, whose Vermont headquarters sits on land claimed by his native group. As of this writing, neither the founders nor Ben and Jerry's Twitter account has responded as to whether or not they will return the land claimed to be stolen. I'm sure if this request was granted, whoever the Nulhegan Band of the Coosuk Abenaki Nation conquered it from would also have a claim on that land.

In 2023, Angela Davis, a famous Marxist, feminist, and political activist, found out that she had an ancestor who arrived in the Americas on the Mayflower (and for those uninformed, they were super White). Since I'm Native American (probably...), that means some of her ancestors oppressed some of mine, killing them, taking their land, and pushing some of them to reservations. Does Angela Davis, who is Black, owe me, who appears White, reparations for her ancestors' treatment of mine? Who, among our ancestors, had more power? Whatever your answers to these questions, I doubt she will do any apologizing to those her ancestors oppressed (nor should she).

As a Native American Hispanic, I could throw a dart at a map of the world, and no matter where it hit, I could find a group that had somehow wronged one of my many ancestors. In turn, wherever the dart landed, that group could probably find one of my ancestors who had wronged them (we'll skip the German heritage for what should be obvious reasons). Who owes who? Who is the oppressor and who is the oppressed? The real answer is it doesn't matter. We are where we are because of the ideas and actions of people who are nearly all dead. Justice, whether to reward or punish, is lost to those who are no longer amongst us. We can only reward or punish those who are still alive. If we maintain the idea that we must right historical wrongs, it means that today, of two babies born at the same time in the same hospital, one could be labeled oppressor and the other victim before they even have the capacity to see, move, or talk. If that sounds like a good idea to you, I suggest we segregate the hospitals by oppressor and victim, so we can start those babies' lives on a socially just path. If that sounds like a recipe for chaos and further injustice, please continue reading.

Who Deserves What?

A thought experiment: Who deserves ownership of my beloved home state, the area currently known as Texas? Does it belong to the first people and offspring to live there? What if those people didn't actually live there but merely walked through it on the way to somewhere else? Does it belong to the first people to settle there, only to be killed or subjugated by other tribes indigenous to North or South America? If the idea of resolving past wrongs is the goal, to whom should the state of Texas belong?

If your answer (as is popular) is to say the land was stolen by Europeans, it was stolen by people (Europeans) who stole it from people (the last Indigenous group to hold it prior to colonization) who stole it from people (whatever poor Indigenous people were killed or removed by those conquered by the Europeans) who stole it. Texas, at one time or another, has been claimed by six separate cultural Indigenous groups, who lived and fought as ferociously with each other as any European nations. Later, six separate nations also claimed Texas at one time or another: Spain, France, Mexico, The Republic of Texas, The United States, and lastly (sort of), the Confederate States of America. The average inhabitant of Texas falls under several of these social groups. Even in trying to return the land to an Indigenous group, we must ask which Indigenous group it should be returned to. I have a feeling more than a few hands will go up.

Luckily, today, the world generally views expansionist military states and naked colonialism with disdain, leaving the world in a more or less stable state, to the detriment of map makers everywhere. Until very recently, the idea of "might makes right" was the leading belief concerning world order, meaning that if a state could forcefully rule a land or group of people, it's their right to. I'm sure you have an idea of how the lines on the map should be drawn, and perhaps somebody else might have a slight problem with that. Much like "one person's terrorist is another's freedom fighter," your idea of justice will collide headlong with somebody else's. You may be willing to enforce your will with violence if necessary, just as your ancestors did, in order to mold the world to what you would like it to be. If not, perhaps your ideals just aren't worth fighting for.

This leads me to a concept I was taught during my schooling: anachronisms. An anachronism is an idea out of time. For example, the idea of women voting fits perfectly in 2023 but would be very confusing in 1623, when nearly nobody voted, as most countries had some type of hereditary ruler hand-picked by God to lead (although if true, it would seem he picked them specifically to see them have at one another for his (or her) sick amusement). Viewing Germany and Japan as friendly nations makes perfect sense today, but not so much in 1942, when companies such as Porsche, Hugo Boss, Mitsubishi, and Kawasaki were manufacturing planes, tanks, and uniforms for Nazis and other dictatorial regimes.

Over time, ideas and situations change, leading the population as a whole to change with it. Ideas that were once held sacrosanct or well thought-out fall by the wayside, leaving room for newer ideas. Trying to hold dead people accountable for modern morality is just as insane as trying to predict what morality will be like in fifty years and trying to plan our thoughts and actions for that. However you view any historical group of people, know in the future others will judge you and find you wanting. Imagine, for example (the first to pop into my head), if there were a religious revival after seeing the results of increased secularization, and the population realized spirituality had positive externalities (externality: side effects unrelated to the original intent). It could be that those in the future would view with disdain and hatred those who cast away the deeply held beliefs of their ancestors. That is, they would hate you, sidelining any of your accomplishments and dismissing your good work because you didn't hold an idea that had not yet developed and would not develop, potentially, until after you were long dead.

Why do we want to hold people accountable for racism and bigotry they didn't personally commit? Because it gives contemporary groups power and allows us to believe we are good people for holding the "correct" ideas. By acknowledging past horrors as bad, you are indicating you're a good person on the right side of history, instead of an average individual trying to selfishly get by day to day. Thus, by calling out and identifying ideas long dead (segregation, internment of ethnic/racial minorities, slavery, colonialism), you are able to feel good about yourself without actually doing anything particularly brave or dangerous.

For example, I tried searching the internet for "percent of the population supporting slavery." Either (A) the question has never been asked in the modern age, or (B) the question was asked, but the results were too one-sided to merit reporting. On the other hand, every day I see various celebrities and activists in the news denouncing slavery, a stance that in 2023 is not very controversial. In the nineteenth century, fighting slavery meant picking up a gun and marching towards an opposing army also armed with rifles, artillery, and even at times machine guns, with the very real possibility of being killed or badly maimed*. Desegregating schools at one point required national guardsmen to escort students through throngs of racist segregationists. I'm not aware of any mainstream group supporting slavery or segregation of spaces (actually, I take back part of that; there are colleges and universities supporting segregation of dorms by race, gender identity, and sexual orientation; look up "themed dorms").

*An organization like this still exists, but smaller by proportion and with significantly less marching. They're called law enforcement. I would encourage others opposing slavery in the modern age to support this anti-slavery organization, unless, of course, you sympathize more with human traffickers, who have been unjustly marginalized by society.

Perspective

The title of this chapter was not intended for any specific group broken down by race, ethnicity, sex, or sexual orientation. It is meant to be a universal appeal to all people whose distant relatives or fellow members of a shared group identity may have treated people in an inhumane or uncourteous way. An average Saudi American should not feel or be held responsible for other Saudis hijacking and crashing four planes in the northeastern American states on 9/11. A Russian American (or US citizen formerly a citizen of the Soviet Union) shouldn't feel accountable for members of the Soviet Union killing or unjustly incarcerating tens of millions of other Soviet citizens. An average female shouldn't feel partially to blame for other females in other parts of the world (or at different times) mutilating female children so they can't get pleasure from intercourse.

If you feel differently, go ahead and get an ancestry test and try to justify the actions of all your ancestors. I know for I fact I couldn't.

I'll be treated as I deserve, not as my father deserved.
— Sergeant Kilrain (fictional), "Gettysburg", 1993, Turner Pictures

Chapter End Notes

I know some would not like me quoting Dr. Martin Luther King Jr. at the beginning of this chapter. Their probable critique is that I have only taken a tiny portion of his beliefs and actions without commenting on the rest, some of which I agree with, and some I do not. For example, the reverend did cheat on his wife, an action I do not support (or would not have supported; I was still a few decades from existing). No matter who you meet or look up to, you will eventually find something about that person you disagree with. No person on the face of the Earth has exactly the same values as you or I do, and to hold out for such an individual is insane. You can value the contributions of contemporary or historical figures without fully agreeing with all of their ideas or actions.

To further this point, I urge anyone to submit to me a figure who is beyond reproach. Keep in mind that this will need to take into account everything the person did publicly and privately. This will also need to take into account everything they didn't do publicly or privately, given their power and platform. For example, if Franklin D. Roosevelt (FDR) didn't have the correct view on internment camps, transgender rights, or the military-industrial complex, this would have to be taken into account to determine if any of his actions were good, or if his monuments should be taken down for the sin of not having the morals of someone living in the third decade of the twenty-first century. Good luck finding that secular saint (if anyone wants to submit the Dalai Lama or Gandhi, that ship has sailed. One slept with teenage girls while he was about eighty, and the other apparently likes having young boys suck on his tongue).

Chapter 14 All People and Groups Have Power

*...the more you hate me, the more you will learn [...] There is no racial bigotry here. I do not look down on n*****s, k***s, w**s, or gr****s. Here you are all equally worthless [...] Do you maggots understand that? Sir, yes, sir.*
— R. Lee Ermey, 1987, Full Metal Jacket, Marine basic training

Ed Buck, a formerly wealthy Democrat donor from West Hollywood, California, was well known for supporting the LGBT community and animal rights issues. He currently sits in prison as a felon for providing and/or injecting methamphetamine into homeless Black men for the purpose of fulfilling his sexual pleasure. Two of these men died while a third overdosed twice in his apartment before he was stopped. It is believed he was able to continuously get away from solicitation, homicide, drug, and rape charges due to his political ties and wealth. I say this not to attack the gay community, nearly none of whom inject homeless Black men with drugs to fulfill their sexual desires; I say this to point out that Mr. Buck had power. He had wealth and connections that enabled him to purchase hard drugs without law enforcement involvement, entice men to his home, and get away with any predictable fallout (for a while at least). He is a member of a group, that is, the LGBT community, that traditionally is said to not have power versus the ruling society. Other groups claiming to not have power include women, religious minorities, and ethnic or racial minority groups.

In 1994, O.J. Simpson, a former NFL player, was tried for the murder of his wife and her friend. It captivated the country for eleven months, with race at the heart of the events (Mr. Simpson was Black, in case you didn't know). After the eleven-month trial, he was acquitted. At the time, around a quarter of the population believed he was innocent and that law enforcement were trying to frame him due to his race. After two decades, only 14% believed he was completely innocent. How was he able to get away with murder (he definitely did it)? He was a wealthy NFL player who could afford the best lawyers money could buy in order to muddle the case against him. Mr. Simpson had two sources of power, either of which could be argued to have been more important. 1) As stated, he was wealthy. 2) He was African American and could marshal racial animosity to his side by insinuating a racist law enforcement apparatus was framing him. Regardless of how racist the police were or were not at the time, I haven't seen any evidence that law enforcement held a gun to Mr. Simpson, handed him a serrated knife, and forced him to kill his (ex)wife and her friend. He remained out of prison due to his power and former position.

In October 1991, Anna Nicole Smith (age twenty-four) was working at an adult establishment when an eighty-six-year-old oil tycoon, J. Howard Marshall, entered the business she "danced" in. Mr. Marshall, who at the time of his death (August 4, 1995, aged ninety) had a net worth of $1.6 billion, began a two-year affair with Ms. Smith. After Mr. Marshall divorced his wife, he married Ms. Smith, thirteen months prior to his death. While the value of the inheritance was contested by numerous parties, at the very least, the widow, Smith, had been left with $8 million in gifts over the course of the "relationship." This was not a relationship between parties that were equally attracted to each other and based on a loving connection. It was a transactional relationship based on both parties wanting something shallow from the other, each having a form of power over the other party. Ms. Smith was attractive at the time, and Mr. Marshall was wealthy beyond most humans' comprehension. Both had power over the other; otherwise, the "relationship" wouldn't have worked, and I would have had to painstakingly sought another anecdote for this chapter. Thank God for stupidity. The world is not separated into groups of people who have power and those who don't. All individuals have power, nearly all of which is approximately equal. Groupings of humanity also have power, and though different, all groups have power over the others. Instead of a pyramid, I see it more as a "checks and balances" from the US Constitution. If you believe differently, I'm going to need someone to explain to me the below situations.

In October 2000, the US House of Representatives enacted House Resolution 605, which encouraged state and city governments to have "amber alerts," whose purpose was to inform the public of an abducted child (aged 0-17) to increase the probability of finding them. Once law

187

enforcement confirms an abduction has taken place, the child is at risk of serious injury or death, there is descriptive information of the child, captor, or captor's vehicle, and the abductee is seventeen or under, the public is informed via cell phone and usually electronic highway signs alerting the public to be on the lookout.

In my adopted home state of Texas, there are also silver alerts, to locate missing persons sixty-five and older who may have impaired mental capacities; clear alerts to locate those eighteen to sixty-four in imminent danger; blue alerts for police officers in similar circumstances; and camo alerts for veterans or current military members with impaired mental faculties. While all of this seems odd, since a single system could cover all these different circumstances, there is ultimately no real harm or difference. Instead, a single alert could cover everyone an amber, clear, or silver alert does, with no distinction for employment or prior military status.

As of October 8, 2023, California SB 673 created an alert that is distinct from an amber alert and with slightly different criteria. It created an "ebony alert." In order for an ebony alert to be issued, the abductee must be (1) African American and (2) between the ages of twelve and twenty-five. The state of California also has a "feather alert" for missing Indigenous persons (indigenous to North America; others don't count) of any age. There are no other current alerts specific to race, ethnicity, religion, sexual orientation, or gender identity, as far as my research has shown for California. If I understand the naming convention, I predict there will soon be a brown alert, rainbow alert, Allah alert, matzo alert, and furry alert. A yellow alert has already been taken to identify those who commit hit and runs, so something more racist will have to be concocted in California for Asian Americans.

How did this happen? There are different criteria for our government to issue alerts based solely on race. If your race is this, you have an alert with your group identity. If not, there is no special distinction. Clearly, the power to influence public policy is not equal. Some more respected professions get distinct alerts, and others get none. Some preferred races get unique alerts, while others are left with a generic one that could apply to anyone.

In truth, I have very little faith in the amber alert system, despite its anecdotal success stories. Every other week or so, I receive alerts for missing people in cities hundreds of miles away from where I live. The fact that an abductor receives the same message likely means they are aware the public and law enforcement are looking for them and can change their appearance or mode of transportation. Making distinctions between age, demographics, and careers of those missing will not likely result in a more positive outcome. That said, it is clear some groups advocating the above alerts had more power than their peers, in order to have special categories to highlight the importance of their own cause. My recommendation? One system, one alert. We don't need a "code black" or "code red" to either encourage (or, to a pessimist, discourage) the public to search for an abducted individual.

Celebration

According to Harvard's (a small private school in Cambridge, Massachusetts, with around 7,000 undergraduate students per year) website, nearly every month of the year is dedicated to a particular demographic. February is Black History Month, March is Women's History Month, April is Arab American Heritage Month, May is Asian American and Pacific Islander Heritage Month (there's only so many months; Asians and Pacific Islanders are basically the same, after all, according to Harvard), May is Jewish American Heritage Month, June is LGBTQ+ Pride Month, July is Disability Pride Month, September is Latinx Heritage Month, October is LGBTQ+ History Month (and simultaneously National Disability Employment Awareness Month), and November is Native American Heritage Month. They also have about a dozen "recognition days" that correspond to particular demographics distinct from the heritage or pride months. I would list them, but you get the point.

I only included the above because of a change in residency I had. Until recently, for me, June was Pride Month, and the other eleven months were the times I could walk through a retail store without seeing tuck-friendly (think Buffalo Bill) one-piece bathing suits. In my new city, there was a second Pride Month in August I hadn't known was a thing. The city I moved to is a college town, and with the national Pride Month in June, there was no way for the students to celebrate with each other unless a second month was created during the school year.

While I appreciate the celebration of me, somehow it seems a little excessive that my city celebrates more than one demographic for one-sixth of the year. Even God (for those faithful) only asked for a little more than one-seventh of the year across all religions I'm familiar with. With my self-identity, seven out of the twelve months in my current city are dedicated to celebrating me, or at least my demographic groupings. There are, of course, groups that are left out, and not even the obvious culprits. There's no Mormon Appreciation Month, Caribbean Pride Month, Albino History Month, Disabled Veterans Month, Eastern European Remembrance Month, and, most importantly, no Survivors of Communism Month. Those groups obviously don't have the same power as the other heritage month groups, or they'd have their own month to celebrate their diversity and historical contributions.

I would also like to add that I think this is all a mistake, as all these months tend to divide us rather than bring us together. If you think I'm wrong, just wait until some psychopath suggests Aryan Pride Month, and good luck justifying excluding it. Hopefully, they don't add an Aryan History Month after potentially getting the first one. (For those ignorant of history, Aryan refers to an ethnocultural self-designation by Indo-Iranian peoples.)

Racism

I have been told by multiple people, including politicians and leading voices from outlets such as the New York Times and Washington Post, that I, because I am a Native American Hispanic, cannot be racist. Because I am not White, I lack the power necessary to use my prejudice against others. No matter how bigoted, shallow, or ignorant I act, I can never be racist. I was also told, when I jokingly accused another female of being sexist against men, that she cannot be sexist because women have no power over men whatsoever. Ignoring for a moment the stupidity of believing women have no power over men, the worldview that you cannot be racist or sexist unless you are a straight, cisgender, White male is nonsense.

Ignorance, bigotry, and hate know no bounds, regardless of race, color, religion, sex (including pregnancy state, sexual preference, or gender identity), national origin, or age. A seventy-eight-year-old female, light-skinned, transgender, pansexual Muslim Inuit can be equally, if not more, racist than any straight White male or any other individual. If this person were to become president, CEO of a company, a landlord, or a murderer, they would have power over others, including the power to end others' lives.

I've recently moved for work, leaving my house unoccupied while I look for renters. Here is an interesting question: If I only accepted women applicants, is it sexist? If I only reviewed applications from Hispanics or Native Americans to the exclusion of all others, is it racist? Does this give me power? The answer is obviously yes, so logically that would mean a Native American Hispanic woman does have power, and I can wield that power to enforce any bigotries I may or may not have.

Under the (flawed) contemporary definition of racism, I must have power for an act of mine to be considered racist. But we are not operating in logical times. Logic is only accepted if it goes in one direction and supports specific, approved ideas. In what world does it make sense that a Hispanic woman can discriminate against any sex or race without it being considered racist or sexist?

A relative of mine worked at a job requiring light physical labor (light for most; I'd probably be sore and complain after day one), moving heavy potted plants. His boss, the manager, had a candid conversation about who they would and would not hire. There were three categories of people this manager would not hire: women, overweight people, and Muslims. Here, bigoted hiring practices did have some minor practical merit. The manager believed women would not be able to perform the physical labor required for the job on the same level as a man. Ditto the rationale for overweight people. The manager also believed Muslims, because they may fast from sunup to sundown during Ramadan, might be physically weaker during this month from a lack of food and thus unable to do the job required.

As I sulked over hearing this in 2022, I asked for the demographics of the manager. These "hiring practices" were from the mind of a Hispanic female. This woman, who had very easily identifiable power, used it to the detriment of no less than three approved minority groups, at least one of which she was a member (I don't know if she was overweight or Muslim). If your opinion of the manager's hiring practices changed when I mentioned her sex and ethnicity, and perhaps you were more open-minded to the thought process that led her to her conclusions, I would say you need some introspection about exactly what type of racism and sexism you approve of and which you don't.

To put it mildly, this is unacceptable discrimination. If a person can do the job when needed, their religion, sex, and BMI score should have no more bearing than the amount of body hair or preference for romantic partners (as long as they're of legal age and species).

Part Two.

After the manager from the above story had moved on, my relative became in charge of hiring. Since my relative had recently purchased a house, he and his wife began inviting people over to socialize. When the former manager was invited over, she brought up the subject of hiring and asked my relative if he had continued her hiring practices after she had departed. Given that she brought this up on her own, she seemed proud of her ability to think critically and solve problems in ways no one else on Earth would have considered... Apparently, she not only was racist and sexist, but had wanted to proselytize her "unique" way of thinking to others so that the world might be a better place. If not, chaos would ensue and perhaps the somewhat heavy plants would simply not get moved, doomed to die and decay while overweight female Muslims paraded around the shop.

A coworker relayed an event to me that occurred at a community college. After class, students lined up to exit while the professor answered students' questions at the podium. One of the students had lost their phone and concluded, with no evidence whatsoever, that one of the other students had stolen it. Believing this, the individual determined the remedy was to stand at the exit and search every student's purse and backpack before letting them leave. The person was described to me as "large and intimidating," which I believe, since I don't believe every person leaving would acquiesce to someone searching their possessions without the tacit threat of bodily harm. I will not reveal this person's race or sex, but I will say the student was not a straight cisgender White male. Yet, this person had a very identifiable power. The student managed to find their phone elsewhere and at least had the decency to apologize publicly to the class the next day. If you believe you know the race and sex of the person who was described to me, it says more about you than it does about me. "Large and intimidating" could apply to any sex or race, unless you believe some races and sexes cannot be strong or intimidating.

In May 2018, a seemingly White teenager from Woods Cross, Utah went to prom wearing a traditional Chinese dress and decided to post the pictures online (as teenagers are wont to do) of her and her date. The hysteria that followed became national news, requiring our "deepest thinkers" to weigh in so other bigoted idiots under twenty don't make the same mistake. Her sin? She was White and therefore appropriating Chinese culture without permission (I'm not exactly sure who is approved to give this permission) by wearing the dress. As far as Google is concerned, cultural appropriation is defined as the unacknowledged or inappropriate adoption of the customs, practices, ideas of one people or society by members of another and typically more dominant people or society. The girl did not have the power to wear whatever she wanted without being labeled a racist; that right was reserved for others.

What does this mean in practice? People perceived as White in the United States cannot act, dress, style themselves, cook, or perform other activities from another culture without being considered an oppressor. Start a taco food truck? Unapproved. Buy a samurai sword? Unspeakably racist. Meticulously learn an instrument and style of music popularized by Black musicians? You might as well put on a white hood and head to Home Depot to pick up some two-by-fours and a pack of matches.

I know the criticism that these stories will generate; if true (which they are), these stories are only anecdotes and don't tell the whole story concerning race and gender in twenty-first-century America. Unfortunately, anecdotes and statistics are all the evidence I know how to provide, and if both are discounted, I no longer have any ability to support the truths I'm trying to reveal. I prefer to let the truth speak for itself and tolerate the views of those who deny what's in front of their own eyes.

To deny all groups have power is to also deny their agency over their own lives. While this normally means that marginalized groups aren't responsible for their current conditions, it also denies that success in these same groups is the result of their own hard work. For example, if a

Hispanic man cannot get ahead because of the systemic oppression he lives under, how do we explain successful Hispanic men? If the answer is that he is only as successful as White men allow him to be, then he hasn't actually achieved anything for himself. He has simply been propped up by the racist culture around him.

You see, pretending people are held back requires you to also believe they can only succeed by allying themselves with their oppressor. Logically then, any Hispanic man who is successful has only achieved their success because White men enabled it. People in approved marginalized groups with achievements and success are robbed of their triumphs.

Under the idea that only straight White men have power is the assumption that any racial, ethnic, or sexual minority only has their position because they have been aided by their oppressors for ominous reasons. Separating the world into victims and oppressors (those with power and those without) is not only moronic but flies in the face of what we can see with our own eyes and hear with our own ears. Who dominates the NBA and NFL? Who has the greatest chance of graduating from MIT? Who makes up our educators? If the answer to all those questions is not White males, then why would this be permitted by a society where White individuals hold all the power and wish to keep all the various marginalized groups down?

Losing Yourself

One of the stranger incidents I've seen is people actually losing their race, ethnicity, sexual orientation, or gender identity if they dare buck the system. When the Smithsonian National Museum of African American History and Culture* first opened in 2016, Supreme Court Justice Clarence Thomas (who is Black) was oddly left out of the various displays and pieces celebrating African American culture and contributions. Why he was originally left out is only known to the curators, but leaving out arguably the most powerful African American in the country spoke volumes about who does and doesn't count as Black in the eyes of those running the institution.

*Currently, only Native Americans and African Americans have their own Smithsonian museums. Women, Asians, Hispanics, Pacific Islanders,

LGBT individuals, and Inuit Americans apparently haven't contributed enough to be deemed worthy of having a museum

    **In all seriousness, their museums are located with everyone else's: the Air and Space Museum, the American History Museum, and the American Art Museum among others. I'm unsure why segregating museums by identity group is important, but about six of my identity groupings don't have one. Again, just wait until some psychopath asks where the White museum is so he can appreciate his people's culture.

    Kyrsten Sinema, senior senator from Arizona, was lauded as the first openly bisexual member of the senate in 2018. There were innumerable positive articles about her dress and appearance as it relates to her orientation, as it was seen as a sign of progress. After opposing legislation supporting Democrat policy issues, her orientation was never mentioned again. She lost her status as LGBT because of her other policy stances, leaving her as just some run-of-the-mill politician holding back progress.

    For all the support Hillary Clinton had as the first serious female candidate for the presidency, Nikki Haley, former governor of South Carolina and ambassador to the UN, had no accolades as a serious candidate for the 2024 presidency. Apparently, no one was hoping for her to break the glass ceiling or looking forward to the potential for history to be made. These figures, while clearly meeting the pre-requisites of their identity, lost it. Why? In order to be included in those groups, you have to agree with the group. If not, you lose your status and become a member of the oppressors. I didn't make the rules and also find this all very strange. Some sanity would be desired, but until then I guess I'll just keep having to keep up with the ever-changing rules as to which individuals do and don't count as marginalized.

Why We Want to Believe Some Have Power and Others Don't

    Why do we maintain the fiction that some groups have power and others don't? Because to be in a victim group means you are not responsible for where you are in life. To be in an oppressor group means you are not, as an individual, responsible for your success. Thus, those successful aren't there because of their own hard work, and those oppressed are only in their situation because of the malicious actions of others. In this narrative (and narrative is the right word), anyone in a "marginalized group" has their poor outcomes excused. If a thieving, drug-using Thai man is arrested for theft, he has the ability to point to systemic racism for keeping him down and forcing him into a life of substance abuse and burglary, and various race-centered organizations will support his claim. If a White woman does the same, she'll probably find no sympathetic ear and instead rightfully be mocked for putting herself in legal jeopardy.

We maintain the fiction because if racism, sexism, homophobia, and transphobia aren't to blame for most bad outcomes, we must then logically find other explanations, and some have difficulty accepting those explanations. In order to prevent bad outcomes, we must understand how we've reached that point, so as to take corrective measures. If we continuously blame largely non-existent, powerful, oppressive forces, we will be unable to fix the problem because we aren't tackling the issues at the heart.

In July 2022, with COVID-19 still a prevalent issue, a separate disease, Monkeypox (which has since been changed to Mpox so as not to stigmatize monkeys), was making its way through New York City. In the first report released that I could find, 336 New Yorkers were infected. Of those, 321 were men, and none were female. The disease seemed for some reason to infect those attending nightclubs and parties, both in the US and Europe. Imagine if you were the health department of New York City. In order to prevent the spread of Monkeypox (er, Mpox), what do you tell your citizens? No amount of systemic homophobia, racism, or sexism explains why this disease seemed to only infect males because there is no systemic homophobia, racism, or sexism that led to this outcome. This outcome was due to the activities of the individual participants that further enabled Monkeypox (er...Mpox) to spread.

It's easy to blame nebulous forces working against you, and it's hard to take responsibility for one's own actions and hold people accountable for the actions they take. But if we can't admit the source of the problem, we're far less likely to solve the problem.

Opting Into Oppression

Around October 2018, Senator Elizabeth Warren released the results of an ancestry/genetics test to prove that she was part Native American. In 1997, she used this self-identity to become the "first woman of color" hired by Harvard Law School. The reason she underwent the test is that it had become a campaign issue in the 2020 election. Having been called "Pocahontas" by then-President Trump, mocking her claimed heritage, she felt obligated to prove her ancestral oppression.

From this test, it was determined she had a Native American ancestor "approximately six to ten generations ago," assuming you believe the validity of the test used. Using the most accommodating figure of six generations, this means she was 1.6% Native American and 98.4% White (no need to figure out which flavor of White, as it turns out they're all basically the same, or so I've been told). At the other end, at ten generations, this would have made her less than 0.1% Native American and over 99.9% White.

If I were to show you a picture of Senator Warren with snow in the background, you would be unable to find her. The senator (whether actually Native American or not) wanted to be Native American, and thus opted into a victim group. This separated her from all others not in a victim group and thus gave her a shield (or sword) she could use whenever the moment called for it.

Why would someone want to be in a victim group? Given the level of oppression (…) Native Americans receive today, why would someone want to be in this group if they could pass themselves off as a member of the supposed oppressors? Because there is status in being in a victim group. There are special rules for members of victim groups, many of which mean being prioritized for coveted jobs or elite schools, amongst other advantages.

Companies needing to fill arbitrary diversity quotas will interview and hire candidates with less experience and credentials if that person is able to check off one of any number of boxes concerning their identity. If lower standards to fill diversity goals weren't needed, there wouldn't even be a need for DEI (diversity, equity, and inclusion) programs, as the most qualified would be hired. It doesn't actually matter if this is fair or not; it is what people do. Every day.

Like all others, Native Americans (which I assume I actually am) have and do contribute just like all others. Their contribution alone in World War II as coded radio operators and paratroopers should cement their impact on current-day America as much as any other group. As the national motto goes, E pluribus unum. (For those currently purchasing lottery tickets, that's Latin for "Out of many, one," approved by act of Congress in 1782).

Additionally, there is celebration of members of racial, ethnic, or sexual minorities that does not exist for the rest of the population.

There is no Male Pride Month, no European Heritage Day (except in the deepest, darkest corners of White supremacist circles), and certainly no parade for heterosexuality (it was tried a time or two and was a total cringe fest). Translation: for some, there is celebration of the self; for others, there is less than nothing; there is only scorn.

As it turns out, there are ways of opting out of the super-lame identity grouping of straight White male. You can find identity in some distant racial group, declare yourself a gender minority, such as nonbinary, or opt into a sexual orientation that doesn't quite accurately describe you, say, by claiming to be pansexual. Thus, a person can move from oppressor to victim without really changing anything about their life. There's no need to go live on a reservation, remove any appendages that you may enjoy having, or even become intimate with people you are not truly attracted to. Thus, the boring, milk-toast, straight White cisgender male can become a nonbinary queer Native American who will be celebrated with marches, have months dedicated to them, and be held up as brave without any actual accomplishments.

Chapter End Notes

Steeped in secrecy, a satchel nicknamed the "nuclear football" is carried with the US president by an aide-de-camp (the president's military secretary). Published literature by high-ranking government officials claims the case has four items in it: a black book of potential courses of action in the case of a major military threat against the United States or its allies, procedures for tapping into the emergency broadcast system, a three-by-five-inch card with authentication codes to use America's nuclear arms, and a list of locations the president and his/her/their cronies can safely evacuate to. The satchel is also rumored to contain communication equipment to transmit any presidential orders.

With this item alone, the President of the United States can order the launch of 400 nuclear-tipped Minutemen III Intercontinental Ballistic Missiles (ICBMs), fourteen Ohio-class ballistic missile submarines (each carrying twenty-four Trident II missiles with eight nuclear warheads per missile), and sixty heavy bombers capable of carrying nuclear missiles or bombs. Since atomic weapons were first used by the United States, the president has been the only person with the authority to order the US military to use these weapons. Given the current US military strength and worldwide reach, whoever wields this tool is, unquestionably, the most powerful person on the planet. The only limit to this raw power is the person holding it and the society allowing it.

From 2008–2016, Barack Obama, the first African American president, had a power no other American had. How could it be said that any grouping of people (tall, redhead, White, gay, Asian, skinny, bald, furry) had more power than him? As a group (since that seems to be how "we" want to define things the further into the 2000s we get), this means that male African Americans at this time had more power than any other demographic group on the face of the planet. I'll finish with this: If the capability to kill billions across the globe does not count as power, what does?

*I chose the quote at the beginning of this chapter because it spoke deeply to my own life experience. Whether in primary school, college, military, or other jobs over the course of my life, I've generally been surrounded by a diversity of people and ideas. I've had myriad bosses and leadership of a different sex, ethnicity, race, or sexual orientation, nearly none of whom struck me as odd or undesirable, since my main goal in those jobs was to make that paper. I've also had bosses and coworkers of my own race and sex who were completely incompetent and deserving of scorn, not for anything related to their demographic groupings but simply because they were individuals with individual character failings. Somehow, that quote from Full Metal Jacket stuck with me because of how constructive it seemed. The message I took from it was that the petty physical distinctions between people do not, or at least should not, matter.

"That's my mechanic. Whose bright idea was it to get rid of him?"
— Amon Leopold Goth, Kommandant SS-Haupsturmführer, "The Butcher of Plaszow," Schindler's List, 1993. Uttered moments before the next shipment went out.

Chapter 15 Respect Your Enemy

"A man can condemn his enemies, but it's wiser to know them."
— Harper Lee, author, 1926-2016

In the winter of 1914, in the midst of World War I, French, British, and German troops, who previously were shooting and machine gunning each other to death with extreme prejudice, took part in an unofficial ceasefire to celebrate a common holiday, Christmas. In no-man's-land, between the trench lines, enemies exchanged gifts, sang carols, and even played that most European of sports, soccer. Despite everyone knowing these very same people had been and would be shooting at them and their comrades the next day, they were able to recognize their common humanity and for a brief moment see a fellow human being instead of an assortment of meat and military equipment attempting to kill them.

In my upbringing, while playing soccer myself, my parents reminded me that the other team was not the enemy, which I so callously called them, but my opponent. The intention was to teach me that those two words have different and important meanings. An opponent is the other team, whose goal is to beat you. An enemy is a hostile force intending to subjugate or kill you. Over the last two decades, I've seen my fellow Americans increasingly regard their political counterparts not as opponents, but as enemies.

I'd like to think I can convince rational adults this is not the case, but sadly there are far too many who have so demonized their opponents that they'll never emerge from this misguided idea. As such, the best I can do is urge respect for those you believe to be your enemy (or, hopefully, opponent).

I've said most of what I've wanted to convey, and sadly there's but little more to this work. I know how controversial some of the ideas I've presented are, and I know many will strongly disagree with what I've put forth. Before finishing, I wanted to convey the notion that it's perfectly fine if you don't agree with everything I've written. I would find it odd if all my ideas, start to finish, were without criticism or accepted as gospel by any sane person walking the earth (we have enough insanity; please don't add to the count).

On the assumption you disagree with something I've put forth, I ask, even if you see me as an opponent or enemy, that you at the very least respect me as a fellow human being. If you believe I'm less than that, perhaps some sort of pig or insect, there are a few historical figures I'd point you to who had similar thoughts on different people. I hope you're more tolerant than them.

I know that somewhere in this world there is another version of me, sitting in a similar chair, perhaps enjoying an adult beverage as they type as I am now. This "other me" is just as smart and well-read and feels as passionately about their side as I do mine. Within their own set of values, they are just as moral, just as hardworking, and equally desiring of a good, meaningful life. That doesn't mean I don't hope they fail; it means I have respect for somebody with ideas that oppose mine — even insane, off-the-wall, completely bonkers ideas.

In the same way, you have opponents and enemies. They are opposite versions of you; passionate that they're in the right and believe you are the enemy. At the same time, they are human, capable of failure, fallacy, and susceptible to being misled and propagandized into believing anything under the sun. Just like you.

In the epic All Quiet on the Western Front, a German soldier in World War I faces the horrors of war versus what his teachers and government told him volunteering meant. After a series of battles, the main character eventually gets trapped in no-man's-land, between his side's trenches and the enemy's. At the same time, he is confronted by an enemy soldier in the same situation. The German soldier promptly stabs the other before he can be stabbed or killed himself. It is only then that he realizes what he is fighting.

The French soldier does not die immediately and instead lingers in the same artillery crater as the German soldier between the two front lines. Realizing what he has done, the German tries to heal and comfort the French soldier, to no avail. The damage had already been done. While in the fight, all the German soldier saw was an opaque enemy armed to the hilt to kill him. What he sees after bayoneting the other soldier to death is their common humanity.

This is not to say that the fight should not have occurred. If peace at any price is your solution, understand that the cost may be more than you can bear. Respecting your enemy does not mean that you capitulate to their will. It means combating them in a humane way and, if victorious, treating them in a way you would reasonably wish to be treated if you lost the fight.

As every election, court ruling, war, and trial show, your side will not always win. You'll be lucky if it's any better than fifty-fifty. This means that, if it hasn't happened yet, at some point, you will be on the losing side. If we rake across the coals each losing side every time this occurs, we're only providing the fodder for when the tables eventually, inevitably turn. If, on the other hand, we are humble in victory and contrite in defeat, we can work through our most contentious issues without every fight being life or death.

As you create a mental image of your opponent, whoever and wherever they may be, do not create a fictitious evil monster bent on your destruction (unless, of course, they are an evil monster bent on your destruction, in which case, I'd recommend a sufficiently powerful firearm; I can recommend some). Once you understand your opponent as they are, you will have a better idea of how to either compromise or defeat them. God help you, you may even realize you're on the wrong side.

If you can't learn to live peacefully side by side with your opponents, there are only a few options left.

I'll leave this sub-chapter with an anecdote. During World War II, from August 23, 1942, to February 2, 1943, the Germans and Soviets were fighting deep in Soviet territory over the city of Stalingrad on the Volga River. The Slavic people, of which Soviets were considered, were one of the hand-picked ethnicities or races Hitler and his fascist regime considered Untermensch (subhuman). As such, they were lesser than their "Aryan" neighbors in every way, in accordance with the racist ideologies in Germany at the time.

On November 19, 1942, the Soviets launched a pincer movement (that is, attacking the left and right sides simultaneously) and eventually encircled* hundreds of thousands of crack German units in the city. In order to accomplish this, prior to the attack, over one million men snuck into the staging areas without the Germans knowing (sort of — they knew but didn't believe it).

Being encircled is a very, very dangerous military outcome. Supplies such as food, reinforcements and ammunition cannot be brought in, panicking units have nowhere to retreat to (versus surrendering), and there is the possibility of losing communication with your own side. If an encircled unit cannot be rescued or breakout to safety, they will inevitably be lost.

The Nazis' mistake was to assume their enemy, due to their race, was incapable of complex military movements or thoughts. Covertly moving a million men, forward staging tanks and attack aircraft, and strategically attacking the weak flanks required intricate planning, details, logistics, reconnaissance, and secrecy. By assuming their enemy was racially inferior and idiotic, the Germans failed to respect their enemy and lost somewhere in the neighborhood of 250,000 men who became surrounded. It ultimately became one of the turning points of World War II, leading to Germany's defeat.

This is not just some obscure military reference from approximately eight decades ago; it is an important lesson for the present. Those you regard as your opponents and enemies are not idiots with poorly developed ideas and motivations. They are people to be regarded with respect, and not to be underestimated. You treat them otherwise at your own peril.

Don't let your own bigotry and biases lead you to mistake your opponents and enemies for being any less capable than you (unless, of course, I'm your opponent; in which case, assume away).

Civility

Over the course of my life, I've met people here or there who disagree with me on one issue or another. I started cataloging these people until I came to a strange realization: to a man (or woman), I eventually come across an issue or opinion with each of these people I disagree with, sometimes very strongly.

I had/have two courses of action for each of these individuals: (1) remain courteous to those I disagree with (and perhaps learn something from them), or (2) break off all ties and publicly shame them for having the audacity to think differently.

Every day, with very few exceptions, I imagine you must do something similar. You work for or with someone you may not like or agree with, provide goods or services to those whose presence you don't enjoy, and perhaps even vote for representatives that don't 100% do what you would like them to do. You may even have friends and family that don't 100% match your worldview. If you don't, I would say you are either in a cult or wildly ignorant of the thoughts of those around you.

Try, if you can, to put yourself in your opponents' shoes and see if you would act any differently in the circumstances. It's very easy to villainize our rivals and equally difficult to see and understand their point of view. You are, after all, the villain in someone else's story. I'm betting your desire would be that they are civil towards you if victorious.

"A king does not kill a king."
— Salah al-Din Yusuf ibn Ayyub (commonly known as Saladin)
after capturing Guy of Lusignan, King of Jerusalem, 1187 AD

Chapter 16 You Are Lucky to Live in the Time and Place You Do

Can it get worse? Oh yes, much worse.
— A Bridge Too Far, MGM Studios, 1977, in reference to the surrounded British 1st Airborne Division at the Battle of Arnhem, September 17–26, 1944

The morning will come when the world is mine, Tomorrow belongs to me
– Act I, Cabaret, 1966 cautionary Broadway Musical about the rise of fascism in the 1930s

Around the Fourth of July, 2023, R&B singer Jill Scott (who oddly shares part of her name with the original writer, Francis Scott Key) sang her version of the US national anthem during the second day of the Essence Festival in New Orleans. As part of her introduction, it was announced over the loudspeaker, "Everyone please rise for the only national anthem we will be recognizing from this day forward." Below are the lyrics to her version:

Oh say can you see by the blood in the streets / That this place doesn't smile on you colored child / Whose blood built this land with sweat and their hands / But we'll die in this place and your memory erased / Oh say, does this truth hold any weight / This is not the land of the free, but the home of the slaves!

As of this writing, Ms. Scott's net worth was approximately $10 million. By this measure, she is wealthier than approximately 98.5% of the United States population while also being wealthier than 99% of the world's people. In addition to singing, she has also acted in well-known film and television roles (none of which I've seen or remember). Why Ms. Scott believes she is not in the land of the free confuses and astounds me, given her personal success. How she tolerates living in such a dystopian hell perplexes me even more, given that her ability to flee elsewhere is unmatched by the average person. If she views herself as a slave for some odd reason, I'm wildly unsure of how to view myself.

If you are an African American with an ancestor who was enslaved, 320,000 White (or close enough) Americans died fighting for the Union to provide your freedom (we'll skip over those maimed; they're kind of a downer).

In 2021, while I was deployed to Africa, seemingly out of nowhere, Juneteenth (June 19) became a US national holiday for which everyone got the day off. It commemorates when 2,000 mostly White Union soldiers entered Texas to free 250,000 enslaved African Americans. I'm happy to rephrase this to read "when 2,000 American soldiers entered Texas to free 250,000 enslaved Americans." I leave it to you to determine if the inclusion of the races of those involved is important or not. Personally, I believe the latter indicates progress; interpret that however you like. If there is insistence that we include the races of those involved, then logically, the races of all the different parties should be important.

Somewhere between 36,000 and 40,000 African American soldiers also died fighting for the Union. Oddly, there were even African Americans voluntarily recruited into the Confederate army towards the end of the war, but with few participating in combat. But few is not none.

If you are one of the approximately 10 million LGBT or 7.6 million Jewish individuals (or some mix of both) living in the United States, realize that there are 300,000 fellow US citizens who never made it back to American shores to ensure that the genocidal, homophobic, sexist, and racist regimes of Adolf Hitler, Benito Mussolini, and Hideki Tojo came to an end and ensured your freedom and survival. Currently, there are only thirty-four out of 195 (17.4%) countries in which same-sex couples can legally get married. There are eleven countries in which you may be executed with extreme prejudice by the state for engaging in the same acts. According to the Jerusalem Post, there are currently only four elderly Jewish individuals in Yemen, the rest having been forced out. In Iraq, as of 2022, that number was three. As of May 27, 2022, in Iraq, making contact with Israel is punishable by death.

If you are female, thank your appropriate deity (or yourself if you don't believe in a higher power) you don't currently live in any of the thirty-one countries that have mutilated more than 200 million women and girls so that they cannot get pleasure from intercourse. There are still countries where women aren't allowed to vote, and even more where social convention stops women from exercising their right to make their voices heard (if you believe there's a country in the West that still does this, please don't attempt to vote, as clearly, you're too stupid to figure out how to do so in an intelligent fashion).

I don't bring these facts up to demand anyone pay homage to any demographic group, excuse poor current or past behavior, or tolerate injustice in the present. I say this so you understand the cost in human suffering and blood for you to be where you are. Lucky you.

What do all of the above oppressions have to do with one another? They speak to the current and past horrors that have taken place and the sacrifices it has taken to reach the place we are now at. Anyone with a brain knows the answer to, "Can it get any worse?" Of course, it can get worse, and of course, it has been worse. That doesn't mean we've arrived at Utopia and that there isn't room for improvement. At any stage of human development, if we had believed things were perfect then, we would have been wrong. We would also be wrong to assume it only ever gets better, and that we can't backslide into something resembling the French Revolution just as the guillotines start coming down on whoever "had it coming."

Howard Zinn (1922–2010) was an American historian, playwright, philosopher, and socialist intellectual who worked at both Spelman College and Boston University. His opus magnum (read: important work) was A People's History of the United States, published in 1980. To this day, it is required reading at a number of high schools, colleges, and universities. Without reading it (or even barely glancing at the Wikipedia article), I can tell his work is a view of American history from a socialist and communist point of view, focusing on exploitation, racism, and class conflict. Despite his deep-seated issues with his country of birth, he decided to remain in the country his entire life, having been born in New York, New York, and expiring in Santa Monica, California, at the age of eighty-seven. Towards the end of his life, the avowed communist was receiving $200,000 per year in royalties from his book alone. At his time of death, that would have put him in the top 10% of income earners.

Whatever issues he highlighted (again, I didn't read his book, or the children's version, A Young People's History of the United States — Wait, should I be making a children's version of this book?) against his home nation, it was not enough to send him packing to the socialist utopia of... uh... (mmmm?) that great socialist utopia that doesn't even have to be named.

Somehow, despite hating his own country and economic system he greatly benefitted from, writing books opposing it, and speaking publicly about its ills and leadership, he remained well respected and free. I would list the nations that would have otherwise incarcerated or executed such a person in the past or present, but it would probably be easier to list the nations and times that this would not have happened. (Note: I don't advocate for the murder or incarceration of rabble-rousers; the purpose of free speech is to vet all ideas against each other to see which are the most moronic so they can be discarded to the ash heap of history).

Much like the deceased Mr. Zinn, many living in the US or other Western countries do not (or did not) understand how lucky they are to live in the time and place that they do. All one need do is turn on social media or read from the mainstream press to find people who genuinely believe they have it bad, with no help or support in sight. They look at their parents as a yardstick and proclaim they had it easier, while they themselves were cursed with being born into twenty-first-century America. These complaints are about how housing is too expensive in our most desired cities, that college education and loans are unaffordable, and that they are oppressed at every turn by bosses, fellow citizens, law enforcement, etc. I know from experience that no matter how good people have it, they will complain.

Our frame of reference is what we know, and for most of us, what we know is abundance and prosperity, even if we cannot recognize it. In earlier eras, being impoverished actually meant death, whereas today it generally means living in a less than desirable area and not being able to afford luxury goods none of us truly need. While it would be nice to have a full Balenciaga bodysuit, complete with "face shield" (a mask with no opening for the mouth or eyes) for... reasons, no one seriously believes they need this multi-thousand-dollar outfit in order to survive.

While serving overseas, I was with an organization of approximately forty Americans that temporarily boarded in a fifteen-story hotel. The hotel would be considered mid-range to slightly lacking by US standards, but for the area, it was the epitome of luxury and style. While outside, homeless children wearing rags begged foreigners for money (I thought they may have been faking it until I saw the shack and oil-drum fire the next morning) along crumbling streets, my fellow US citizens complained about their accommodations. They complained about the speed at which housekeeping came by, that the smoothies at the bar were made with mix instead of fresh fruit, that they had to have a roommate in their accommodations, and how hot the coach bus was before the AC had time to circulate, while outside the locals either biked, walked barefoot, or rode improvised un-airconditioned buses, apparently crafted with old US military equipment. They even complained that only one member had their towels folded into animal shapes and placed on their bed (that individual tipped the housekeeping staff).

While working at a bar in a trendy, artistic part of town, I came across a photographer in his late 20s living with his parents. One subject the gentleman brought up was that he was unable to find a house or apartment he could afford. He then voiced he believed it was "the system's" fault and that nefarious forces were aligned against him getting inexpensive housing. I then offered my services to help him find an apartment, while at the same moment pulling out my phone to pull up an app dedicated to apartments and real estate (I would name the app, but unfortunately, the particular company has not paid me to do so… yet). Once the photographer saw me searching, he became particular about why he could not find housing. You see, he had requirements for his housing; it had to be at or below a particular rent/mortgage, be conveniently located so his commute wouldn't be bad, and be in a safe neighborhood with good amenities, while at the same time being walkable to hip, trendy areas. Additionally, he needed an x number of rooms, x square footage, preferably with an Olympic-size pool with scantily clad female drink attendants (all right, I made that last part up, but the rest is true). You see, it wasn't that my new friend couldn't find housing; it was that he could not find housing he wanted that he could afford.

Where We Are

The current environment in the West is the result of millennia of human development, culminating in it being the most desirable place to work, raise families, and live out our lives. If it were not, people would be fleeing from the West, instead of to it, to those other, more desirable places. The dividends from the economic and social hurdles overcome have been laid at your feet from birth. The problem, as I see it, is that people do not recognize how truly fortunate they are. If you want to see which society is working, see where people risk life and limb to go.

I don't think North Korea, Venezuela, Syria, or the Democratic Republic of the Congo have a serious illegal immigration problem. People don't flock to the US, Australia, and Western Europe because they're systemically racist, unequal, and unjust. They risk their lives and freedom because they rightly know that it's here they have the best chance of living happy lives for themselves and their families.

For those who believe those immigrants (legal or not) tolerate the West simply for economic gain, ask yourself why that economic gain is in the places they flee to and not in the countries they flee from.

Muhammad Ali, famous boxer and activist, spent years advocating for left-wing causes, joined the Nation of Islam, and protested the Vietnam War by refusing to be drafted, resulting in him being barred from boxing for over 3 years. His advocacy was pointedly race-related, identifying himself most strongly as a Black man in a culturally dominant White society. In the 1970s, Mr. Ali famously fought George Foreman for the heavyweight title in Zaire in an event aptly named the Rumble in the Jungle. Upon his return, he was asked by a reporter what he thought of Africa. He replied, "Thank God my granddaddy got on that boat." Again, if you don't like this truth, your problem is with the deceased Mr. Ali (1942–2016), not myself. I am only recounting what others have said from their own experiences, having seen with their own eyes what the rest of the world is like.

If you don't like that I've said what others have, based on their own experience, then close your eyes and place your hands over your ears so you don't hear any other facts that may harm your delicate nature. For all others, I thank you for your open-minded nature and urge you to read on. You're almost done.

In all seriousness, I have family members still alive who can remember a time in which they were barred from certain public pools in my home city. The Ku Klux Klan, in addition to irrationally hating African Americans and Jews, also hated and hate members of my own religion, Catholicism. The fact that I'm of mixed race (and have dated those not of the same race/ethnicity) until very recent times was grounds for ridicule and exclusion for both me and my parents. That bigotry is so far on the fringes today, it is honestly difficult to locate. This is not to say those problems don't to this day exist; it's to say those problems are largely absent and are truly (rightly) marginalized views.

My goal in this chapter is to provide a realistic assessment of where we are right now. All around us is propaganda desperate to convince us that it has never been worse and that we as a society have sins we must pay for. "They" do this for myriad reasons; the most easily understood is money. For media, if it bleeds, it leads, and the most amount of attention and eyeballs don't go to the cute puppy up for adoption or the local Girl Scout cookie sale outside Walmart.

We, the American people, must be driven to paranoia and outrage so we feel compelled to continue watching and listening to the problems of the country and the world, rather than live our lives in happiness. Behind the obvious money angle is a less understood motivation: the need to have something to fight for. 98.3% of Americans would know what to do if out of nowhere a Reichsführer-SS Officer came around the corner riding a Tiger tank (and with 45% of households owning firearms, he better stay in his tank). They would also know the appropriate response if Robert E. Lee were to break time and space and appear before them riding a horse, attempting to ensure escaped slaves were returned to their "rightful owners." Unfortunately, they probably wouldn't know what to do if Mao Zedong, Joseph Stalin, or Pol Pot knocked on the door to "reorganize agriculture," but we'll just chalk that up to bad education.

Today, however, these obvious villains are largely absent, or perceived to be absent. Because of humanity's Western-led progress, the obvious bad guys have been largely thrown into the deepest seas or had long falls from short ropes, assuming we got to them before they beat us to it. But that hasn't meant our brains, shaped by evolution, don't look for villains.

What makes a hero? An individual who must struggle against an appropriate oppressive force. Heroes cannot exist in a vacuum; they must have something with which to fight against and to rise to the occasion. But what if there doesn't exist a truly oppressive force? By necessity, one must be found or made up. We need something to fight against; it's in our nature. It could be a fight against leaders, a fight against a rival group, nature itself, or even simply a fight against ourselves. We are not content to believe everything is fine.

Greta Thunberg, born January 3, 2003, is a Swedish environmental activist who speaks passionately about climate change. She has been included on the Forbes list of "The World's Most Powerful Women" and nominated for the Nobel Peace Prize in 2019, 2020, and 2021, joining Benito Mussolini (1935), Adolf Hitler (1939), Joseph Stalin (1945, 1948), Fidel Castro (2001), Hugo Chavez (2005), and Vladimir Putin (2014). She has also been medically diagnosed with Asperger's syndrome, obsessive-compulsive disorder (OCD), and selective mutism (look it up).

When she first heard about climate change in 2011 at the age of eight, she became so depressed she stopped talking and lost twenty-two pounds in two months from a self-imposed diet (she is also currently vegetarian). At the age of fifteen, she withdrew from school to protest in support of action against climate change, claiming government leaders were robbing her of a future. She refuses to fly unless "it's an emergency" and sailed from Europe to North America to give a speech at the UN to speak about climate change. However, the boat's crew had to fly between Europe and the United States, completely negating the carbon Ms. Thunberg saved by not flying herself.

As of this writing, there is no carbon database calculating the carbon cost of her accommodations (probably a hotel) she stayed at while visiting New York, transportation to and from the UN where she gave her speech (to include the carbon cost of the required infrastructure), or what it took to construct the boat that brought her from Europe to the US. Whatever the cost was, no doubt it could have been less to the detriment of the planet. How dare she (After all, why not just have a virtual climate conference?).

Normally, I would list a series of public policy positions she holds that would cause problems, but as it turns out, I only need to name one: she wishes the population of the world had zero carbon emissions. Not net zero, not reduced emissions, but none. This would go beyond taking us back to the Dark Ages, as even in the Dark Ages, people were allowed to light candles and cook using wood-burning ovens. Even modern windmills, hydroelectric dams, and solar panels require components necessitating plastics and other petrochemicals for manufacturing and transportation. Eliminating the extraction and use of fossil fuels would have a worse effect than the intentional detonation of every nuclear bomb on the planet. At least in that case, some part of society would survive. Without petroleum-based products, we would be unable to even get food to where people are, and most of the population of the world would starve to death in a couple of months. If someone wanted to test this suicidally stupid idea, I'd recommend a small city or state, say... Sweden.

The truth is that even under the worst-case scenarios involving climate change, Ms. Thunberg would be fine unless she put her face against the sand on a beach and stayed there for thirty years or so. She has robbed herself of a useful education and has allowed herself to be a tool of the environmental movement. To that end, she will find wealth, popularity, and a desirable future at the cost of her integrity (unless she believes what she's saying, in which case she's just crazy).

For any critics who have made it this far into this work, I would like to mount a defense of my choice of words. Regardless of what is or is not between someone's legs, if they do or say irrational or silly things, I call them crazy. Everyone still above ground knows people, either those they know personally or popular figures, they consider crazy. For those wishing to debate the issue of who can call whom crazy, I'll provide contact information so we can debate why a woman (me) can't call another woman crazy.

Point being, Ms. Thunberg needed something to fight, a cause that would give her life true meaning. It's easy to fight greed, corruption, and homicidal dictators because they are so easily identified by their bad qualities. No one watching Star Wars has any issues identifying who the bad guys are (but let's be real; "stormtrooper" is a super cool name for combat troops, historical issues aside). We are designed to have to struggle against something. We need an obstacle to overcome or a goal to meet to give our lives meaning. For some, it's the number of followers on Instagram. For others, it's the total in their bank accounts. And for a few of our shallower members of humanity, it's the number of notches on our bedpost or lipstick case.

Note: for those who believe critiquing a mentally ill female teenager/ young adult is uncouth, know that I would criticize anyone (and have) with her particular advocacy, regardless of their age, sex, race, sexual orientation, or mental faculties, assuming they were putting themselves out there publicly to forcibly change the way I live (I have a feeling if I tried to change the laws where she lives to require her to consume meat, she might have a problem with me).

If the advocates for White supremacy (again, if you can find them) had as their representative a ninety-seven-year-old autistic Lithuanian woman, I would also publicly oppose them, as my issue is not with their various identity groupings and disabilities, but with their ideas.

I know this was a lot of space to dedicate to one person or cause, but there is a point to it. Like many others, the example above provides a case study into why people don't want to believe they have it as good as they do. People's lives need meaning, and believing things are on the brink of catastrophe allows them to fight it and be the hero in their own story. If everything's okay, then even moving the needle isn't going to do much more than make it slightly more okay.

Our shared cultural stories usually have an obvious villain or oppressive force that must be overcome by the hero. People want to be that hero because it is unique, celebrated, and is (usually) thought to require an exceptionally courageous person who can do what others cannot.

Here is normally where I'd cite statistics about decreasing poverty rates, accessibility to goods in developing countries, and the cratering number of deaths due to war since the end of World War II to highlight progress made, but it's not necessary. You already know or should know that the twentieth and twenty-first centuries have vastly improved the conditions of all of humanity. If you don't, tell me the time and place you'd rather live, and I'll paint you a picture you're likely to find deeply disturbing.

Pessimism in the United States and the West in general has reached a fevered pitch. Bad and incorrect ideas have permeated the culture to such a degree that "we" collectively believe it has never been worse. Racism is worse, the economy is awful, and intolerance of each other in general is escalating. (I actually agree racism has gotten worse in the last two decades, but not in the ways most say.)

By almost every measure, it has never been better. We have a more educated population than at any time in America's history. Our most poverty-stricken citizens are much more likely to be obese than malnourished. With the exception of rampant drug use and overdoses in the last few years, lifespans have been increasing every decade since as far out as the 1950s. Racism, sexism, homophobia, and transphobia are at historic lows, and certainly better than in the rest of the world. I know this because I have seen the world with my own eyes. Don't trust me, ask others who have seen it; you're likely to get very similar observations.

Has racism, sexism, homophobia, and transphobia been eliminated in the West? Certainly not. Do they exist at their lowest levels in human history? The answer is unquestioningly yes. If you doubt me on this, simply ask older relatives or open a Wikipedia article.

I was conversing with a friend around 2010 who suggested the country had never been more divided. I simply told him there was a time in which Americans organized millions of troops to shoot at one another during the Civil War, at which point my friend agreed that there was, in fact, a time in which we were more divided.

I have seen large portions of the world and have studied many parts that I've not set foot on. I can assure you, no matter how bad you think it is where you are, it gets worse, a lot worse. 98% of the females in the African country I was deployed to had their clitorises removed in their youth so they wouldn't get pleasure from sex. In various Middle Eastern countries I've worked in, the punishment for same-sex activity is death. I've seen racism so rampant in foreign countries that people are openly denied entry into businesses based solely on their skin color or because they were not from that country. I've seen establishments in overseas downtown areas that openly rent young females for the evening for $20 to strangers with no questions asked. These examples are not the exception; they are the norm for humanity here, today.

Without even seeking out the sewers of how bad humanity can act, I've seen and heard enough to know it gets more awful than I hope you can imagine. I know it's hard to hear because you may not feel like you are lucky. Gas, rent, relationships, depression, vices — I understand it's

215

tough to see how it could get worse. But you only know how good you have it when you lose it or see the alternative. Look it up, or even better, see these places in person. The horror of reality and seeing how bad it can get will shock you into accepting how good you have it. And if you can't see it, you are lost. By desiring to believe you are a victim with the world painting crosshairs on the back of your head, you can't see that this is largely a figment of your imagination.

Are there people who want me to leave the country for being a US-born Hispanic? Absolutely. Are there also people who believe the world is flat or that they are Jesus Christ reborn? Also yes. The point I'm trying to make in those examples is that, yes, there are legitimate bigots and crazies, but they are of an inconsequential size and lack any real power. The only power they have is the power that we give them by highlighting their causes and providing the attention they seek.

See it from the bigoted racist's point of view (if you can find one): while you believe they are the cause of your problems, they believe you are the cause of their problems. And if you feel uncomfortable putting yourself into the mind of a bigot, just pretend that they're a criminal needing empathy in the face of an unjust system. I'm not giving anyone a pass (and certainly not simpletons who judge people by their group identity), and honestly, there's a very strong likelihood I'm more judgmental than you are.

Like Chapter 13, You Are Not Responsible for Racism and Bigotry You Did Not Commit, this chapter's title is not pointed at any particular race, ethnicity, sex, sexual orientation, or gender identity. It is intended to be universal, a truth that spans all groupings of people.

Chapter End Notes

As I close this chapter and approach the end of this work, I understand what critics will say. Yes, it's better than it was, but there is still much for which we must "do the work." Immediately after or preceding that phrase will be a laundry list of perceived social injustices that still exist. They'll surround incarceration rates, immigration enforcement, or perceived intractability of portions of the population refusing to adhere to the latest dogma. All of that's fine, and there are still issues that need to be worked out, but that doesn't take away from the fact that it's never been better.

If our complaints and most serious issues were presented to the trailblazers of history, they'd likely laugh in our faces that we've progressed so much we're arguing over such trivial things. I doubt that Rosa Parks would care that a Caucasian girl wore dreads to prom or that Cesar Chavez would concern himself with an Italian couple owning a taco truck, but I could be mistaken. Almost no one wants to admit the time in which they live is easier than what has come before or that they're living in an enviable place. Our minds seemingly don't want to confront this because the next logical question will be "Then why do things seem so hard?"

There is an answer to this question I hope by this point you can answer yourself.

> "If a fellow isn't thankful for what he's got, he isn't likely to be thankful for what he's going to get."
> — Frank Clark, US congressman, D-Pennsylvania, 1860-1936*

*For those questioning why I would quote an avowed racist, find me a person in 1900 who wasn't a racist and I'll quote them next time.

What I've Gotten Wrong

> "Let's be honest about journalists: we find a lot of ways of being wrong."
> — EJ Dionne Jr., Washington Post columnist

The only people who don't make mistakes are those who are no longer among us. So long as we draw breath, we will continue to make errors in judgment and hold ideas that are factually false. Over my life, I've been wrong on many things, some small and inconsequential, some large and life changing. The views I have now will probably change over the remainder of my life as I realize some of the things I've thought were correct are actually incorrect, no matter how much I want them to be true. Wisdom comes from recognizing where we fall short and allowing our minds to be open to ideas we may have originally dismissed as wrong or bad.

This chapter highlights a small subset of those things I was wrong about. I don't just want others to recognize the truth when it's presented to them; I want that for myself too. Throughout my schooling, I believed only merit defined where a person ended up. The lazy and slothful would end up with lower grades and worse jobs in the future. Those industrious and self-controlled would rise through the ranks and then end up with a good job and a prosperous life at the other end. I put no stock in social connections or activities outside of effort alone.

While in college, there was a leadership training organization with prestigious leadership positions one had to apply for. These positions on the surface allowed an individual to have power over others and develop leadership skills. Since joining this organization, I felt destined to get one of these prestigious positions and thus grow. I had failed to recognize how deeply social connections mattered and that merit and achievement alone were insufficient to get these jobs. I felt at the time that the position was mine and that I had earned it through hard work. When I found out I hadn't gotten the position, my world shattered. A fundamental building block for how I viewed the world had been destroyed, replaced by a new one: merit and hard work alone are not enough to achieve success; social connections also matter.

As I matured, I became aware of a long list of other inputs. Accidents of birth location, parents, luck, and even religion (one of the girls I liked in my youth simply went to a different church, and the different church's members socialized apart). Even with all these other influences dictating life outcomes, I still maintain that hard work and merit offer the best odds at living a fulfilling life. While a homeless heroin addict in California can still beg for more money than some of the hardest-working individuals in Africa earn, that African can still lead a better and more fulfilling life, even if his or her income is significantly less.

At this point, it should come as no surprise that in my youth, I desired (and did) to enter the US military. I believed in American values, and even though I knew our country had obviously erred in the past, I still believed the causes were generally just. While in high school from 2002–2006, I supported the wars in Iraq and Afghanistan. For Afghanistan, I believed we were righteous in getting revenge for September 11, and for

Iraq, I believed we were in the right to end destabilizing dictatorships. While I hadn't internalized the phrase at the time, an early version of "never again" echoed through my mind, pushing interventionism for those I perceived to be generating chaos in the world.

I had failed to understand that we cannot impose values on others without cost. The Middle East and the Arabian Peninsula have different values than the West. Understand, even small cultural differences can cause huge rifts. In large portions of the world, there is no perceived issue with marrying first cousins or having multiple wives. In others, I kid you not, there doesn't exist an age of consent. My error was thinking that (1) those living in cultures far different from mine were oppressed and (2) all that was needed for a better world was to liberate those people from their dictatorial leadership, and freedom would ensue. I did not appreciate that not all people and cultures necessarily want the same things. Some place more value on religion, family cohesion, or traditional values than the West does.

In the case of Iraq and Afghanistan, it wasn't enough to free the people from their current leaders. Those leaders came to power because the culture around them enabled and tolerated it. Simply removing the man in charge at the moment did nothing to change the culture that put that person there, and moving one strongman out simply left a power vacuum that needed to be filled. While I believe in the long term it is possible to change a culture, it takes actions the West is unwilling to engage in at the moment due to the perceived harshness. For example, if there exists a tradition of child brides you want to do away with, making the practice illegal and jailing those engaging in it would be required. If women aren't allowed in school, then building schools and forcing parents to send their children there would need to be done at the end of a rifle to ensure parity between the sexes regarding education. Simply leaving those decisions to the culture you've "liberated" will not yield the results you want. Of course, the opposite dystopia is tolerating traditions and practices you yourself abhor.

Additionally, in my youth, I opposed legalizing marijuana, believing it to be a sign of socially destructive activity. I didn't equate it with alcohol and didn't even ponder how marijuana compares to harder, legal drugs. As I came across functional friends and family who smoked or otherwise consumed THC-based products, over time I realized it wasn't the destructive force I believed it to be, but rather regarded it as comparable to alcohol (although the body count from alcohol seems much higher). In addition, early in my life, I had a strong commitment to authority, as the career paths I was trying to go down relied on clean criminal background histories lacking abuse of alcohol and illegal drug use, among other illicit activity.

As I matured, I learned that the rules are just strong suggestions. When I mentioned this to a close relative, they disagreed with me, insisting that following the rules was absolute. When I asked if they ever sped, they simply answered yes. When I asked why, they answered that it was because a driver, for safety, needs to move at the speed of traffic. My response? Following the speed limit is a suggestion, and while you can be punished for breaking the law, the consequence of not operating intelligently (such as by driving at the speed of traffic versus the speed limit) is potential injury or death, assuming traffic is moving faster than the speed limit. Thus, over time, I realized that while authority is important, it isn't absolute. The history books are filled with people acquiescing to authority, only to find themselves taking part in horrific activities they otherwise would not have unless told to. While I recognized the Nuremberg defense of "just following orders" works 99.8% of the time, I also learned that when the time came that I had to answer for my actions, I could not use the defense of "because other people told me to."

There was also a time I believed no one was above the law. Without naming names (some of which you can figure out), over the course of my life, I have seen many wealthy, well-connected, or powerful figures escape any consequences for their illegal or immoral actions. Some were the children of wealthy parents, others were successful and powerful celebrities, and many were just run-of-the-mill politicians whose policy positions or letter next to their name (D/R) was apparently more important than their ability to follow mutually agreed-upon rules. Sadly, what I've learned over my lifetime is that there are levels to justice. Nearly all people (call it 90%) fall under a level I call "plebs," whom the law will help or prosecute in line with current norms. The next tier up is what I call "privileged" (about 9.99%), for whom wealth can steer justice, say by hiring good lawyers or being able to settle out of court. Above this and at the top are the "elite" (.01%), those who don't have to steer justice or pay anyone. These "elite" have a pass because of who they are, who they're associated with, and the power they have. Law enforcement will look the other way (or be directed to) from their transgressions; individuals will run interference or become willing scapegoats; and ultimately, justice will not prevail (this "pass" does have limits). If you doubt this, just start googling celebrities or politician names to see their transgressions and what their punishments were. I have a feeling whatever you find, you'll determine that had you done the same, the outcome would have been far worse.

Lastly, in my youth and naivete, I assumed mature, adult individuals would be able to use the democratic process to select the best of us to lead the country in a direction most beneficial and in line with our collective values. As the 2016 presidential election geared up, I was presented with candidates that seemed more associated with hereditary monarchies than a functional democracy. Prior to the first primaries, it was believed the presidential election would ultimately come down to a third Bush versus a second Clinton. The powers that be pushed these two as the people best able to lead the country who just so happened to have spouses or relatives who had previously held the post. While neither of these two were elected, I've noticed remarkable concern from my fellow Americans that the best representatives are not being offered to us. Sadly, we've gotten to the point where our potential representatives aren't even willing to debate each other in a meaningful way.

While critiquing this system, I would also like to note that it seems to be the best we have until we hook up a computer to rule us, and it determines we're too dangerous to rule ourselves or continue existing. The mature adults who both vote and run for public office are clearly lacking, being replaced by shortsighted constituents and representatives with seemingly room-temperature IQs (some quite literally; you know who I'm talking about). As an aside, we tend to get the type of representatives we deserve, not the ones we need. Those running for political office prioritize votes, not good ideas, when it comes time for them to vote or govern.

I hope, after exposing some of the things I believed to be correct that were wrong, you will look inwardly at some of those beliefs you hold and ponder their accuracy. At times, this can be difficult because the truth may attack a core tenet of yours. I have no doubt over the course of your life, your values and attitudes have changed in ways that if you met your past self, you'd have some charged language concerning their beliefs.

"My good friends, for the second time in our history, a British Prime Minister has returned from Germany bringing peace with honor. I believe it is peace for our time. Go home and get a nice quiet sleep."
— Neville Chamberlain, British prime minister, September 30, 1938, after ceding portions of Czechoslovakia to Nazi Germany. Eleven months later, Germany invaded Poland, starting World War II.

Conclusion

The main theme tying all the chapters together is truth. You don't have to like that I've pointed out what is accurate, and I don't expect blind acceptance of what I've stated simply because pen was put to paper (technically typed; my handwriting is awful). You may want the world to be different, but that is different from accepting things as they are. Rather than pretending to live in a fictional world with fictional stories, deal with what is real. You'll find it easier to get to where you want if you have a firm understanding of the problem. If you find fiction easier to deal with, please confine your insanity to yourself and those like-minded (if you wore some type of sign, that would be helpful to others).

For critics, you may notice a lack of specific, data-driven statistics proving my points, for the most part. This was done for a reason: even if I cited statistics in a careful, irrefutable, and methodical manner, those same critics would dismiss them outright, regardless of objective facts, and rely instead on cherry-picked statistics (or worse yet, nothing) more favorable to what they believe. Other writers of contemporary books have cited tomes of statistics and incontrovertible facts, all to be ignored by those not wanting to believe the truth that's right in front of them. Since I perceived that method ineffective, I decided to go a different route. I decided to tell you things that are so obviously true that to believe the opposite you would have to be mad. Those I'm trying to reveal the truth to are not those madmen (mad people?), but reasonable individuals willing to believe what they know to be true, or who can accept the truth when it is presented to them.

Ideally, what would be revealed by those denying reality would be a long list of people whose ideas and opinions should be looked at with skepticism rather than being given the benefit of the doubt. Unfortunately, it seems that is not the case. Denying reality has become a mark of those devoted to the cause, to the detriment of all else. What is an accurate label for someone who, when presented with the truth, still refuses to believe it, despite all evidence and common sense to the contrary? Willfully ignorant? Mad? Dogmatic? The actual label doesn't matter. What matters is that this person cannot be convinced with facts and may have to be driven to sanity by other means (such as appeals to emotion or endorsements from celebrities — luckily, they'll do nearly anything so long as the paycheck is big enough). At some point, it must simply be accepted that some cannot be convinced by any means, and those souls will simply be lost, believing something factually incorrect.

Generalities

In nearly every chapter, I've made what I call generalities. These statements concern broad truths and are not meant to be absolute. For example, if I said that males are taller than females, you are to interpret this as "on average, males are taller than females." Of course, there are some females taller than the average male, and some exceptionally taller than most males, but that doesn't take away from the truth that, on average, males are taller than females. I'm not trying to argue that tall females don't exist; rather, I'm trying to identify objective truth and perhaps find out why it is the case.

Many would take some of my observations and generalizations as stereotypes. By definition, a stereotype is a generalized belief about a particular category of people. Some bigoted individuals use these stereotypes to paint with a broad-brush entire categories of people and judge individuals by their group identity. For example, some misandrists (people who dislike, despise, or are strongly prejudiced against men) believe that because men commit most violent crimes (which is, of course, true), all men are violent or should be treated as though they will be violent. There is a difference in identifying an objective fact and using it in unfair and malicious ways.

What we lose by denying generalities exist is the ability to correctly identify root causes because we don't like what that root cause actually is. By doing this, we eliminate our ability to consider all options and ideas because we have not allowed ourselves to think "bad thoughts." For example, it is generally true that the homeless have much higher rates of hard-drug use and alcoholism than the average person. This substance abuse is what makes incorporating these individuals back into normal society so difficult, as housing such people relies on them being able to take care of a residence, adhere to socially agreed-upon rules, and (gasp) perhaps pay rent and utilities. Most would consider the idea of a substance-using homeless person a harmful stereotype, but it is true, even if it isn't true for even half of those living on the street. By making it impermissible to talk about substance abuse, we eliminate any solution that relies on that diagnosis of the problem, and the problem doesn't get solved. Many would rather maintain their worldview than actually solve the problem if it otherwise means changing their outlook.

Generalities (or stereotypes) don't generally materialize out of nowhere. There are reasons these generalities came into existence, and not simply because racist or sexist individuals wanted to make fun of large groupings of people. I know the stereotypes surrounding my identity groupings, and they are largely accurate. I would not hold these generalities to an individual, say, by assuming a Hispanic individual has mowed lawns for employment (although, go figure, I did in my youth), because an individual is just that, an individual.

Reality

While in training as an air battle manager in the Air Force, a fellow trainee and I were comparing our government to a chessboard. I asserted that the queen piece is comparable to the president — able to act swiftly and the most powerful piece on the board (that said, losing the piece isn't the end of the world, as has happened multiple times). Congress is like the king — slow to act and largely useless for timely action, but lose that piece, and the game is lost.

My friend then asked me what we were. He then suggested, "The bishop? A rook perhaps?"

My response: We're not even pawns; we are the felt on which pawns glide.

Nearly everything I've written above is as true and correct as I can recall. While I may have changed a name, relation, or inconsequential detail, it was done only to protect those I know the stories came from. If you believe I made up all or large segments of the above stories, you are sadly incorrect. If it helps your mental well-being, feel free to imagine that this is all fiction and should be moved to a different corner of the bookstore. You may hug the stuffed animals providing you comfort and talk to friends blindly agreeing with you — anything to avoid facing the facts — but know that there is a reality you must either deal with or face the consequences of because you are incapable of dealing with the truth.

Lies and falsehoods are told every day. Neither I nor anybody else can tell you fact from fiction. You must determine it on your own with only the information readily available to you. You, your loved ones, and people you've never met will be the victims or beneficiaries of your assessments and chosen actions. Please do not abdicate your duty to think and act to others simply because they are charismatic, claim to be experts, or are on TV. You, not they, will be paying the vast majority of the price or reaping the rewards of the actions or inactions you take.

I would like to end this book with a note on those truths I've revealed. I didn't make them true. I don't necessarily wish this is how the world works, nor do I necessarily think it's fair. In terms of equality, it's not fair that males are generally stronger than females. It's not fair that some are born into cultures with destructive traditions and lifestyles while others are not. While I've intermixed my opinions on some of those truths I've revealed, this isn't meant to be a book about my opinion; this book is about a reality we find uncomfortable to accept. If you don't like what I've revealed because it is true, your problem shouldn't be with me, but with reality itself (and good luck canceling that).

If my sin is revealing what is true, then I propose you turn to those spouting fiction; there's definitely no shortage of those. Understand that I live in the same world as you, subject to the same rules. I understand that, as was joked about in the sitcom Seinfeld, "The female body is a work of art. The male body is... utilitarian." This means people are more drawn to the female form, while the male body is more or less only practical for the physical labor and combat it may or may not have to take part in. The male sex, generally, is not as sought after for its physical attractiveness because that's ultimately not its purpose.

Whether viewed as a man or woman, I am subject to this overall truth, and must accept it in order to make the best possible decisions to get whatever it is I want (I leave it to you to determine what that might be). How does this affect me? Outside of a (male) gay bar, no one is going to buy me drinks. I will be expected to make the first move in any potential relationship, whether fair or unfair. My perceived value, to either potential partners or society, will always be more closely tied to my income and career rather than my physical appearance (thank God).

Additionally, money won't solve nearly any of the problems I have. Most of the issues in my life are self-created, and I must live with the consequences of decisions I've made over the course of my existence, with no real opposing force hindering my success other than perhaps nature itself. All that is to say, for better or worse, I am subject to all these truths and more, whether I like them or not.

Individual truth (or "my truth") does not exist, except in your imagination. There is one reality we are all living in. While your perception of the motivations of others and events may differ, ultimately, all of us are living in the same world with the same events occurring around us. We may choose to live in an imagined world, divorced from reality, but understand all choices have consequences. If we left truth up to each individual person, we'd get an endless number of fantasies bearing no relation to reality, all in conflict with one another. If you choose to ignore the real world, replacing it with the one you wish were true, you'll likely never fix the problems you wish to solve.

I can think of no greater hell than desiring to fix a problem but never grasping how to do it, no matter how much time, effort, and resources are dedicated to it, because you fail to understand the nature of the problem. Not accepting reality has a cost. Personally, I have no problem with people wishing to live in a fantasy land of their own creation. All around us are people who believe they are smarter, better looking, or more skilled than they actually are. In many ways, this is harmless and allows us to navigate the world in a more tolerable way. It becomes an issue when it spills into the public sphere and forces others to buy into that fantasy.

In my neighborhood are scores of people who think they are either the president of the United States, the queen of England, or Jesus Christ reborn. It only becomes an issue when those same people demand "Hail to the Chief" be played as they enter a room, mandate I curtsy, or require me to worship them as the son or daughter of God. While you may find it comforting and fashionable to live in a fictional world and force others to buy into it, know that someday someone else's fiction may be placed on you if it hasn't already, and you will be forced to live a story you know to be false. The language you use and actions you take will be used against you in the same way you have done against others.

I live by the mantra of treating others the way I would want to be treated, knowing I will inevitably be on the losing side again. I'd encourage you to do the same.

What Is Truth?

Over the course of this book, including the title, I've used the word truth without defining it or referencing traditional philosophical definitions or debates. Endless tomes, lectures, and entire lives and careers have been dedicated to questions and answers concerning "What is true?" I'm sorry to be the wet blanket, but I have no interest in this deep, seemingly unanswerable question. It could be that we are in the imagination of a turtle flying through space just as much as our perceived reality is nothing but us playing a virtual reality game — immortal beings entertaining ourselves and killing some time. Rather than ponder the endless potentials, I've chosen to only concern myself with what I can see in front of me and leave the rest to fate.

For the purpose of this work, I define truth as that which is in accordance with fact or reality. The rapid scientific development over the past few centuries has relied on objective facts and observations that could be learned by a single person and taught to others via a common language and writing. Understand that even a single word such as truth can have multiple definitions (and most do) and interpretations. The word gay, for example, has denoted something that is happy (such as when the Flintstones theme song declared "we'll have a gay old time"), lighthearted, and carefree; or, in modern times, usually denotes someone within the LGBT community.

I defined the word truth so you would understand what I am trying to communicate when I say something is true, rather than leave it up to the interpretation of the reader. You may think I'm grossly oversimplifying the word, or on the other hand, you may be wondering why I would dedicate any space whatsoever to define so simple a word and concept. Both of these outlooks are perfectly fine. If you approach this book using the definition I provided, you will better understand what I'm trying to say, rather than try and interpret my words in a way you wish to.

Feel free to interpret my words any way you wish, but if (after I've defined how I'm using the word) you choose your own interpretation, you're essentially just talking to yourself, as you apparently have no interest in the ideas I'm trying to pass along and would rather insert your own beliefs about what I'm trying to say. Half the problem with the modern age is that we are not effectively communicating with each other because we use vague, open-ended language and interpret that language in a way convenient to us.

For example, "pro-life" groups are not necessarily pro-life in all situations, as many in this camp also support the death penalty. Many "pro-choice" individuals are not necessarily pro-choice if the choice involves the purchase of firearms or requiring everyone to be vaccinated against all diseases. Those pushing for inclusivity are not pushing for inclusivity for all; rather, the push is only to include whichever groups happen to be in vogue.

What Truth Isn't

Truth is not a feeling you have about what is occurring around you. If I felt that the sky was green, it wouldn't mean that it is true that the sky is green. The sky still remains blue (or black) even if I believe it's true that the sky is green. If you thought the sky was green, you'd be wrong, along with anyone else agreeing with you. You may believe you're an animal and not a human being, but this again would be untrue. You may believe it all you like, but that simply means you're wrong and unable or unwilling to believe the truth when it's presented to you.

You likewise may believe that this is the most racist, homophobic, and sexist time in human history, and you would also be wildly incorrect. Much like anyone can claim to be anything they please, anyone can claim anything is true or untrue. The act of saying how you perceive events or the world around you doesn't make it so, even if you want it to for one reason or another. Anyone seriously believing their children see monsters under the bed or in the closet should know it is the child's imagination, not supernatural monsters preying upon the least mature of us for their own sick, twisted pleasure.

Why We Want to Deny Truth

Reality is hard. Fiction has the ability to soften that edge into something we want to believe is true. It allows us to be the heroes in our own story, easily identify the villains, and make sense of a mostly random and chaotic universe. Accepting the truth means admitting things we don't necessarily want to, either about ourselves, others, or the situation we find ourselves in.

An old schoolmate of mine called one day concerned about her male friend, who I'll refer to as Rob (who I assume to be in his early twenties). Rob had become infatuated with a girl he'd never met (who we'll call Jane) on a dating app, who was claiming to be a twenty-seven-year-old female. Out of the blue, a person claiming to be Jane's father texted Rob announcing that Jane was in fact thirteen and had been in a car accident. The man then claimed that if Rob sent $2,000 to cover the cost of the car wreck, he would not contact Rob again. A few weeks later, after Rob sent the money, the man again contacted Rob, claiming Jane required surgery, and requested an additional $1,000. After Rob sent the money, the man again contacted him claiming that his thirteen-year-old daughter had died, and requested another $1,000 in funeral costs.

Around the same time, an FBI "sergeant" texted Rob, claiming to be from some sort of child protection task force and wanting to talk to him. You already know what is happening because you are not involved and can objectively determine what Rob has gotten himself into. Rob could not see it because admitting he was being scammed required him to admit that Jane didn't exist, had never existed, and was simply a method of coaxing him out of money. In order to arrive at the correct solution, Rob would have to admit to himself that there was never a Jane, no accident, no death, and certainly no FBI agent texting him to talk about the exploitation of minors. All of it was a scam to coerce my schoolmate's friend out of whatever money could be gathered.

Likely, the situation will resolve itself with the only consequences being Rob will be out $3,000 and need to continue searching for an appropriate female partner. More men and women will fall for this trick, not because they're not intelligent, but because they want to believe in the fiction. The fiction they want to believe in? That they had found someone special. Admitting at any point that it was all a setup would mean admitting that there was never anyone real on the other end of the line, just some stranger (and probably a dude) looking for easy money. It would also mean you'd have to admit to yourself you fell for an obvious trick.

While that example is pretty straightforward, there are endless other fictions people want to believe because to admit the opposite were true would cause... distress, to say the least. While researching for this book, I came across a rather odd headline: "I'm a lesbian marrying a man, Friends don't understand: My sexual orientation never changed. I simply fell in love with a very unexpected person." Given the source I collected this from, I would find it odd if it were satire or an outright lie. The writer makes it very clear she is not bisexual. If I understand her writing, she claims to have an attraction to only one man (in the same way most gay men fall in love with just one woman to the exclusion of all others). The woman so wanted to keep her closely held identity, she neglected to acknowledge what that identity even meant, even if it was obvious to nearly everyone else.

Reality escaped her, and she continued believing she was unique and transcended labels — a lesbian who fell in love with a man. I honestly wish I had more space to dedicate to stories of people getting it wrong, and perhaps in the future I will, but that will have to wait. To the main point, if we can't maintain our own fiction, we are forced to see what we didn't want to be true, and for many, that is a bridge they will not or cannot cross.

How do I know this to be true? Because there are things over the course of my life I've learned that, in hindsight, were obvious. The only reason I couldn't see it was because some conscious or subconscious part of me didn't want it to be true. Acknowledging what I'd learned was difficult, but afterwards, I became more aware of what was occurring around me. A sense of calm followed in a way I believe most mature adults experience.

The ideas in the numbered chapters above are, to some, both accurate and verboten (German for forbidden) to talk about or consider. They cannot be believed because cornerstones in a certain person's worldview will be destroyed in the process, requiring a new worldview to be created. Going from believing criminals steal because they want instead of need requires generating a new worldview, shifting thieves from downtrodden victims to victimizers in need of apprehension and potentially incarceration. Going from believing society is at fault to the individual is at fault for the outcome of their own life requires shifting blame and scorn to individuals rather than grand societal events outside of a person's control.

Why Are These Truths Uncomfortable?

Each of us has a value system, and in that value system are core beliefs that prop up all the other ideas relying on it. An example of this may be that the wealthy didn't earn their wealth. All other ideas, advocacy, and worldview rely on this initial thought. With that idea as the foundation, one could advocate for a redistribution of wealth, since the wealthy don't deserve it anyway (but where, oh where, will the money go?). When someone or something challenges that core belief, most people become defensive to the extreme. The reason: if the foundational belief is incorrect, logically, all the ideas stemming from that are no longer valid (or perhaps simply less valid).

If, for example, most wealthy people did earn their money, it becomes infinitely harder to try and argue that their wealth should be redistributed. With so much riding on these core beliefs, they are very difficult to dislodge from people's minds. New explanations to describe the world must be created, and those explanations are usually not what people want to hear or believe. The ideas I've presented are a full-on attack of closely held beliefs for millions in the US and the West in general. I've revealed what many people don't want to believe because doing so requires an individual either (A) to form a new worldview or (B) to believe in something they know is false.

While I know many who don't care if they believe something false, there are those who cannot live with themselves if they commit to ideas that are incorrect or don't make logical sense. "Knowing" the truth is what sets these people apart in their own minds, and they can only see themselves as this elite intellectual giant by being logically consistent. People orient themselves in the world based on these core beliefs. They define their situation and the situations of those around them based on those beliefs. If the core belief is altered or abandoned, a logically consistent person is now required to reposition themselves in their own mind.

For example, if you had just invaded Poland based on the belief that you were racially superior, you must reorient yourself if Dr. Scientist walks up and says with 100% certainty that there are no qualities that make your race "better" than the people you just got done invading. Now the invasion can't be viewed as nature taking its course, with the strongest prevailing, but must be seen for what it is: a naked power grab based on nothing more than the desire to rule more people and larger swaths of land. All those soldiers and the citizens initially supporting the war may not be big fans of a power grab; whereas before, it simply seemed like destiny. Most importantly, you must now come to terms with the fact that you are the bad guy, having brutally murdered those in your way, killing fathers, women, children, and oppressing those not killed in the process.

These and many other truths are uncomfortable because they attack core beliefs and the ideas that rely on those beliefs being true. A new worldview must be created, with new beliefs and new assumptions forming different ideas. People fear where those ideas may lead due to the fact that it probably conflicts with the prior long-held ideological beliefs. At the end of the Cold War, millions of communists woke up one day to news that capitalism had won and that their belief in the superiority of their system was false. Many never reached this conclusion, as it was too difficult to change their core beliefs after a lifetime of faith in the system. It was easier to lie to themselves and blame the failure on something, anything, else to explain what was evident around them.

Identity

The least interesting things about ourselves are the identity-level characteristics we largely don't have any control over. I hope that if I were to reveal to you what I have accomplished in my life, your first reaction would not be "You've done so well as a Hispanic person," or "That's not particularly exceptional for a male." Our skin-deep identities and orientations seem to have overwhelmed any sense of true accomplishment, instead replaced by a "How much of a victim am I?" hierarchy.

This victim status doesn't concern itself with the individual, but rather the group. For anyone that starts their sentence with "As a (blank), (blank), (blank)" before providing their opinion, what they're really communicating is "My idea is valid because of my group identity, and thus cannot be questioned, not because the idea makes sense." This leads to insane ideas such as that women can never understand men, Asians can never understand Native Americans, or that pansexual people cannot understand straight people since they can never truly understand the lived experience.

In some ways this is true, in that we cannot truly feel what another human being is experiencing. In a much stronger sense, this same idea neglects that we can empathize or may have had similar things happen to us. Some may look at me and assume I have not experienced racism or sexism, which, of course, I have, like nearly everyone. In my view, a particularly studious person can know far more about a culture or group of people than a person living in that group, even if they did not live inside the skin of that person. Likewise, a member of this group may not in fact know anything about their group identity, instead simply living their lives ignorant of how their group identity affects their life, if it even does.

Even if your identity were the most interesting thing about you, would you want it to be? Are you John's gay friend or are you John's friend who owns that trendy bar? Do you want to be known as the Black guy at the office or the guy who is leading in sales? Would you rather be known as the female pilot or simply as the pilot? Here's an interesting question: Am I more interesting being straight or bisexual? Do I have more merit as a Native American or White person? Whose thoughts and ideas should we be more supportive of, a straight cisgender white male or a veteran, Native, Hispanic, transgender, lesbian of color to a single parent?

Ask any logistician, and they will probably look at you perplexed. Their first question would be how your sex, skin tone, gender identity, race, ethnicity, religion, height, or weight has any impact on the ideas you put forth. My question would be the same.

What I Hope You've Gained

How do I know the things I've written are largely correct? From my own life experience and the experiences of those around me. Countless times, I reread the numbered chapters' titles, attempting to play the part of the "red team*" in order to challenge what I had previously written. I had friends, family, and strangers read the titles to see if anything jumped out at them as flagrantly false. Finally, I tried what I considered to be a slightly more scientific approach and read the titles as if they were saying the opposite: "Males and females work the same," "Choices don't have consequences," "You are not lucky to live in the time and place you do."

For each of the chapters, I swapped truth for perceived untruth and was left with falsehoods and insanity.

*"Blue/red teaming" is a drill where members of the same side act as either themselves or the opponent in order to plan for what the actual opponent will do. For example, if I were to plan the D-Day invasions in World War II, I would assign an ally the role of playing as the Axis (red) during training to plan for what the actual Axis forces might do so the Allies (blue) would be prepared for the Axis reaction.

You already knew or suspected everything I've revealed on either a conscious or subconscious level. I haven't revealed anything a part of you didn't already know, even if you are or were unwilling to admit it because of what that would mean. What I hope has occurred is that you've been able to separate what you want to be true from what is actually true and can tell the difference between them.

There's nothing wrong with having a utopian vision of the future you wish we were at, but if you apply that vision to the present, you will not get the result you want. You will instead only perceive what you want to be true, and see only what you want to see, ignoring evidence to the contrary.

A Challenge and a Warning

One of the numbered chapters above is a near and total fabrication. You must determine which one it is on your own (or cheat and read a review, assuming one exists, if you're not up to the challenge) and take from it what I am actually trying to convey. I will not spell this out to you because if I have to, you've missed the point entirely and are truly lost. (If you somehow got this far and can't guess the chapter instantly, you are an anomaly. I don't know how you can both read and not walk into oncoming traffic due to stupidity.)

I know what you're asking yourself: What is the cost of ignoring these truths? As stated sporadically throughout the course of this work, you will make suboptimal decisions based on incorrect base assumptions. For example, let's say you were a female trying to attract a male partner and had to put more time into either (A) the gym or (B) work. If you assume men and women desire the same thing, you may be tempted to

235

attain greater wealth by dedicating more time to work, since you look around and see young attractive women gravitating towards wealthy men, and thus assume men are also greatly attracted by the material wealth of their potential partners. This would be a mistake and likely limit the number of male suitors versus going to the gym. You don't have to like that reality any more than I do, but ignoring it will not get you what you want.

If you were in charge of dealing with a city's crime, if you assume crime's primary purpose is taking care of basic human needs, you will not be able to tackle the problem because you don't understand why it's occurring and what's going through the minds of those committing the crimes. Instead, you are likely to tolerate crime and grasp at solutions that do nothing to solve the problem and may even make the situation worse (say, by limiting arrests of those stealing under $1,000 of merchandise). Crime will run rampant, and at some point, there is no coming back, as what's needed to solve the problem will have fled to greener pastures (even if those pastures are in Texas and slightly more arid than expected). If you believe a degree is a degree is a degree, you may make the mistake of majoring in a field with laughably limited job opportunities and a very costly tuition. After the school administrators have been paid, professors have authorized the cap and gown to be worn down the aisle, and shortly after you depart the adolescent theme park colleges have become, the bill finally comes due. Only by ignoring perfectly sound advice will the consequences be recognized at a stage in which it's too late to do anything except pay what's due. Of course, there is a chance someone else gets stuck with the bill.

Last Call

Behind your eyes lies a machine capable of solving quadratic equations simply by looking into the sky as an object falls so you may catch it. Your "gut," which is actually located between your ears, lets you know when something is off before your conscious mind can. Throughout this book, I've only told you what you already knew on some level. It is the gift nature has bestowed upon you, the ability to recognize patterns and learn from them so you don't make avoidable errors. You ignore this gift at your own peril.

Last time I checked, this is America. Use your own best judgment. Good luck.

> *No matter what happens next, don't be too hard on yourself. Even now, after all you've done, you can still go home. Lucky you.*
> — Captain Martin Walker, sole survivor, Delta Force Recon Detachment (fictional)

Safe Book Burning Procedures

WARNING: Prior to casting this book into any open flame or otherwise incinerating it, consult your local fire marshal concerning the legality and ensure there are no current burn bans in effect. If, while participating in a book burning, law enforcement has detained or arrested you, make sure to consult with your public defender, private lawyer, or local ACLU representative prior to making any spoken or written statements to law enforcement. If you yourself are a member of the ACLU who has been detained while incinerating any texts or electronic devices containing this audiobook, please stand by. A fund is being created to provide bail-related resources to ensure you are freed as quickly as possible. For those wishing to contribute, the fund will also provide an additional signed copy of the book and a pack of matches to those unjustly detained. Additional shipping and handling charges only apply if you'd like the copy presoaked in lighter fluid for easier burning.

Special bulk discounts and credit purchases apply for ten or more copies. Don't be left empty-handed at the next rally! Burn today, pay later!

www.ingramcontent.com/pod-product-compliance
Lightning Source LLC
Chambersburg PA
CBHW052125270326
41930CB00012B/2765